Becoming Urban Cyclists

Becoming Urban Cyclists:
From Socialization to Skills

Edited by
Matthieu Adam
and Nathalie Ortar

University of Chester Press

First published 2021
by University of Chester Press
Parkgate Road
Chester CH1 4BJ

Printed and bound in the UK by the
LIS Print Unit
University of Chester
Cover designed by the LIS Graphics Team
University of Chester

This collection © University of Chester, 2021
Individual contributions © their respective authors

The right of Matthieu Adam and Nathalie Ortar to be identified as the joint editors of this work has been asserted in accordance with sections 77 and 78 of the Copyright, Designs and Patents Act 1988

The moral rights of the authors have been asserted in accordance with sections 77 and 78 of the Copyright, Designs and Patents Act 1988

All Rights Reserved
No part of this publication may be reproduced, stored in a retrieval system or transmitted in any form or by any means without the prior permission of the copyright owner, other than as permitted by UK copyright legislation or under the terms and conditions of a recognised copyright licensing scheme

A catalogue record of this book is available from the British Library

ISBN 978-1-910481-17-2

CONTENTS

List of Figures	vii
List of Tables	ix
Acknowledgements	xii
Notes on Contributors	xiii
Introduction *Matthieu Adam and Nathalie Ortar*	xviii
Chapter 1 Becoming an Urban Cycling Space *Peter Cox*	1
Chapter 2 Conducting Interviews with Maps and Videos to Capture Cyclists' Skills and Expertise *Matthieu Adam, Nathalie Ortar, Luc Merchez, Georges-Henry Laffont and Hervé Rivano*	18
Chapter 3 Key Events, Motivations and Prior Experience in E-Bike Adoption *Dimitri Marincek*	44
Chapter 4 The Effects of a Promotional Campaign on the Practice of Utility Cycling: Bike-to-work in Switzerland *Patrick Rérat*	72

Chapter 5
Promoting Urban Cycling: An Ecolinguistic   103
and Discursive Approach
M. Cristina Caimotto

Chapter 6
Adult Beginner Cyclists in French Cities   129
Thomas Buhler

Chapter 7
Immigration Background and Cycling –   150
Findings from Germany
Janina Welsch

Chapter 8
What Makes Women Stop or Start Cycling   188
in France?
David Sayagh, Clément Dusong and Francis Papon

Chapter 9
Appropriating the Bicycle: Repair and   215
Maintenance Skills and the Bicycle-Cyclist
Relationship
Margot Abord de Chatillon

Afterword   244
Rachel Aldred

LIST OF FIGURES

Figure 2.1: Theoretical cyclability in the Lyon area (Luc Merchez, 2019). 25

Figure 2.2: Methodological and analytical set-up. 27

Figure 2.3: Cameras on a private bike (left) and a Vélo'v (right) (Matthieu Adam, 2018). 29

Figure 2.4: Shots filmed by our participants (Véléval Project, 2018). 31

Figure 3.1: Conceptual model of the adoption of the e-bike—adapted from Chatterjee et al. (2012); Jones et al. (2015). 49

Figure 3.2: Restorative cycling trajectory. 61

Figure 3.3: Resilient cycling trajectory. 61

Figure 4.1: The system of Velomobility (Rérat, 2021; images taken from pixabay.com). 75

Figure 4.2: Motivations to participate in bike-to-work according to the number of years of participation (maximum of three answers per participant). 81

Figure 4.3: Parade at the end of bike-to-work 2017 at the Federal Institute of Technology and the University of Lausanne (source: EPFL, 2017). 94

Figure 4.4: Parade at the end of bike-to-work 2018 at the Federal Institute of Technology and the University of Lausanne (source: EPFL, 2018). 95

Figure 5.1: Interdiscursive alignment adapted from Mautner (2010a). — 109

Figure 5.2: A popular, grassroots visual created by a Twitter user (Engineer Like a Girl, 1 May 2020, 12:09 a.m., Twitter post, 2020). — 123

Figure 6.1: Distribution of the level of cycling habits among the French urban population (2018). — 136

Figure 6.2: Flows of people persisting or changing profile category between March 2018 and March 2019. — 144

Figure 7.1: Percentage of the population with an immigration background between 2005 and 2018 (source: Statistisches Bundesamt, 2019). — 153

Figure 7.2: Rank of transport means by importance for everyday transport, status for oneself and status for the general society (source: own illustration based on data from ILS-study/Klausing, 2015). — 174

Figure 9.1: Self-assessment by survey participants of the condition of their most used bicycle according to the city of residence. — 223

Figure 9.2: Self-assessment by survey participants of how at ease they are with bicycle repair according to their frequency of bicycle use. — 224

LIST OF TABLES

Table 3.1: Interviewee characteristics.   55

Table 4.1: Impact of participation in bike-to-work on perceptions of the commuting trip among people who did not previously cycle to work.   85

Table 4.2: Effects of the bike-to-work event on cycling practice.   94

Table 5.1: The occurrences of "deserve" in context in the "Mayor's Transport Strategy" (Mayor of London, 2018) giving the preceding or succeeding seven words in the report.   120

Table 6.1: Six statements composing our "SRBAI+id" test of a habit for six transport modes.   135

Table 6.2: Five profiles resulting from the combination of the three criteria: current use, cycling skills and intentions (with ABCs highlighted).   138

Table 6.3: Socio-economic features of the five cycling-related profiles.   140

Table 6.4: Persistence in bicycle use for groups of cyclists in 2018 (P1 and P2) and percentage of cycling newcomers for the other three groups.   143

Table 7.1: Population with an immigration background in Germany ($N = 20.8$ million) by main countries of origin, i.e. their own or their parents' country of birth (source: Statistisches Bundesamt, 2019).   154

Table 7.2: Characteristics of population by immigration background and immigrant generation (source: Statistisches Bundesamt, 2019).	155
Table 7.3: Household size and income by immigration background (source: Statistisches Bundesamt, 2019).	156
Table 7.4: Sample characteristics by immigration background (source: BMVI/MiT, 2017).	161
Table 7.5: Bicycle availability by immigration background and gender (source: BMVI/MiT, 2017).	162
Table 7.6: Cycling attitude and traffic situation assessment by immigration background (source: BMVI/MiT, 2017).	163
Table 7.7: Bicycle use by immigration background and gender (source: BMVI/MiT, 2017).	164
Table 7.8: Country/region of reference by immigration background/generation and average duration of stay (source: ILS-study, 2010; see Welsch, 2019).	165
Table 7.9: Sample characteristics by immigration background/generation (source: ILS-study, 2010; see Welsch, 2019).	166
Table 7.10: Preconditions for cycling by immigration background/generation (source: ILS-study, 2010; see Welsch, 2019).	167

List of Tables

Table 7.11: Bicycle use by immigration background/generation and gender (source: ILS-study, 2010; see Welsch, 2019). — 168

Table 7.12: Share of responses by reason by immigration background/generation (multiple entries) (source: ILS-study, 2010; see Welsch, 2019). — 169

Table 7.13: Mobility socialization (factor/item average) by immigration background and generation (source: ILS-study, 2010; see Welsch, 2019). — 170

Table 7.14: Parameter estimation for bicycle use (at least weekly: yes/no) (source: ILS-study, 2010; see Welsch, 2019). — 171

Table 7.15: Rank for importance of transport means (source: ILS-study/Klausing, 2015). — 173

Table 7.16: Rank for status of transport means — self (source: ILS-study/Klausing, 2015). — 173

Table 7.17: Rank for status of transport means — society (source: ILS-study/Klausing, 2015). — 174

Table 9.1: Interviews conducted in Lyon and Melbourne. — 222

ACKNOWLEDGEMENTS

This book would not have been possible without the scientific, editorial and linguistic support of Peter Cox. We therefore thank him warmly for his time and crucial input! We also thank Sarah Griffiths and colleagues at the University of Chester as well as the authors and the participants of the workshop that preceded this book.

NOTES ON CONTRIBUTORS

Margot Abord de Chatillon is a PhD researcher in urban mobility based at the LAET (ENTPE, Lyon) and the Lirsa (Interdisciplinary Research Laboratory in Action-Oriented Sciences, Cnam, Paris). Her work focuses on bicycle repair and maintenance and on the role of material objects in cycling practices, through an international case study in the cities of Lyon and Melbourne. https://orcid.org/0000-0001-5653-6072

Matthieu Adam is a Research Fellow in Urban Studies at CNRS (National Centre for Scientific Research) for the research unit UMR 5600 "Environment City Society" (EVS), Lyon, France. He works on the study of public policies and social practices involved in greening the production of urban space. His research, which borrows from radical geography and critical sociology, focuses primarily on urban cycling, and secondarily on sustainable urban projects and on policies of territorial attractiveness. With Émeline Comby, he edited the book *Le Capital dans la cité : une encyclopédie critique de la ville* (Éditions Amsterdam, 2020).

Rachel Aldred is Professor of Transport and Director of the Active Travel Academy at the University of Westminster. She has published more than 50 peer-reviewed journal papers on active travel and related subjects, and her work has won prizes including in 2016 the Economic and Social Research Council Prize for Outstanding Impact in Public Policy.

Thomas Buhler is trained in urban engineering and first worked as a Planner in France and the Czech Republic. Since 2013, he has been an Associate Professor at the University of Franche-Comté in France, in the Department of Geography and Planning. He is currently a member of the research unit "Theorizing and Modeling for Development" (ThéMA). His research concerns the study of planning discourse, mobility policies and behaviour, and the study of conflicts in the case of wind-energy projects.

M. Cristina Caimotto is Assistant Professor of English Linguistics and Translation in the Department of Culture, Politics and Society at the University of Turin, Italy. Her research interests include political discourse and environmental discourse, with a focus on ideology. She is the author of *Discourses of Cycling, Road Users and Sustainability: An Ecolinguistic Investigation* (Palgrave, 2020), a study that searches for a positive new discourse that would inspire and encourage cycling as a habitual means of transport, rather than simply exposing ecologically destructive discourse. She is also a cycling advocate.

Peter Cox is Professor of Sociology in the Department of Social and Political Science at the University of Chester. His research covers a wide range of topics within the sociology and politics of cycling. He has published and edited a number of books including *The Politics of Cycling Infrastructure* [with Till Koglin] (Policy Press, 2020), *Cycling: A Sociology of Vélomobility* (Routledge, 2019) and *Cycling Cultures* (University of Chester Press, 2015).

Clément Dusong gained his PhD through the Laboratory for Economic and Social Dynamics of Transport (DEST) within the Department for Planning, Mobility and Environment (AME) at the University of Gustave Eiffel in Marne-la-Vallée, France. His thesis studies cycling evolution in the Île-de-France region, with a particular focus on Paris inner suburbs behaviour. He is especially interested in the inequalities of practice within territories and social groups. Currently, he works at the Academy of Active Mobilities (ADMA) as an expert trainer to improve the inclusion of active modes in mobility policies in France.

Georges-Henry Laffont is a trained Geographer, has a PhD in Urban Planning and is a Lecturer in Urban Planning at the National School

Notes on Contributors

of Architecture of Saint-Étienne (France). Member of research units UMR 5600 "Environment City Society" (EVS) and UMR 7324 "Cities, Territories, Environment and Society" (CITERES), his work focuses on the capacity of images, discourses, objects and devices of contemporary production of space to affect individuals, groups and societies. He is also interested in urban lifestyles and their resilience in the context of transitions.

Dimitri Marincek is a PhD student and Graduate Assistant at the University of Lausanne, Switzerland, where he is also a member of the Observatory for Cycling and Active Mobilities (OUVEMA). He is working on electrically assisted bicycles (e-bikes) and their users. His research is inspired by biographical approaches to mobility and the concept of a lifelong cycling trajectory. He is also active in bicycle planning research in Switzerland.

Luc Merchez has a PhD in Geography, is Senior Lecturer (MCF) at École Normale Supérieure de Lyon (France), a member of the UMR 5600 EVS and of the LabEX Intelligence des Mondes Urbains. For the past several years, he has been interested in urban mobilities in conjunction with socio-spatial inequalities (ANR VEL'INNOV project), as well as accessibility issues (especially food accessibility). He specializes in the field of Geographic Information Systems (GIS) and geostatistical analyses, in particular at infra-urban scales. His research also focuses on geovisualization issues (types of representations, interactivity, …).

Nathalie Ortar is Senior Researcher in Anthropology at the ENTPE-University of Lyon, France and member of the "Urban Planning, Economy and Transportation" (LAET) research unit. Her research has mainly focused on the links between dwelling and spatial mobility. Since 2010, she has been leading research on the changes in social practices that occur in the ways of living in a context of injunctions to mobility and energy transition. Her last book *Ethnographies of Power: A Political Anthropology of Energy* (2021) is available through open access.

Francis Papon is Director of the Laboratory DEST in the Planning, Mobilities and Environment Department at the University Gustave Eiffel.

Patrick Rérat is a full Professor of Geography of Mobilities of the University of Lausanne, Switzerland, where he is also the founding co-director of the Observatory for Cycling and Active Mobilities (OUVEMA). His research focuses on the various dimensions of cycling practices and the politics of velomobility. His latest book is entitled *Cycling to Work. An analysis of the Practice of Utility Cycling* (Springer, 2021).

Hervé Rivano is a Computer Scientist and Professor at the French National Institute of Applied Sciences (INSA Lyon). He leads the joint Inria–INSA Lyon Agora research team of the CITI laboratory and is a member of the executive board of Lyon Urban School. His research activity focuses on network infrastructures underlying digital urban systems. In particular, he has been working on the design of low-cost environmental sensor networks to collect dense data on anthropocene phenomena such as air pollution and urban heat islands. He is also interested in the instrumentation required for the implementation of dynamic and predictive urban infrastructures, in particular for decarbonized transportation modes.

David Sayagh is Lecturer at the University Paris-Saclay. He holds a PhD in Sociology from the University of Paris-Est (now University of Gustave Eiffel). His research focuses on bicycle socialization and more generally on the links between urban, mobility, sport, health and ecological socializations. He is currently working on the international research project "Vélotactique":
(https://cyclops.hypotheses.org/velotactique)

Notes on Contributors

Janina Welsch is a Researcher in the Mobilities and Space Research Group at the ILS Research Institute for Regional and Urban Development GmbH in Dortmund, Germany. Her research interests evolve around ways and aspects of sustainable mobility transformations, mobility management and on the study of mobility behaviour of different population groups. In her PhD she focused on the mobility behaviour of people with different family origins, often described in German statistics as people with an immigration background.

INTRODUCTION
Matthieu Adam and Nathalie Ortar

Ironically, it is a health crisis that has furthered the cause of cycling—a means of transport promoted for its physical and mental health benefits (Bourne et al., 2018; Götschi et al., 2016; Humphreys et al., 2013). Indeed, one of the side effects of the Covid-19 crisis has been to prompt the authorities and ordinary citizens to think again about the use of public space, including roads, in order to develop efficient and safe transport solutions that take into account social distancing. From Berlin to Montreal, from Bogota to London, many city authorities have decided to develop bike solutions because cycling is an individual mode that avoids close contact. They have accordingly adopted a "tactical urbanism" (Baron, 2019) as it allows rapid but malleable and reversible installations through trial-and-error experimentation and adaptation.

Since the turn of the 21st century, in countries of the Global North, cycling has progressively outgrown its policy categorization as a leisure or sports activity to now be considered as a means of transport for utilitarian purposes (Aldred & Jungnickel, 2012). It has become both a legitimate practice and a credible urban alternative to the car, public transport or walking. Starting generally from a very low percentage of modal share, cycling has surged in many major cities, increasing between 2001 and 2015 by factors of 2.5 in Paris, by 3.5 in London, by 4 in Lyon and by 6.5 in Brussels (Héran, 2018). In the wake of the inhabitants of Amsterdam (Feddes, 2019) and Copenhagen (Colville-Andersen, 2018), which have been worldwide references for cycling cities since the 1970s, increasing numbers of European and North American city dwellers are taking up cycling as a means of transport.

The basic design of the safety bicycle has changed little in over a century (Cox & Van de Walle, 2007) and it can be described as "a new old thing" (Vivanco, 2013). However, the development of dock-based

Introduction

or dockless bike sharing (Chen et al., 2020; Fishman, 2016) and more recently the incorporation of the bicycle into the "gig economy" with its multitude of bike messengers in precarious employment (Altenried, 2019; Kidder, 2016) has renewed the practices and image of cycling in cities. The electrification of a proportion of vehicles (Fishman & Cherry, 2016) and the rediscovery of the utility of cargo bikes (Cox & Rzewnicki, 2015) as well as adult tricycles have allowed the diversification of uses and enabled less athletic people or people with impairments to take up cycling.

Cycling is presented by elected officials, urban professionals from the public and private sectors, associations and NGOs, or scholars, as one of the major means to address environmental issues in the field of daily mobility (Parkin, 2012). Low environmental impact, minimized traffic congestion, relatively light and cheap infrastructure requirements, coupled with the versatility provided by cycles of a range of designs are all requisite qualities for a means of transport for the energy transition.

Over recent years, cycling has become an important issue for public authorities in many countries and the subject of national and local action plans. In France, for example, a national cycling plan including not only incentives to develop new infrastructure, but also bike repairs, as well as the training of bicycle mechanics, was about to be enacted before the Covid-19 outbreak and has been extended during the crisis. Local relays have been set up with some municipalities offering financial aid (several hundred euros) for the purchase of utility and electric bicycles or organizing cycling promotion campaigns. Although allocated budgets remain small compared to those for automobile transport (roads, parking spaces), cycling is being progressively integrated into mobility and urban planning programmes. Temporary cycle lanes or "slow streets" (streets shared by pedestrians, cyclists and motorists, with very low speed limits) are burgeoning. These new infrastructures are part of tactical urbanism whose effect is to transform cities by trying out new solutions and some bike lanes could become permanent. They have attracted new users, particularly those fleeing public transport. In this exceptional context, some started pedalling, becoming urban cyclists, characterized by a wide variety of practices (often analysed separately) ranging from commuting to utility trips (shopping, taking children to school, etc.) and from leisure trips to top-flight sport.

The Art and Life of the Urban Cyclist
Why use the expression "becoming urban cyclists?" What is at issue here is not so much a generation "becoming" urban cyclists for the first time, but instead a population becoming urban cyclists "again". The recent development of city cycling in Europe and North America is not a beginning but a comeback after a sharp decline between 1950 and 1970 and decades of abandonment (Héran, 2014; Pucher & Buehler, 2012).

Becoming an urban cyclist requires a variety of skills and a set of knowledge. These include the need to know how to pedal and move forward safely, merge with traffic, fit in with other users, gain access to dedicated cycling infrastructure, navigate in a known or unknown city/neighbourhood (with or without a guiding device), maintain and repair a bike, find a space to park and secure a bicycle, etc. Those skills and expertise are achieved through different forms of socialization.

"Becoming" expresses our interest for the process by which people acquire the skills and knowledge necessary for cycling in the city, a process that might vary with culture, gender and social space, but also with topography, residential as well as occupational location, the social environment in which the cyclist grew up, and more. But city cycling is not just a question of acquiring additional skills or knowledge because their very acquisition transforms people in their own eyes and changes how other road users perceive and consider them (Aldred, 2010, 2013).

"Becoming an urban cyclist" is therefore not only about acquiring a set of skills to get on a bike, pedal and weave in and out between the cars but it also changes people's perception of space,

Introduction

time and the city, as well as of other road users; it changes their way of moving and interacting with others. It leads to the discovery of new places, new physical and mental sensations and emotions (Ortar, 2019). "Becoming" therefore questions what it takes to become someone else. Riding a bike for everyday transport influences the city dweller's identity (Steinbach et al., 2011), as do external perceptions of their cycling (Aldred, 2013). This book therefore aims at describing who becomes an urban cyclist and how, and how this in turn contributes to shaping specific identities, perceptions and practices.

Urban Cycling and Inequalities
While urban cycling is a common practice, there are substantial territorial variations (Cox, 2019; Horton et al., 2016) between countries and between rural and urban areas. Early studies indicate that education received at school and in the family as well as gender (Shaw et al., 2020), peers and the geography of places all matter for becoming an urban cyclist. The required competencies differ, seeing that in "low-cycling" cities cyclists are expected to perform in the same way as motorists despite strikingly different affordances and divergent capabilities (Larsen, 2017; Spinney, 2007). The modal share thus seems to depend on local mobility norms, geography, public policies, gender, age and social class.

Moreover, the redevelopment of cycling mobility is socially and spatially unequal (Cox & Koglin, 2020; Fuller & Winters, 2017; Goodman & Aldred, 2018; Stehlin, 2019). First, the interests, abilities and possibilities of using the bicycle to get around vary with gender, age, health, social class, economic resources and socialization. Secondly, policies and cycling infrastructure, as well as road cyclability, vary considerably between areas. These two factors work together to produce complex socio-spatial inequalities.

In countries of the Global North, infrastructure—cycleways, cycle tracks and cycle lanes (Stehlin, 2019), shared-bike terminals (Duarte, 2016)—are mainly located in neighbourhoods with the highest economically and culturally resourced populations. As shown by quantitative studies, in Europe, this is especially visible in the centres of big cities as almost everywhere in the Global North, the modal share of cycling is correlated with socio-occupational category (Rérat et al., 2019; Steinbach et al., 2011), income (Fuller & Winters, 2017) or education level (Goodman & Aldred, 2018). Those who become urban cyclists are more often executive personnel and professionals or technicians and equivalent staff rather than office workers or labourers. City cycling is also gendered; urban cyclists are almost everywhere predominantly male (see Song et al., 2019 for a literature review). In France, around 60% of urban cyclists are men (concordant figures between mobility studies [enquêtes ménages déplacements], national census figures, and manual counts carried out by local authorities). In the United Kingdom, men are twice as likely as women are to travel by bicycle (Goodman & Aldred, 2018). The gender gap seems to be lower in cities and countries where the modal share is high, such as Denmark or The Netherlands (Aldred et al., 2016; Boterman, 2018). Yet, this is not valid for all populations: in The Netherlands, for example, teenage girls (Soemers, 2016) and women from recent immigration (Kaplan et al., 2018) cycle less than their male counterparts (see also Welsch and Buhler in this volume). In addition, when the modal share rises but remains low, the correlation between an increase in modal share and progress in gender equality is not automatic (Aldred et al., 2016).

Social inequalities and unequal geographical cyclability combine to produce complex and contrasting situations. On the one hand, the development of cycling infrastructure leads to an increase in cycling practices (Burk, 2017; Pucher & Buehler, 2012). On the other hand, infrastructure is most often built where cycling is identified as important by elected officials and planners. Cycling facilities and measured and observed practices therefore tend to reinforce each other as the density of infrastructure is correlated with the increase in modal share (Burk, 2017). In addition, the areas

Introduction

with the highest modal share are also those where the gender, education and social class distributions of cyclists are the most egalitarian (Aldred et al., 2016; Fitch et al., 2019; Garrard et al., 2012; Goodman & Aldred, 2018). Improvements in the cyclability and the diversity of practices and users also seem to be correlated. High-quality cycling infrastructure facilitates the use of bicycles by a wider audience (including vulnerable users): their development therefore seems to be a factor that increases the number of urban cyclists while reducing class, education and gender inequalities.

Biographical Approaches to Understanding Practices
Mastering a practice is a learning process and it takes time to acquire the requisite skills to "carry it out". Practices themselves are made up of many heterogeneous elements (Reckwitz, 2002) that Shove et al. (2012) group as "materials", "competences" and "meanings". "Materials" "include things, technologies, tangible physical entities and the stuff of which objects are made". Regarding cycling, material also includes environments (weather, road, topography) and "biological bodies" (Cox, 2019; Larsen, 2017). "Competences" refer to skills, expertise and techniques (Shove et al., 2012). For Larsen (2017), cycling competences include steering and balancing skills, and knowledge of the local traffic systems which implies that some people do not (yet) have the necessary competences to ride in a particular environment (Larsen, 2014; Spinney, 2007). By "meanings", Shove et al. (2012) refer to "symbolic meanings, ideas and aspirations" attached to specific practices within a broader context. In the case of cycling, the association is contradictory. It is portrayed as dangerous (Horton et al., 2007) and a source of stigmatization in some cases (Aldred & Jungnickel, 2012) but simultaneously as a source of freedom and well-being (Cox, 2019; Larsen, 2017). Those three elements are interconnected and influence each other. The trajectories of practices hinge on the connections between these three elements. Moreover, they change their meaning and popularity when the connections between them

are remade by innovation, policy, political movement, or fashion or consumer preferences (Shove et al., 2012).

Competence and meaning are linked to socialization. Studies of "mobility biographies" (see Müggenburg et al., 2015 for a literature review) underline the important role of socialization in the choice of modes and in the construction of mobility strategies. They also allow us to question the role played by materiality. The concept of socialization is generally defined as the repetitive dynamic of learning by individuals throughout their existence; learning which enables social coexistence as well as immersion within groups with which they share a sense of belonging, for example the family group or a work collective (Darmon, 2006). Who transmits what and how during socialization is decisive and makes it possible to specify the action of social norms, the modes of transmission as well as the references for effective action which mark out the history of individual socialization. Research on socialization distinguishes primary socialization, passed down through parental education, and secondary socialization acquired through individuals' successive experiences (Darmon, 2006; Lahire, 2013).

Studies of mobility highlight the influence of primary and secondary socialization on modal choices, on individual strategies of displacement, and on the social image of users and modes (Baslington, 2008; Kaufmann et al., 2015; Ortar et al., 2018; Rau & Manton, 2016; Sattlegger & Rau, 2016). The literature has shown that the initial learning of biking and continuous experience of it increasingly influence the skills of urban cyclists and build their identity as cyclists (Aldred, 2013). Starting to ride a bike daily is also the result of a multiplicity of events (Müggenburg et al., 2015) and socialization. Although research and monitoring carried out by national or local authorities highlight sex and social status of those cycling and where they ride, we still know relatively little about the effects of socialization and their interactions with instrumental parameters (gender, social background, income, places lived in, age) on the adoption or not of the bike on a daily basis. Links

Introduction

between changes in spatial organization (new infrastructure, new regulations) or transport policies (incentive or restrictive measures) and individual behaviour are weakly understood, although they are determining factors for adopting or abandoning the practice. For all these reasons, we believe that biographical approaches are necessary to understand the development of city cycling and obviously to answer the question: How does one become an urban cyclist?

Enlightening Cyclists' Practices, Socialization and Skills
This volume follows a workshop organized in Lyon (France) in February 2020 that brought together researchers from different backgrounds (sociology, anthropology and geography), studying different cities and countries (Australia, France, Germany, Switzerland, United Kingdom) and using various quantitative and qualitative methods. The choice of a multidisciplinary approach stems from several considerations. Firstly, research work on mobility learning and socialization is still scarce but emerges jointly from several disciplinary fields: sociology (Kaufmann, 2011), psychology (Baslington, 2008), geography (Donnelly et al., 2017), and even transport engineering (Manton & Rau, 2016). This book forms part of this general movement and expands its scope. While knowledge about cycling in the city is still lacking, especially with regard to socialization and skills, to restrict the inquiry to one discipline would amount to closing down an emerging field of research before it has fully opened up. Second, at the intersection of individual possibilities, spatial infrastructure of geographical areas, and social practices, city cycling is intrinsically an interdisciplinary theme. No discipline can therefore claim to exhaust the subject; each brings its methods and postulates, enhancing the reflection of readers and the future research this book will help to inspire. This interdisciplinarity is also visible in each of the chapters as, whatever their scientific background, all the authors draw on plural and varied theoretical and methodological resources.

Becoming Urban Cyclists

The volume focuses on the acquisition of skills and competences to supplement existing work linking cycling practices to individual life courses (Freudendal-Pedersen, 2015; Füssl & Haupt, 2017) or to gender (Song et al., 2019; Vogel et al., 2014). The objective is to shed light on geographical and sociological differences in order to help understand what is likely to facilitate or curb urban cycling practices.

The chapters treat both socialization to bicycle mobility (learning of the practice as such: how to ride, fit in with the traffic, park, etc.) and socialization through bicycle mobility (how cycling leads to learning about a city or about other road users, how it changes people's identity, etc.).

In the first chapter, starting from the Covid-19 pandemic which has created the need to develop contactless means of transport without creating congestion, Cox explores how during the 19th and the beginning of the 20th century the cyclability was created, how it collapses in most countries to re-emerge since the turn of the 21st century. Through a historical, political and comparative analysis, Cox describes how the acceleration and intensification of action to transform urban mobilities during the pandemic was made possible.

Adam et al. deal with the lived dimension of the cyclability of geographical areas and present the method that its authors used to access the perceptions of cyclists. Cyclability refers to the capacity of spaces to accommodate, facilitate and ensure the safety of cycling practices. Scientists and urban planners mostly use GIS-based methods for their evaluations. The indicators used are based on projections of factors already identified to increase or decrease people's ability to cycle in a given place. These evaluations are then compared with the actual experience of 40 commuters in the cities of Lyon and Saint-Étienne (France) and their appreciation of the territory in order to provide a "thick" understanding. It combined three methodological tools: measurement of trips by GPS tracking, analysis of video recordings from on-bike cameras, and interviews, during which tracking and videos were used to elicit reflection. The

Introduction

chapter analyses the strengths and weaknesses of the method and highlights how it affords access to the wealth of material that can shed light on the capacity of local authority areas to facilitate or hinder people's plans to become urban cyclists.

For observers of urban cycling, the rise of e-biking in developed countries is the most salient phenomenon of the last decade (Fishman & Cherry, 2016). Purchases of e-bikes are increasing and markets are growing rapidly. Marincek applies the conceptual framework of Chatterjee et al. (2012) to explore factors that prompt city dwellers in Switzerland to adopt e-biking. In particular, he is looking for "turning points", changes in life course (transport-related or not) that can trigger e-bike purchase. Through his biographical approach with 24 e-bike users in Lausanne, he analyses the role of key events, motivations, and prior experience of mobility in starting cycling or returning to cycling with the e-bike. He shows how influence of contextual events, biographical events and partner-related events can all influence choices. To recruit new or returning urban cyclists, Marincek proposes to use his results to target policies and, for example, focus the promotion of e-bikes on the key events he identifies.

With developing infrastructure and planning for bikes, awareness campaigns are a common tool for promoting utility cycling. In Switzerland, a yearly bike to work action brings together more than 50,000 commuters who commit to cycling to work in May and/or June as often as possible. Rérat addresses the various impacts of such a promotion campaign on the practice of utility cycling with a focus on skills and competences. Using data from a questionnaire survey with 14,000 participants in the 2016 bike-to-work action, Rérat uses Kaufmann's (2011) conceptualization of motility to show how the intervention attracts both new and not-so-regular utility cyclists for commuting trips. It is also a time when cycling potential may be improved by adapting their new bike or e-bike and equipment (rainwear, etc.). The structure of the bike-to-work scheme around work teams of colleagues is an especially effective means to exchange experiences that lead to new skills (choice of routes, behaviour in motorized traffic). Rérat's survey also highlights the need for urban planning for cycling to make cycling attractive, efficient and safe for a large and diverse range of users.

Caimotto takes an ecolinguistic approach to cycling, analysing discursive production in various cycling-related documentations: UK newspaper articles, institutional documents (UK and all Europe) and transcriptions of spoken discourse from the Cycling Cultures in a Mass Motorized Society project (Aldred, 2012, 2015). In doing so, she helps us to understand the different ways in which cycling promotion disseminates values, and their social and political implications. On the one hand, her results show that people who cycle are more inclined than average to appreciate narratives celebrating nature and to pay close attention to climate and environmental change. On the other hand, she highlights a marketization of cycling promotion that sometimes looks like business discourse, i.e. presenting the economic advantages as the most relevant ones (ahead of well-being, the environment, etc.). Caimotto correlates discourses to varying motivations to show how each is likely to attract different populations, depending on their connotation. Discourses (and images) used by elected officials, cyclists' associations or town planners draw different profiles of the future urban cyclists they imagine. Finally, Caimotto defends discourse that gives pride of place to the association between cycling, well-being and environmental protection.

Buhler works on what he calls adult beginner cyclists, i.e. people cycling for utility purposes on a rather regular basis but with low cycling skills. Studying various French cities using a quantitative transport panel survey, he estimates that adult beginner cyclists represent between 1.8% and 3% of the French urban population (i.e. between 600,000 and 1,000,000 cyclists). This number suggests that there is a large pool of French cyclists whose acquisition of better knowledge and skills could see them cycling on a daily basis, that

Introduction

is, they would become "true" urban cyclists. To go further, Buhler investigates who these adult beginner cyclists are and what makes them special. The data reveal no particular sociological profile. However, a second key result of his research shows that two-thirds of these adult beginners quit cycling during the year of the survey. This underlines the fact that beginners, even though adults, are a very vulnerable category of cyclists on which mobility policies and cycling associations should focus.

Among potential adult beginner cyclists are populations from immigrant backgrounds. Using data from the German national travel survey, a quantitative telephone survey conducted in Offenbach (in the western part of Germany), and qualitative interviews, Welsch focuses on the differences in cycling behaviour and socialization between people from immigrant and non-immigrant backgrounds. She shows that people not from a recent immigrant background are more likely to cycle. The fact that persons of the second generation cycle more readily (i.e. have basic cycling skills) than persons of the first generation, especially women, could indicate a kind of "transport assimilation" (using Welsch's words). However, this "assimilation" does not seem to be confirmed by the data about the frequency of bicycle use, which is as low for the first as for the second generation. Moreover, the second generation is even less likely to cycle on a weekly basis. Qualitative interviews with people with a Turkish background show that, according to perceived status in society, they consider that the bicycle ranks low on the scale, i.e. it is associated with poverty (whereas the car is the attribute of upward social mobility). Finally, Welsch advocates dedicated programmes like cycling courses for immigrant women that increase the proportion of people with cycling skills and a sustainable transport system that would be more inclusive.

Addressing the gender issue, Sayagh, Dusong and Papon note that almost everywhere women cycle less than men (Garrard et al., 2012). They use quantitative interviews conducted in the French metropolises of Montpellier and Strasbourg and in the inner

Becoming Urban Cyclists

suburbs of Paris. Drawing on the approach of Bonham and Wilson (2012), they focus on the key events that induce changes in "bicycle biographies": changes in physical condition, changes in social relations or family structure, moving house or place of work, etc. By doing so, Sayagh, Dusong and Papon try to answer the question: What makes women stop or start cycling in France? Crossing the variables of gender and age, they highlight the decline in cycling by women during their teens and link it to factors like body and identity changes, which in turn are shaped by social injunctions to be "feminine" or by getting access to a moped or a car. In adulthood, women often stop cycling when they become pregnant and do not go back to it when the children are growing up because they become their "taxi drivers". Moreover, when moving to an area of residence perceived as less bike-friendly, women are more likely to abandon cycling than men. While health problems may be a reason to stop cycling, they may also lead to take-up or resumption, e.g. for losing weight or on "doctor's orders". Going over a number of factors that cause people to stop or (re)start cycling, this chapter suggests that mobility biographies should influence the perception of different means of transport, of corporal and spatial dispositions of persons, of ecological concern, and of competencies and feelings of competence to ride and repair a bike.

Abord de Chatillon deals with bicycle maintenance and repair practices. Because cycling means minimally having a bicycle in a proper state-of-repair, becoming an urban cyclist requires knowing how to manage a breakdown or a simple adjustment. In addition, knowledge and mastery of bicycle mechanics contributes to shaping the urban cyclists' bodily relationship with their bicycle while riding. Unlike with cars, many people repair their own bicycles and very diverse repair and maintenance practices coexist. In her chapter, Abord de Chatillon compares attitudes between cyclists who are inexperienced in repairing and maintaining their bikes and those for whom repair and maintenance are easy and frequent activities. Using qualitative interviews from Melbourne (Australia) and Lyon

Introduction

(France), she sheds light on the process of acquisition of repair skills. She shows how learning to repair and maintain a bicycle in a workshop can lead to switching from the "bike-as-an-alien" to the bike as an appropriated machine, transforming the relationship between cyclists and their cycles. Reciprocally, cycling practices lead to a better mechanical knowledge of the bicycle and a better ability to repair and maintain it. This chapter thus demonstrates the entanglement between cycling practices and repair practices: the more capable you are of fixing your bike, the more likely you are to become a determined urban cyclist.

Together these narratives show that becoming urban cyclists proceeds by weaving strands of knowledge, of experience, of place, self-perceptions and socially constructed identities together. All of these further interact with the physical realities of urban space. Ultimately, becoming urban cyclists is shown as a process that cannot be formed through any single intervention, but engaging with the multiple dimensions of its practice to enrich our understanding of its complexity can provide pointers towards better interventions.

References

Aldred, R. (2010). "On the outside": Constructing cycling citizenship. *Social & Cultural Geography*, 11(1), 35–52. https://doi.org/10.1080/14649360903414593

Aldred, R. (2012). Cycling cultures: Summary of key findings and recommendations. https://westminsterresearch.westminster.ac.uk/item/8z5y3/cycling-cultures-summary-of-key-findings-and-recommendations

Aldred, R. (2013). Incompetent or too competent? Negotiating everyday cycling identities in a motor dominated society. *Mobilities*, 8(2), 252–271.

Aldred, R. (2015). A matter of utility? Rationalizing cycling, cycling rationalities. *Mobilities*, 10(5), 686–705.

Aldred, R., & Jungnickel, K. (2012). Constructing mobile places between "leisure" and "transport": A case study of two group cycle rides. *Sociology*, 46(3), 523–539.

Aldred, R., Woodcock, J., & Goodman, A. (2016). Does more cycling mean more diversity in cycling? *Transport Reviews, 36*(1), 28–44.

Altenried, M. (2019). On the last mile: Logistical urbanism and the transformation of labour. *Work Organisation, Labour & Globalisation, 13*(1), 114–129.

Baron, N. (2019, December). Bike mobilities, democratic revival and the local fix. Valencia, from corruption epicentre to Mediterranean cycle capital. *Belgeo. Revue Belge de Géographie, 4*. https://doi.org/10.4000/belgeo.36436

Baslington, H. (2008). Travel socialization: A social theory of travel mode behavior. *International Journal of Sustainable Transportation, 2*(2), 91–114. https://doi.org/10.1080/15568310601187193

Bonham, J., & Wilson, A. (2012). Bicycling and the life course: The start-stop-start experiences of women cycling. *International Journal of Sustainable Transportation, 6*(4), 195–213. https://doi.org/10.1080/15568318.2011.585219

Boterman, W. R. (2018). Carrying class and gender: Cargo bikes as symbolic markers of egalitarian gender roles of urban middle classes in Dutch inner cities. *Social & Cultural Geography, 21*(2), 245–264. https://doi.org/10.1080/14649365.2018.1489975

Bourne, J. E., Sauchelli, S., Perry, R., Page, A., Leary, A., England, C., & Cooper, A. R. (2018). Health benefits of electrically-assisted cycling: A systematic review. *International Journal of Behavioral Nutrition and Physical Activity, 15*(1), 116. https://doi.org/10.1186/s12966-018-0751-8

Burk, D. (2017). Infrastructure, social practice, and environmentalism: The case of bicycle-commuting. *Social Forces, 95*(3), 1209–1236. https://doi.org/10.1093/sf/sow100

Chatterjee, K., Sherwin, H., Jain, J., Christensen, J., & Marsh, S. (2012). Conceptual model to explain turning points in travel behavior application to bicycle use. *Transportation Research Record, 2322*(1), 82–90. https://doi.org/10.3141/2322-09

Chen, Z., van Lierop, D., & Ettema, D. (2020). Dockless bike-sharing systems: What are the implications? *Transport Reviews, 40*(3), 333–353. https://doi.org/10.1080/01441647.2019.1710306

Colville-Andersen, M. (2018). *Copenhagenize: The definitive guide to global bicycle urbanism*. Island Press.

Introduction

Cox, P. (2019). *Cycling: A sociology of velomobility*. Routledge.
Cox, P., & Koglin, T. (2020). *The politics of cycling infrastructure: Spaces and (in)equality*. Policy Press.
Cox, P., & Rzewnicki, R. (2015). Cargo bikes: Distributing consumer goods. In P. Cox (Ed.), *Cycling cultures* (pp. 130–151). University of Chester Press.
Cox, P., & Van de Walle, F. (2007). Bicycles don't evolve: Velomobiles and the modelling of transport technologies. In D. Horton, P. Rosen, & P. Cox (Eds.), *Cycling and Society* (pp. 129–148). Routledge. https://doi.org/10.4324/9781315575735-12
Darmon, M. (2006). *La socialisation*. Armand Colin.
Donnelly, L., Garfinkel, I., Brooks-Gunn, J., Wagner, B. G., James, S., & McLanahan, S. (2017). Geography of intergenerational mobility and child development. *Proceedings of the National Academy of Sciences, 114*(35): 9320–9325. https://doi.org/10.1073/pnas.1700945114
Duarte, F. (2016). Disassembling bike-sharing systems: Surveillance, advertising, and the social inequalities of a global technological assemblage. *Journal of Urban Technology, 23*(2), 103–115. https://doi.org/10.1080/10630732.2015.1102421
Feddes, F. (2019). *Bike city Amsterdam: How Amsterdam became the cycling capital of the world*. Uitgeverij Bas Lubberhuizen.
Fishman, E. (2016). Bikeshare: A review of recent literature. *Transport Reviews, 36*(1), 92–113. https://doi.org/10.1080/01441647.2015.1033036
Fishman, E., & Cherry, C. (2016). E-bikes in the mainstream: Reviewing a decade of research. *Transport Reviews, 36*(1), 72–91. https://doi.org/10.1080/01441647.2015.1069907
Fitch, D. T., Rhemtulla, M., & Handy, S. L. (2019). The relation of the road environment and bicycling attitudes to usual travel mode to school in teenagers. *Transportation Research. Part A, Policy and Practice, 123*, 35–53. https://doi.org/10.1016/j.tra.2018.06.013
Freudendal-Pedersen, M. (2015). Whose commons are mobilities spaces? – the case of Copenhagen's cyclists. *ACME an International e-Journal for Critical Geographies, 14*(2), 598–621.
Fuller, D., & Winters, M. (2017). Income inequalities in bike score and bicycling to work in Canada. *Journal of Transport & Health, 7*, 264–268. https://doi.org/10.1016/j.jth.2017.09.005

Füssl, E., & Haupt, J. (2017). Understanding cyclist identity and related interaction strategies. A novel approach to traffic research. *Transportation Research. Part F, Traffic Psychology and Behaviour, 46*, 329–341. https://doi.org/10.1016/j.trf.2016.08.003

Garrard, J., Handy, S., & Dill, J. (2012). Women and cycling. In J. Pucher, & R. Buehler (Eds.), *City cycling* (pp. 211–234). MIT Press.

Goodman, A., & Aldred, R. (2018). Inequalities in utility and leisure cycling in England, and variation by local cycling prevalence. *Transportation Research. Part F, Traffic Psychology and Behaviour, 56*, 381–391. https://doi.org/10.1016/j.trf.2018.05.001

Götschi, T., Garrard, J., & Giles-Corti, B. (2016). Cycling as a part of daily life: A review of health perspectives. *Transport Reviews, 36*(1), 45–71. https://doi.org/10.1080/01441647.2015.1057877

Héran, F. (2014). *Le retour de la bicyclette : une histoire des déplacements urbains en Europe, de 1817 à 2050*. La Découverte.

Héran, F. (2018). *Système vélo*. Forum Vies Mobiles. https://fr.forumviesmobiles.org/reperes/systeme-velo-12437

Horton, D., Cox, P., & Rosen, P. (2007). Introduction: Cycling and society. In D. Horton, P. Rosen, & P. Cox (Eds.), *Cycling and society* (pp. 1–24). Routledge.

Humphreys, D. K., Goodman, A., & Ogilvie, D. (2013). Associations between active commuting and physical and mental wellbeing. *Preventive Medicine, 57*(2), 135–139. https://doi.org/10.1016/j.ypmed.2013.04.008

Kaplan, S., Wrzesinska, D. K., & Prato, C. G. (2018). The role of culture and needs in the cycling habits of female immigrants from a driving-oriented to a cycling-oriented country. *Transportation Research Record, 2672*(3), 155–165. https://doi.org/10.1177/0361198118793242

Kaufmann, V. (2011). *Rethinking the city: Urban dynamics and motility*. Routledge.

Kaufmann, V., Ravalet, E., & Dupuit, É. (Eds.). (2015). *Motilité & mobilité : mode d'emploi*. Éditions Alphil.

Kidder, J. L. (2016). Hollywood, bike messengers, and the new economy. *Critical Sociology, 42*(2), 307–322. https://doi.org/10.1177/0896920513516024

Lahire, B. (2013). *Dans les plis singuliers du social : individus, institutions, socialisations*. Collection Laboratoire des sciences sociales. La Découverte.

Introduction

Larsen, J. (2014). (Auto)ethnography and cycling. *International Journal of Social Research Methodology*, *17*(1), 59–71. https://doi.org/10.1080/13645579.2014.854015

Larsen, J. (2017). The making of a pro-cycling city: Social practices and bicycle mobilities. *Environment and Planning A: Economy and Space*, *49*(4): 876–92. https://doi.org/10.1177/0308518x16682732

Larsen, J. (2018). Commuting, exercise and sport: An ethnography of long-distance bike commuting. *Social & Cultural Geography*, *19*(1), 39–58. https://doi.org/10.1080/14649365.2016.1249399

Müggenburg, H., Busch-Geertsema, A., & Lanzendorf, M. (2015). Mobility biographies: A review of achievements and challenges of the mobility biographies approach and a framework for further research. *Journal of Transport Geography*, *46*, 151–163. https://doi.org/10.1016/j.jtrangeo.2015.06.004

Ortar, N. (2019). What the e-bike tells us about the anthropology of energy. In S. Abram, B. R. Winthereik, & T. Yarrow (Eds.), *Electrifying anthropology. Exploring electrical practices and infrastructures* (pp. 83–99). Bloomsbury.

Ortar, N., Salzbrunn, M., & Stock, M. (Éds.). (2018). *Migrations, circulations, mobilités. Nouveaux enjeux épistémologiques et conceptuels à l'épreuve du terrain*. Presses Universitaires de Provence.

Parkin, J. (2012). *Cycling and sustainability*. Emerald.

Pucher, J., & Buehler, R., (Eds.). (2012). *City cycling*. MIT Press.

Rau, H., & Manton, R. (2016). Life events and mobility milestones: Advances in mobility biography theory and research. *Journal of Transport Geography*, *52*(C), 51–60.

Reckwitz, A. (2002). Toward a theory of social practices: A development in culturalist theorizing. *European Journal of Social Theory*, *5*(2), 243–263. https://doi.org/10.1177/13684310222225432

Rérat, P., Giacomel, G., & Martin, A. (2019). *Au travail à vélo... : La pratique utilitaire de la bicyclette en Suisse*. Éditions Alphil.

Sattlegger, L., & Rau, H. (2016). Carlessness in a car-centric world: A reconstructive approach to qualitative mobility biographies research. *Journal of Transport Geography*, *53*, 22–31.

Shaw, C., Russell, M., Keall, M., MacBride-Stewart, S., Wild, K., Reeves, D., Bentley, R., & Woodward, A. (2020, September). Beyond the bicycle: Seeing the context of the gender gap in cycling. *Journal of Transport & Health, 18,* 100871. https://doi.org/10.1016/j.jth.2020.100871

Shove, E., Pantzar, M., & Watson, M. (2012). *The dynamics of social practice: Everyday life and how it changes.* Sage.

Soemers, J. (2016). *Steps towards an active future. A study on the influences on transport mode choice to school among Dutch adolescents.* [Unpublished Master's thesis]. Utrecht University.

Song, L., Kirschen, M., & Taylor, J. (2019). Women on wheels: Gender and cycling in Solo, Indonesia. *Singapore Journal of Tropical Geography, 40*(1), 140–157. https://doi.org/10.1111/sjtg.12257

Spinney, J. (2007). Cycling the city: Non-place and the sensory construction of meaning in a mobile practice. In D. Horton, P. Rosen, & P. Cox, *Cycling and Society* (pp. 25–45). Ashgate.

Stehlin, J. G. (2019). *Cyclescapes of the unequal city: Bicycle infrastructure and uneven development.* University of Minnesota Press.

Steinbach, R., Green, J., Datta, J., & Edwards, P. (2011). Cycling and the city: A case study of how gendered, ethnic and class identities can shape healthy transport choices. *Social Science & Medicine, 72*(7), 1123–1130. https://doi.org/10.1016/j.socscimed.2011.01.033

Vivanco, L. A. (2013). *Reconsidering the bicycle: An anthropological perspective on a new (old) thing.* Routledge.

Vogel, M., Hamon, R., Lozenguez, G., Merchez, L., Abry, P., Barnier, J., Borgnat, P., Flandrin, P., Mallon, I., & Robardet, C. (2014). From bicycle sharing system movements to users: A typology of Vélo'v cyclists in Lyon based on large-scale behavioural dataset. *Journal of Transport Geography, 41,* 280–291. https://doi.org/10.1016/j.jtrangeo.2014.07.005

CHAPTER 1
BECOMING AN URBAN CYCLING SPACE
Peter Cox

Introduction

Within a few short weeks from the authors of this volume meeting together to share their ideas in February 2020, the situations about which they were writing individually and collectively were dramatically reshaped by the need to respond to Covid-19. Social spaces and spaces of urban mobilities shifted from being viewed as sources of conviviality and of positive anticipation to locations of threat and risk (Cresswell, 2021). Across Europe, lockdowns restricted travel and constrained outdoor activity, although conditions and restrictions varied country by country (Salazar, 2021). Simultaneously, cycle travel was rapidly identified as a vital area for support: cycle suppliers and maintenance were classified as essential retail (Bicycle Association, 2021; Morley, 2020).

Work practices shifted. Where possible, white-collar jobs moved to work from home, immediately cutting out a significant portion of urban and sub-urban travel. Other workplaces closed: workers furloughed or unemployed had lives immensely disrupted. Again, once ingrained travel practices were undone in a matter of days. Essential work and tasks of social reproduction still required continued travel, but the pandemic reshaped travel possibilities, especially for those previously reliant on public transport. Primarily, two parallel dimensions of urban travel affected by the pandemic required addressing rapidly. First, urban journeys that would normally have taken place by public transport needed to be replaced in light of the hugely diminished capacity of mass transport systems under physical distancing precautions. Shifts to home working may have decreased travel but did not mean that mass transport systems were no longer required. Passenger fears of viral contamination were matched by transport operators' and public authorities' fears of losing passengers to increased motoring. Second, lockdowns were recognized to have significant disbenefits for physical and mental health, both of which could be addressed by active travel. The multiple benefits previously recognized in numerous advocacy documents (ECF, 2017) and academic studies (for example, Buehler & Pucher, 2021) were made strikingly visible. But increased rates of walking and cycling required more space for safely distanced travel. Simultaneously, the rapid drop in car traffic and on-street parking revealed the scale of urban space normally occupied by private motorized travel. Responding to need and opportunity, a range of infrastructural interventions were rapidly implemented.

As of March 2021, about a year after the majority of lockdowns commenced, the European Cyclists' Federation (ECF) Covid-19 measures tracker (https://ecf.com/dashboard) counted 2,571.84km of new infrastructure measures planned across Europe, of which 1,419.88km had already been implemented, combined with budgetary allocations of €1,172,742,723. In their global overview of new cycling measures implemented in response to the pandemic, Combs and Pardo (2021) recorded 1,313 discrete actions in 524 cities, states or provinces globally by the end of 2020. Undoubtedly, this has been the most rapid transformation of city spaces for cycling to date, but these changes did not appear by accident or through serendipitous generosity and farsightedness of planners and policy makers (Ponkshe, 2020). Rather, they should be understood as a continuation of more than 100 years of interaction between cyclists and the places in which they ride. Causative agency for change, this chapter will show, lies both in those who plan infrastructure and in the cyclists themselves: cities shape cycling and cyclists shape cities.

The Covid-19 pandemic crisis has not entirely created a new relation between cyclists and the city. Instead, existing relations are intensified and patterns of change dramatically accelerated (Batty, 2020). Importantly as we shall see, patterns of change are not unidirectional. Conflicts over urban space, mobility and legitimacy are also intensified. Divergent forces impel different models of change, producing contending, often irreconcilable outcomes.

In these processes, we find that the rapid transformations of city spaces have dramatically altered both perceptions of the spaces in which cyclists ride the city and the possibilities of becoming an urban cyclist: for better and for worse. To understand these changes and impacts better, the chapter first looks back in a wider historic context to show the double process of cyclists adapting to existing European cities and how, in turn, the presence of cyclists changed the cities themselves. It then examines some of the adaptations produced in response to the pandemic and the ways in which this has made cities appear different spaces for cycling. Finally, it examines some of the emergent policy frameworks produced during this time and their implications for future relations between cyclists and other forms of urban mobility.

Contended Histories of Urban Cycling in the 19th and Early 20th Centuries

There was no automatic alignment between city and the bicycle in its early years. The high-wheeler was not a machine for easy stop-start riding. Tricycles suggested more sedate (and less gendered) possibilities of travel, better adapted to urban life, but until the advent of mass production, all cycles (bicycles and tricycles) remained expensive, hand-built luxuries. Their users had to make the case for their use in shared public space. They did not arrive into pre-existing urban mobility scapes as we understand them today. Urban roads were not primarily circulatory spaces: this emerging 19th-century use was in tragic conflict with their prior understanding as ambulatory spaces, as growing concerns over street deaths, especially of children, testified.

Many cities remained unsure of how to treat this new intruder, some (like Vienna) choosing to outlaw it altogether. In the UK, organized user groups—and, of course, these were the clubs of social elites—used their positions to argue for tolerance and recognition as an equal conveyance to any horse-drawn carriage (Lightwood, 1928). Changing employment patterns and places, together with increased traffic by omnibus and tramcar reshaped the urban street into a circulatory space. It was in this context that the safety bicycle came into its own in the 1890s. Immediately, cyclists became protestors and advocates for road improvements, for equalization of traffic codes and laws (Epperson, 2014; Reid, 2014). From the very earliest years therefore, cities became spaces for cyclists through the actions of cyclists themselves.

Oldenziel et al. (2016) valuably chart the diverse experience of European cities in their different relationships with cycling over the course of the 20th century; it is unwise to oversimplify the complex patterns of interaction of social and political forces and modes and powers of governance that shape specific cities' experiences of cycling and cyclists' experiences of those cities. Nevertheless, some broader observations can usefully be made, drawing primarily on data from the UK (see Cox, 2012). The physical dominance of motor vehicles had become highly apparent in the 1930s through the rapid growth of road traffic casualties among pedestrians and cyclists. The dominant position of motor traffic was further enhanced by its repeated prioritization in traffic planning models and in the light-touch regulation enacted to curb motor dominance or punish motoring transgressions. Urban streets had become primarily circulatory spaces, despite the relatively low numbers of motor vehicles in comparison to cycles. The advent of mass private motoring in the post-war years, especially in the boom of the 1960s brought the conflicts to a head.

By the late 1960s, it was becoming clear that cities across Western Europe, designed around mediaeval patterns of walking plus animal traction vehicles, could not cope with mass motorization. City squares that had formerly been markets and meeting places had become car parks; streets were no longer safe to walk in. At the same time, there was growing global concern with the impact of human life on the environment and the effects of pollution, particularly noticeable in urban areas. Added to this mix of forces, youth movements of the 1960s, and the events of 1968 in particular, had begun to re-imagine the city as a vibrant place, articulated most clearly in Lefebvre's (1968) analysis of the "Right to the City". They had also discovered the power of citizen action: the idea that people themselves could make changes directly, not just relying on the slow process of parliaments.

The problem for urban administrations was how to deal with increasingly congested, polluted and unsafe cities. Pedestrianization of city centres and investment in public transport systems comprised one set of responses. Another way of addressing these problems (and not entirely incompatible with the previous) was to insist that cities should be rebuilt in order to accommodate the car. As long as the car equated with modernity, this was entirely logical, and governments encouraged travel by car as a symbol of success. However, the cost of this rebuilding appeared too high for many citizens. It meant the destruction of exactly those things that they treasured about the city, its historic pattern buildings and layout, and its communities. Protests against urban motorways such as those in Paris culminated in mass protest not only against the proposed construction but also as mobilizations of cyclists specifically for a different kind of city development. The 3 April 1972 "Bike-In" demonstration (mobilizing the then common protest language and form of the sit-in) focused its concern on the proposal for a four-lane highway along the left bank of the Seine (Bess, 2003; Samuel, 2006). Fully 18 months before the energy crisis of 1973 prompted more recalcitrant governments to think about their increasing reliance on cheap oil, cyclists had acted as urban travellers to demand redress to what they saw as the usurping of the city by the car. They were not the only voices and cycling protests were usually integrated within other identities of collectively organized protests, rather than as stand- (or ride-)alone expressions of dissent. The newly formed Friends of the Earth/Amis de la Terre in both France and England was particularly important as a catalyst. Protest actions to highlight the dangers faced by urban

Becoming Urban Cyclists

cycle travellers in cities dominated by motor vehicles, alongside the presentation of concrete proposals for improvements to make for better riding and walking conditions showed both sides of the desire for change. Of course, such involvement with local authorities could only happen where there was sufficient access for activists to inaugurate dialogue with decision makers and sufficient and willing agency within local government to initiate change.

Waves of urban protests in the 1970s led to formations of national co-ordinating bodies to articulate the voices of cycle travellers as cyclists. Fietersbond in The Netherlands and the ADFC in West Germany both coalesced as special interest groups for cyclists from wider initiatives concerned with urban change. In Canada, Montreal's Le Monde à Bicyclette was founded in 1975 using street theatre and "die-ins", where cyclists lay down on the roads or in city squares beside their bikes mimicking road casualties. Other much older and longstanding groups such as the CTC in the UK and the Danish Cyclists' Federation were challenged and invigorated to rethink their role with respect to city cycling. These latter examples provide clear illustration of the divergent roles that cycle activism could take. The Danish Cyclists' Federation wholeheartedly endorsed protests as a means of confrontation, not negotiation, with civic authorities, organizing mass protests and demanding changes to planning priorities. Membership numbers grew from 3,000 in 1975 to 25,000 in 1980 (Cox, 2015). In the UK the CTC (at national level) ultimately left it to other coalitions to campaign for cycling as urban travel, electing to centralize concern for cycling as a leisure pursuit, although, importantly, local CTC groups did form significant parts of urban transport action groups. For years, cyclists had adapted to the gradual processes of change resulting from the growth of private motoring and its stealthy takeover of public city spaces. From the 1980s, growing and organized voices demanded changes to the ways in which cities regulated space (or regulated its use at all) and sought the restoration of urban life for non-motorized activity on a human scale.

Becoming an Urban Cycling Space

Individual city transitions from the domination of motor traffic were made in some specific cases—most notably perhaps in Amsterdam and Copenhagen. Comparative study of the two cases shows no simple or single policy or even policy framework as responsible (Koglin et al., 2021). Instead, a complex of factors was, and continues to be involved. Whatever prior history either city had as a centre of cycling activity earlier in the 20th century, there was no inevitability that they would then turn from the trajectory of motor domination that had been commonly initiated in the 1960s.

Amsterdam's emergence with a 21st-century reputation as a cycling city was contingent on shifting and unplanned factors (Feddes et al., 2019). It was not the product of a linear and logical sequence of reforms. Continuity in the direction of change depended on the constant vigilance and action of participants in the city's planning processes. The role of advocates themselves, able to re-imagine the city (and not just in terms of cycling) was crucial. Cycling as a dominant mobility strand emerged out of a broader rethinking of urban priorities. These were especially visible as cycling stood as an adjunct to growing concern with environmentalism and a wider human ecology (Rosen, 2002). Pro-cycling policies were achieved, not primarily in the pursuit of cycling policies in and of themselves, but as part of a wider agenda of urban regeneration and renewal. When expertise was required to design and to plan for modal shift to encourage cycle traffic back to the city, organized advocate groups were able to supply personnel. This pattern mimics observations of activist knowledge and expertise in more recent studies on climate protests. Corry and Reiner (2021) find high levels of policy engagement in their study of radical climate activists, often erroneously described by opponents as hopelessly idealistic. Far from being disengaged with the minutiae of policy process and change, investigation reveals high levels of knowledge of the issues and practicalities involved—often more than those administratively responsible.

Becoming Urban Cyclists

Among cycling activists, this pattern of deep engagement with policy and planning has a long history. For example, cycling advocates have campaigned for and initiated road improvements and signage for public safety since the 19th century. Citizen advocates are a necessary part of political life, shaping the city through their actions, both visibly protesting and in more hidden ways through advice and engagement, often as vital contributors to unremarked committees (see Emanuel, 2020). As noted above, detailed study of the Amsterdam case reveals how activists were incorporated into city planning processes relatively early on specifically to provide insights not available within existing management. However, this crucially requires an open policy-making process that is able and willing to engage with and incorporate perspectives outside its own. Without permeable borders in the administrative structures that can allow for flow between full-time, professional urban administrators and knowledgeable citizens who bring their own expertise to bear on the problems, and without space for meaningful dialogue between these two groups, progress cannot be made.

In her studies of advocacy, action and policy, Aldred (2012a, 2012b, 2013) reveals how changing policy regimes differ in the effects that they have on outcomes. In particular, the different systems of administration imposed in London, and their widely contrasting organizational processes have, by turns, encouraged and frustrated dialogue between administrators and those whose mobilities are shaped by their actions. Without consistency and a long-term strategy that exists beyond electoral cycles, the possibilities of citizen action and meaningful change are very much reduced despite the rhetoric that may surround policy innovations (Purnell, 2012).

Changing Demands on Cities: Changing Demands of Cities

Cities become spaces for cyclists, therefore, by a complex set of interactions between citizens and polity. This is considerably facilitated where cities have competence and accountability, in line with broader agendas for sustainability. Indeed, it is in the context of a wider consideration of sustainable urban development, especially in response to climate change imperatives (While & Whitehead, 2013), that the most significant shifts, which have restructured urban mobilities for cycling have taken place recently. This trend is part of a discursive shift around sustainability that has moved attention to the city as a site for sustainability (Angelo & Wachsmuth, 2020), but also one which correlates with international attention on cities as the locus of change. The corollary of this approach, however, is that where there is insufficient democratic decentralization to cities, it is hard to bring about meaningful change (Pieterse, 2019).

Nevertheless, reflecting this broader agenda shift of an expanded concern for sustainability post 2000, an increasingly professionalized process of advocacy and lobbying has been built up. It is backed by substantial academic analysis, in order to link cycling and sustainability agendas (social and environmental) and to ensure that shifts towards cycling are an inescapable dimension of current patterns of urban change (see e.g. Bonham & Johnson, 2015; Buehler & Pucher, 2021; Gerike & Parkin, 2015; Golub et al., 2016; Parkin, 2012; Zuev et al., 2021). Simultaneously, of course, advocacy has constantly reinvented itself through grassroots countercultural actions, not dependent on official justifications or professional legitimation of any kind. However, for the purposes of this discussion I want to focus on the implications of the growth of cycling in transport discourse as part of a package of re-imagined urban sustainability.

The downside of the professionalization is that cycling has become, as Spinney (2021) eloquently describes, a way to "fix" wider problems of urban unsustainability—social, environmental and economic. This critique pivots on the danger that successful interventions to increase cycling nevertheless succeed ultimately in sustaining undesirable, exploitative economic relations embedded in the city as a model of capital reproduction (Spinney, 2021). A second and allied approach is concerned with the way in which, even when social and environmental sustainabilities are centralized, the dominance of technocratic approaches inherent in much transport planning subjectifies human activity (Cox, 2020). Creating the right conditions through careful planning agendas will prompt an automatic reaction for citizen travellers. Behaviour changes, it is assumed, will occur because of the sufficient accumulation of triggers: the right infrastructure and the right social and moral pressures. Here the human experience becomes a behaviourist experiment. These difficulties become doubly pertinent in the face of changes enacted by urban administrations as part of the response to Covid-19, as we will see below.

Covid-19: Remaking the Cycling City
Combs and Pardo (2021, p. 2) observe that "where previously pedestrian and bicycle infrastructure projects took years if not decades to plan, fund, and build, agencies were starting to introduce temporary measures that went from inception to installation in a matter of weeks and sometimes days", frequently as a result of emergency powers given to local leaders. Rapidity of intervention and apparent lack of transparency or accountability have equally prompted a backlash against interventions, whether justified or not (Aldred, 2020; Lewis, 2020; Wall, 2020). Rather than concentrating on the controversy and its justifications, the task here is to consider the ways in which cities have remade themselves to encourage cyclists and how city designs shape how cycle users, especially those newly encouraged by the relative lack of motor traffic, learn to ride the city. Importantly we ask whether pandemic-prompted interventions might also be means by which cycling can address the broader complex of crisis facing urban life beyond Covid-19.

Over a third of the responses in Combs and Pardo's survey of Covid-19 mobility measures involve either reallocation of one or more traffic lanes to walking and cycling, or partial or full street closures to facilitate walking and cycling. Importantly, allocating a car-width lane to cycle traffic creates a very different space for movement than the conventional 1.5m segregated cycle lane. As

Becoming an Urban Cycling Space

Spinney (2021) points out, narrow lanes create a particular type of movement: linear, uniform in velocity and asocial, in that they are not designed for side-by-side travel, a mode that remains the privilege of urban car motoring. The reallocation of full lane width, or even full road use, is a much more significant move than might first appear. It allows for a multiplicity of types of use and of users, it facilitates the diversity of uses and users such as cargo bikes, recumbents, tricycles and other wheeled modes that are created as "abnormal" by conventional cycle facility design. Significantly, Spinney also points out the ways in which this multiplicity of activities allows for urban mobilities not framed within the productivist utilitarianism that values cycle journeys primarily as commuting trips responsible for economic reproduction (2021).

Dominant analyses of space allocation for urban mobility proceed on the basis of scarcity: space as a precious resource that must be eked out between competing users. What this does not consider is the vastly differential consumption of space required by urban motoring. Removing the unexamined and frequently unchallenged central obstacle allows a re-imagining of the urban space and realization that if car traffic is not made central, that street space is not a scarce commodity but sufficient for human scale use—as its historical formation suggests. Remarkably, the tide of opinion and analysis would have appeared to be turning even prior to the pandemic. The International Transport Forum analysis for the OECD, *Reversing Car Dependency* (ITF, 2021) drew from roundtable discussions in Paris in December 2019. Its central thesis is that the consumption of urban space by cars is no longer tenable: "The cost to society is too high to ignore" (ITF, 2021, p. 9). While the report as a whole continues to analyse through a model of scarcity, it is clear that that scarcity of urban space is created by the presence of urban motoring, and the outcomes are focused on means by which over-reliance on motor vehicles can be reduced.

Reimagining city space through a different lens has the advantage of opening up the purposes and modes of urban mobility.

Becoming Urban Cyclists

No longer need allocation be justified in utilitarian-productivist terms, in which justification for interventions comes through the most cost-effective use of space and that which contributes most to economic reproduction. Urban mobilities are also about interaction, playfulness—disutility: all those qualities that make life desirable rather than simply a repetitive production of labour in service of an abstract economy. What would city cycling spaces look like if they were designed as more than the most efficient means to avoid lingering (which is ultimately what efficient movement from A to B entails)? One of the continued problems of becoming urban cyclists is the constant risk, as encountered by professionalized cycle advocacy, that in order to appear legitimate, cycling is reduced to a means through which the city secures economic benefits. Whether in terms of more efficient traffic circulation, better air quality, more liveable (and therefore economically valuable) neighbourhoods, reduced health care costs: each of these recognized benefits of cycling that might justify intervention and infrastructure delivery is wedded to the maintenance and reproduction of urban forms that may already be problematic.

For example, Kern's work on *The Feminist City* (2020) urges us to consider profound gendering of cityscapes and urban experience in the way that they reproduce inequalities rather than opening spaces of possibility and equality (Kern, 2020). Similar analyses are made by Ravensbergen et al. (2019), Lubitow et al. (2019) and Lam (2020). To these concerns with gender equity, we might also think more deeply about the deeper implications of climate change and sustainability. While urban cycling has a profoundly important role to play in lessening carbon emissions from transport, the question needs to be asked whether its utilitarian efficiency as urban transport is merely a means to prolong fundamentally untenable economic models of growth (Cox, forthcoming, 2021; Spinney, 2021).

Turning these concerns to a more positive perspective, the most successful and accepted schemes were those that built on existing interventions, such as in Barcelona, Milan and Paris.

Becoming an Urban Cycling Space

Notably cycling here has been part of a broader re-imagining of the purpose and organization of the city itself, as a place to live and work: consequently, the 70% reported growth in cycling numbers in Paris during the first two pandemic lockdowns comes as little surprise. A final observation on pandemic interventions is pertinent here. Acceleration and intensification of action to transform urban mobilities during the pandemic can only occur meaningfully (and with any chance of long-term change) where there is already activity, even if only background. Activity cannot only be one sided. If there is minimal existing meaningful dialogue between city authorities and civil society agency then any changes are likely to be widely experienced as an imposition upon a public, rather than a materialization of collective desire. Intervention must be about democratizing public spaces, making them belong to all and to include all. This will require confronting the degree to which private motoring, popularly but erroneously viewed as allowing mobility for all, actually serves as a powerful exclusionary presence in contemporary cities. That existing urban cyclists have pioneered possibilities for urban travel even when without infrastructure and support, means that it becomes easier for others to experience the possibilities of the city by bike in lockdown conditions. Existing social anxieties have always been projected onto mobile subjects especially cyclists (Gant & Hoffman, 2013). To experience this today is nothing new. Cycling the city and becoming an urban cyclist is not an alien identity. Finally, as urban cycling moves out of a frame of transport, counter-intuitively it becomes more valuable, not less. The pandemic has provided opportunity for urban transformations but from initial analyses, the most powerful agency for urban cycling comes from the recognition that the multiple crises of Covid-19, climate change, gender and racial inequalities, social exclusions through age and ability are interwoven and interact through the fabric of cities. Cities are spaces of human dwelling—to become an urban cyclist for the 21st century is to re-imagine the urban journey space as an opportunity for all.

Becoming Urban Cyclists

Note: Material on the history of urban cycle campaigns has been adapted from P. Cox, (2017) "Fahrräder, Proteste und Wandel: Radfahrer als Gestalter von Städten und Maschinen" in B. Gundler & F. Steinbeck (Eds.). *Balanceakte: 200 Jahre Zweirad. Technik – Kultur – Mobilität*. Munich: Deutsches Museum [German only].

References

Aldred, R. (2012a). Governing transport from welfare state to hollow state: The case of cycling in the UK. *Journal of Transport Policy, 23*, 95–102.

Aldred, R. (2012b). The role of advocacy and activism. In J. Parkin (Ed.), *Cycling and sustainability* (pp. 83–108). Emerald.

Aldred, R. (2013). Who are Londoners on bikes and what do they want? Negotiating identity and issue definition in a "pop-up" cycle campaign. *Journal of Transport Geography, 30*, 94–201. https://doi.org/10.1016/j.jtrangeo.2013.01.005

Aldred R. (2020). Built environment interventions to increase active travel: A critical review and discussion. *Current Environmental Health Reports 6*(4), 309–315.

Angelo, H., & Wachsmuth, D. (2020). Why does everyone think cities can save the planet? *Urban Studies, 57*(11), 2201–2221. https://doi.org/10.1177/0042098020919081

Batty, M. (2020). The Coronavirus crisis: What will the post-pandemic city look like? *EPB: Urban Analytics and City Science, 47*(4), 547–552. DOI: 10.1177/2399808320926912

Bess, M. (2003). *The light green society: Ecology and technological modernity in France, 1960–2000*. University of Chicago Press.

Bicycle Association. (2021). https://www.bicycleassociation.org.uk/news-press/covid-19-cycling-hub/

Bonham, J., & Johnson, M. (Eds.). (2015). *Cycling futures*. University of Adelaide Press.

Buehler, R., & Pucher, J. (Eds.). (2021). *Cycling for sustainable cities*. MIT Press.

Combs, T. S., & Pardo, C. F. (2021). Shifting streets COVID-19 mobility data: Findings from a global dataset and a research agenda for transport planning and policy, *Transportation Research Interdisciplinary Perspectives, 9*. https://doi.org/10.1016/j.trip.2021.100322

Corry, O., & Reiner, D. (2021). Protests and policies: How radical social movement activists engage with climate policy dilemmas. *Sociology, 55*(1), 197–217. https://doi.org/10.1177/0038038520943107

Cox, P. (2012). "A denial of our boasted civilisation": Cyclists and conflicts over road use in Britain, 1926–1935. *Transfers, 2*(3), 4–30.

Cox, P. (2015, 13–14 February). *Cycling, environmentalism and change in 1970s Britain*. Paper delivered at Mobility and Environment Conference. Kerschensteiner Kolleg, Deutsches Museum, Munich.

Cox, P. (2020). Theorising infrastructure: A politics of spaces and edges. In T. Koglin & P. Cox (Eds.), *The politics of cycling infrastructure* (pp. 15–34). Policy Press.

Cox, P. (forthcoming, 2021). Vélomobility is to degrowth as automobility is to growth. *Applied Mobilities [Special issue on Autonomobilities]*.

Cresswell, T. (2021). Valuing mobility in a post COVID-19 world. *Mobilities, 16*(1), 51–65. DOI: 10.1080/17450101.2020.1863550

ECF – European Cyclists' Federation. (2017). *EU Cycling Strategy. Recommendations for delivering green growth and an effective mobility system in 2030*. https://ecf.com/eu_cycling_strategy

Emanuel, M. (2020). Conflictual politics of sustainability: Cycling organisations and the Øresund crossing. In T. Koglin & P. Cox (Eds.), *The politics of cycling infrastructure: Spaces and (in)equality* (pp. 157–178). Policy Press.

Epperson, B. (2014). *Bicycles in American highway planning: The critical years of decision-making, 1969–1991*. McFarland & Co.

Feddes, F., de Lange, M., & te Brömmelstroet, M. (2019). Hard work in paradise: The contested making of Amsterdam as a cycling city. In P. Cox & T. Koglin (Eds.), *The politics of cycling infrastructure: Spaces and (in)equality* (pp. 133–156). Policy Press.

Gant, J. J., & Hoffman, N. J. (2013). *Wheel fever. How Wisconsin became a great bicycling state*. Wisconsin Historical Press.

Gerike, R., & Parkin, J. (Eds.). (2015). *Cycling futures*. Ashgate.

Golub, A., Hoffman, M. L., Lugo, A., & Sandoval, G. F. (2016). *Bicycle justice and urban transformation. Biking for all?* Routledge.

ITF – International Transport Forum. (2021). *Reversing car dependency: Summary and conclusions*. ITF Roundtable Reports, No. 181. OECD Publishing.

Kern, L. (2020). *Feminist city: Claiming space in a man-made world*. Verso.

Koglin, T., te Brömmelstroet, M., & van Wee, B. (2021). Cycling in Copenhagen and Amsterdam. In R. Beuehler & J. Pucher (Eds.), *Cycling for sustainable cities*. MIT Press.

Lam, T. F. (2020). Cycling London: An intersectional feminist perspective. In T. P. Uteng, H. R. Christensen, & L. Levin (Eds.), *Gendering smart mobilities*. Routledge.

Lefebvre, H. (1968). *Le droit à la ville*. Anthropos.

Lewis, T. (2020, 1 November). Car-free neighbourhoods: The unlikely new frontline in the culture wars. *The Observer*. https://www.theguardian.com/lifeandstyle/2020/nov/01/car-free-neighbourhoods-the-unlikely-new-frontline-in-the-culture-wars

Lightwood, J. T. (1928). *The Cyclists' Touring Club: Being the romance of fifty years' cycling*. CTC.

Lubitow, A., Tompkins, K., & Feldman, M. (2019). Sustainable cycling for all? Race and gender-based bicycling inequalities in Portland, Oregon. *City & Community*, 18(4), 1181–1202. https://doi.org/10.1111/cico.12470

Morley, R. (2020). *UK bike shops can remain open during COVID-19 lockdown*. bikebiz. https: //www.bikebiz.com/uk-bike-shops-can-remain-open-during-covid-19-lockdown/

Oldenziel, R., Emanuel, M., Albert de la Bruheze, A., & Veraart, F. (Eds.). (2016). *Cycling cities: The European experience: 100 hundred years of policy and practice*. Foundation for the History of Technology, pp. 100–112.

Parkin, J., (Ed.). (2012). *Cycling and sustainability*. Emerald.

Pieterse, E. (2019). Urban governance and spatial transformation ambitions in Johannesburg. *Journal of Urban Affairs*, 41(1), 20–38.

Ponkshe, A. (2020). Transportation must reform in the post-pandemic era. In A. Ratho & P. L. John (Eds.), *Rethinking cities in a post-Covid-19 world* (pp. 44–51). ORF and *Global Policy Journal*.

Purnell S. (2012). *Pedal power: How Boris Johnson failed London's cyclists*. Kindle edition, Aurum Press.

Ravensbergen, L., Buliung, R., & Laliberté, N. (2019). Towards feminist geographies of cycling. *Geography Compass*, 13(7). e12461. doi:10.1111/gec3.12461

Reid, C. (2014). *Roads were not built for cars*. Front Page.

Rosen, P. (2002). "Up the Vélorution: Appropriating the bicycle and the politics of technology". SATSU Working paper N24 2002. Subsequently published in R. Eglash, J. Bleecker, J. Croissant, R. Fouché & G. Di Chiro (Eds.), *Appropriating technology*. University of Minnesota Press. https://www.york.ac.uk/media/satsu/documents-papers/Rosen-2002-velorution.pdf

Salazar, N. B. (2021). Existential vs. essential mobilities: Insights from before, during and after a crisis. *Mobilities*, *16*(1), 20–34. https://doi.org/10.1080/17450101.2020.1866320

Samuel, P. (2006). *Histoire des Amis de la Terre 1970–1989: Vingt ans au cœur de l'écologie*. https://www.amisdelaterre.org/wp-content/uploads/2012/08/histoire-des-at-1970-1989.pdf

Spinney, J. (2021). *Understanding urban cycling: Exploring the relationship between mobility, sustainability and capital*. Routledge.

Wall, T. (2020, 20 September). The new road rage: Bitter rows break out over UK's low-traffic neighbourhoods. *The Observer*. https://www.theguardian.com/world/2020/sep/20/the-new-road-rage-bitter-rows-break-out-over-uks-low-traffic-neighbourhoods

While, A., & Whitehead, M. (2013). Cities, urbanisation and climate change. *Urban Studies*, *50*(7), 1325–1331. https://doi.org/10.1177/0042098013480963

Zuev, D., Psarikidou, K., & Popan, C. (Eds.). (2021). *Cycling societies*. Routledge.

CHAPTER 2
CONDUCTING INTERVIEWS WITH MAPS AND VIDEOS TO CAPTURE CYCLISTS' SKILLS AND EXPERTISE

Matthieu Adam, Nathalie Ortar, Luc Merchez, Georges-Henry Laffont and Hervé Rivano

Introduction

Cyclability has come into wide usage both in academic work (transport geography, regional development) and in operational urban planning to refer to the variable capacity of spaces to accommodate and facilitate cycling safely. Like walkability that inspired it, cyclability characterizes an urban environment's potential for cycling. The literature (Nielsen & Skov-Petersen, 2018; Winters et al., 2016) claims that the more cyclable a place is—the urban environment generally, a district or a street—the greater the number of cyclists and the more they will use this setting for their trips. Cyclability is a useful concept for three reasons: (i) much of the work on urban cycling is undertaken from a planning perspective (and cyclability is a planning tool); (ii) an increasing number of studies suggest that more people take up cycling when the right infrastructure is available; and (iii) cyclability can be mapped.

As with walkability (Raulin et al., 2016) the literature does not come up with any stable and shared definition. The idea is defined negatively by the indicators characterizing it. Most academic work on cyclability (Papon et al., 2015; M. Winters et al., 2016) measures it (on the scale of a city, district or street) based on the material and functional characteristics of the spaces in question. These qualities include the road type (speed limits, width, flow of motor vehicles, shared-use or pedestrian zones, etc.), the existence, type and quality of cycling facilities (separate from or along the road, cycle lane or track, separators, width, state-of-repair), the slope (direction, gradient) and the types of intersection.

Scientific or expert appraisals of cyclability are generally constructed around indicators based on the quantification of factors that raise, or on the contrary lower, the potential for cycling in a given location. Evaluation tools, which are heavily dependent on the scale at which environmental factors are assessed, rely on the collection of data from various sources (collection of direct observations, self-assessment surveys, GIS data) and even combinations of them (Kellstedt et al., 2020). We refer here primarily to GIS-based methods like Bike Score® (M. Winters et al., 2013) as illustrated in section A.2. Such evaluations still need to be compared and contrasted with cyclists' experiences.

Conversely, studies focusing on cycling practices often make little connection with the physical characteristics of the area (Madsen & Lahrmann, 2016; Noël, 2003) although there are exceptions (Cox, 2019). They relate, for example, to social and cultural identities (Freudendal-Pedersen, 2015b; Füssl & Haupt, 2016) or cross-compare motivations (La Branche, 2012; Soulas & Papon, 2003), preferences (Lusk et al., 2014) and behaviours that relate to social characteristics, especially in the case of bike share users (Vogel et al., 2014). Other works address the question of routines (Larsen, 2014; 2016) or rhythms (Augé, 2010; Cook & Edensor, 2014), route choice depending on otherness and the relations with other users (Carré, 2001; Freudendal-Pedersen, 2015a; Ortar, 2019; Wood et al., 2009) or perceived safety (Lawson et al., 2013). The increasingly copious literature means that we are increasingly well informed about the profiles of urban cyclists and their motivations as well as the spaces to which they give precedence when they have a choice. We know, for instance, that the development of cyclable infrastructure boosts cycling and contributes to a more diverse sociological profile of cyclists, or that most cyclists look to ride wherever possible clear of motorized vehicles (for safety and comfort). We also identify shortcomings both in terms of knowledge and of methodological construction therefore, save for a few exceptions (such as Larsen, 2014, and Spinney, 2011, cf. below), studies are based essentially on analysis of cyclists' discourse and are rarely set against practice as observed in situ.

The Véléval Project is designed to compare and contrast two areas of investigation: the planning conception of cyclability, characterized here as theoretical, and a detailed understanding of cyclists' practices and representations, characterizing what we call "cyclability as experienced". The project brings together researchers in sociology, geography, urban planning and development, and computer studies. To build up tension between practices, representations and the cyclability of spaces, the survey focuses on the biographical and physical features that influence what cyclists feel and how that affects whether they feel "at ease" or not. It includes both factors that influence the choice of route on the city scale and the expertise involved in passing through certain points or following certain routes. Both of these are singular. Motility (Kaufmann, 2011; Kaufmann et al., 2004) encompasses social conditions of access, skills, understood as the way people organize, and plans, that is what they want to do. In this project, we look at the expertise surrounding proficiency in cycling and handling the spatial surroundings and the related socialization. Expertise is understood here as a set of human knowledge and abilities, whether consciously held or not, that enables a technique to be implemented. It includes a range of tacit knowledge as well as explicit abilities (Cox, 2019). Expertise invariably depends on people's relationships with one another and on people's relations with the laws of matter (Chamoux, 2010; Delbos & Jorion, 2019).

Our hypothesis is that cycling practices are as much about physical aptitude as culture. Practices are composed of many different components (Reckwitz, 2002). Shove and her colleagues (2012) group them into materials, competencies and meanings. "Materials include: things, technologies, tangible physical entities, and the stuff of which objects are made. Competences encompass:

skill, know-how, and technique; and meanings include: symbolic meanings, ideas and aspirations" (Williams et al., 2019, p. 745). Shove, like Jensen & Lanng (2016) emphasizes the importance of design—as physical rather than symbolic objects—in carrying out practices. Larsen (2018), drawing on the work by Pink (2011) about establishing cycling practice, includes the environment like the weather, roads, topography and "biological bodies" in this list of considerations in the analysis of cycling practices. This approach to practices relates them explicitly to geographical characteristics taken into account in mapping cyclability. This leads us to postulate that it is possible to identify cyclability as experienced, informed by cyclists' practices and reflexivity.

The underlying aim is to contribute to identifying what Lugo (2013) and Nello-Deakin and Nikolaeva (2020) call "human infrastructure" of cyclable cities. This is by identifying both social and geographical features that mean cyclists can "be at ease cycling in the city" with the aim of planning conditions for extending the practice.

In designing our survey protocol, we began with the observation that it was difficult to achieve any subtle understanding of a mobility practice based solely on semi-directive interviews, as these sources cannot readily be used for evaluating the quality of the spaces for travel. Accordingly, we opted to use and cross compare three methodological tools: measurement of trips using GPS tracking, analysis of images filmed by on-board digital cameras and memory reactivation interviews, in which the tracking and videos make it easier to encourage feedback about the experience. These three methodological tools are commonly used to analyse cycling practices. Systematic review shows that among the methods used for studying cyclists' choice of routes, some 40% use GPS tracking (not collected via smartphones), 20% interviews and just 3% videos (Pritchard, 2018). Our arrangement is innovative through combining these tools and enables us to question the relevance and limitations of theoretical mapping approaches to cyclability. This chapter reviews this methodological experiment by explaining its theoretical underpinning, setting out the protocol and finally highlighting its qualities and flaws.

First, we discuss the relations between facilities and cyclists' experiences and detail the specific features of cyclability and the cyclability policies of our two study areas, the metropolitan council areas of Lyon and Saint-Étienne. Second, we present the memory reactivation process, utilizing GPS video and maps to elicit interview responses. Finally, we provide feedback and evaluation of the method after field testing.

Understanding Cyclability Through Cyclists' Practices and Representations
Lyon and Saint-Étienne: Contrasting Locations
The two survey areas were selected for a contrast of urban settings (size, topography, pollution) and cyclability policies (facilities and support for mobility).

Lyon is a metropolitan area with policies to promote cycling actively, where the practice is on the increase and the modal share of cycling for commuting is comparatively high for a French city (5.9% compared with a French average of 1.9% according to the national statistics office, Insee (Adam, 2017)). Although there are three steep hills, the city is generally flat. The bike share scheme (Vélo'v) is widely used.

Saint-Étienne is a medium-sized city where cycling policy is not greatly developed, facilities (cycleways, cycle tracks and lanes, bike parking, etc.) are of limited quantity and quality and the modal share is low (less than 1%). Although the surrounding area is quite hilly, the city centre itself has few inclines. The Vélivert self-service bike share scheme is not widely used.

Participants, (21 in Lyon, 18 in Saint-Étienne) were "utility" cyclists, who use their bikes to commute to their place of work or education. The participants have varied sociological profiles (age, sex, occupation) and cycling practices (trip length, recurrence or variability and times of day; how long they have been cyclists; use of their own bike or a shared bike; pedal cycle or e-bike).

Theoretical Cyclability of the Study Areas as a Starting Point
Measuring cyclability as a theoretical assessment is particularly useful at the scale of the whole city area. We define theoretical cyclability as the attempt to bring the multidimensional idea of cyclability down to a single hypothetical quantitative score independent of the reports of users or experts. This can then be compared and contrasted with experienced cyclability, that is, not as quantified theoretically, but as perceived, characterized and evaluated by cyclists themselves. Theoretical cyclability rests on the compilation of a series of indicators that are more or less comparable from one method to another. For some (Wang & Akar, 2018), indicators are derived from actual practices, particularly by using geostatistical processing to bring out the salient environmental factors through the comparison of GPS tracking as observed with the theoretically shortest routes. For others (Winters, 2011; Winters et al., 2013), indicators are derived directly by way of discourse analysis, statistical analysis of questionnaires or from cyclists' representations of what impacts their practice favourably. Both methods show a degree of convergence not limited to the indicators used (see the five determinants used in our study below).

The main strategies seek to measure cyclability in a given setting using a zone-based approach. Two leading families of factors can be identified (Wang & Akar, 2018): factors related to the natural environment (topography, weather conditions, etc.) and factors related to the built environment and its component parts (road and cycle network, land use, safety features, aesthetics, etc.).

Based on the state-of-the-art and tried-and-tested methods (Hartanto et al., 2017; Krenn et al., 2015; Winters et al., 2013), the hope is to transpose and adapt existing approaches to the case of French cities to produce multi-scale maps of cyclability. These are based on the development of a composite index, a score that can be interpreted and compared across spaces and over time and whether working at the highest resolution (a place and its immediate surroundings), on the scale of the municipal area as a whole, or at intermediate district levels.

Without justifying their identification or detailed composition here, five determinants were selected and most involve a combination of more than one indicator:

- separate cycle tracks and routes;
- cyclable facilities;
- spaces conducive to cycling (watersides and wooded areas);
- road network characteristics (apart from cycle lanes);
- gradients.

We calculated a cyclability score for 100m x 100m squares. It is a composite index combining the scores of the five environmental determinants listed above within a 250m radius. Selection of a 250m neighbourhood size is arbitrary, but generally defined as the distance (deviation) cyclists are ready to cover to find a more suitable facility for their trip. For each of the determinants, the squares are given a mark from one to 10. The aggregate cyclability index is the mean of the scores for each determinant (unweighted).

Figure 2.1 maps the cyclability index for the Lyon area (Lyon-Villeurbanne and the first ring of municipalities) on a 100m grid. Maps of this kind can be used for examining cyclability along a route, or for a given district, but are not designed for characterizing the cyclability of a single stretch of cycle track or a specific site, such as an intersection.

This evaluation tool is valid for non-micro scales, unlike the more plentiful methods that target the immediate environment (such as the cyclist's field of vision). More broadly, there is no consensus on these instruments, understandable given the diversity of cultural and geographical contexts in which bike journeys in urban settings are examined. Definitions of cyclability remain vague. However, as Kellstedt et al. argue (2020), "A universal definition of cyclability

Conducting Interviews with Maps and Videos

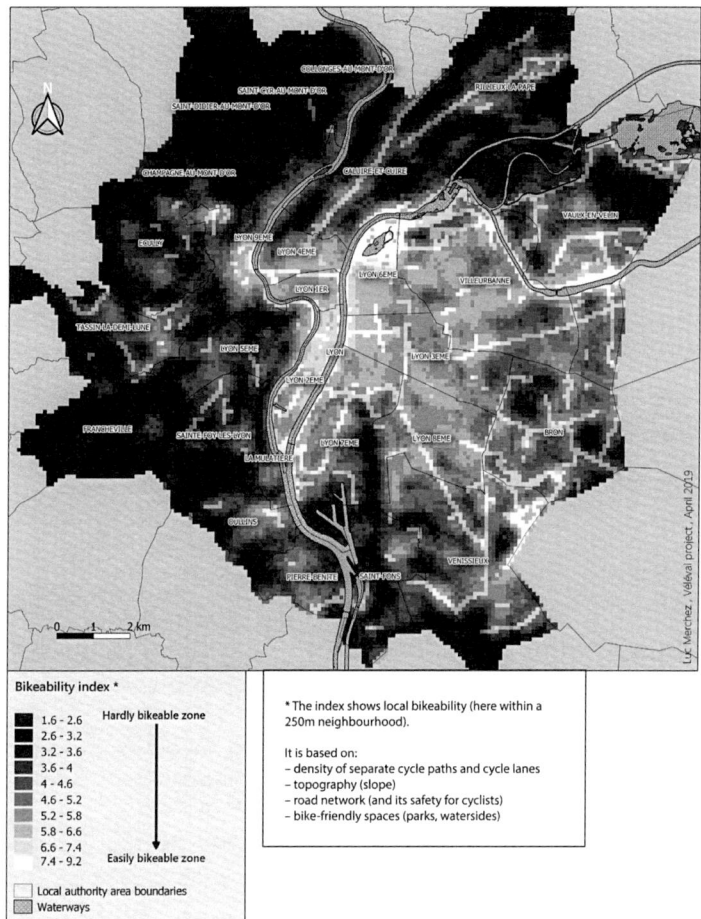

Figure 2.1: Theoretical cyclability in the Lyon area (Luc Merchez, 2019).

may drive the development of more streamlined tools", and conversely, more streamlined tools may assist greater agreement on cyclability.

The value of these approaches lies in their capacity to provide relative comparison. The exclusively numerical (and reproducible) mode of computation can be used to compare the variable cyclable character of two cities, or to measure the impact of certain developments over time. Here, even if it is possible to query the validity of such indexes by limiting ourselves to quantitative methods (e.g. by cross comparing GPS tracking to evaluate how much they minimize cyclability scores) the idea is also to have the maps open to debate by comparing them with what cyclists feel during memory reactivation interviews (cf. section B). As the maps may be unreadable to the uninitiated, the method used in the interviews, described below, is based on information that is easier to understand, such as routes and video (Drevon et al., 2017) of journeys. The cyclability score produced is a relative and not an absolute value.

Monitoring Cyclists' Practices to Produce a Situated Discourse
Our method combines analyses of mobility tracking (captured by GPS camera provided to participants) and analyses of interviews using these data as elicitation tools (Figure 2.2).

The aim is to compare and contrast analyses of GPS tracking and videos with the rider perceptions by memory reactivation in the course of an interview. GPS and video elicitation combine to allow insight into participants' representations and justifications. After initial data collection and processing to produce the items shown to the participants (maps of their practices, video excerpts and area cyclability maps), interviews were arranged. In the interviews, participants were shown both their GPS tracking and journey video to get them to talk about all aspects of their mobility by bike.

The memory reactivation interview, akin to a "reality test", is designed to elicit a "discourse of existence" (Chalas, 2000) by mobilizing the reflexive capacity of participants to access the representations of their mobility practices (Bailleul & Feildel, 2011). Véléval is innovative in using elicitation through two parallel forms: GPS route tracking data and action recorded by video. We thus exploit the mobility tracking and videos to foster reflexivity on practices and to produce a situated discourse (see below). The

Conducting Interviews with Maps and Videos

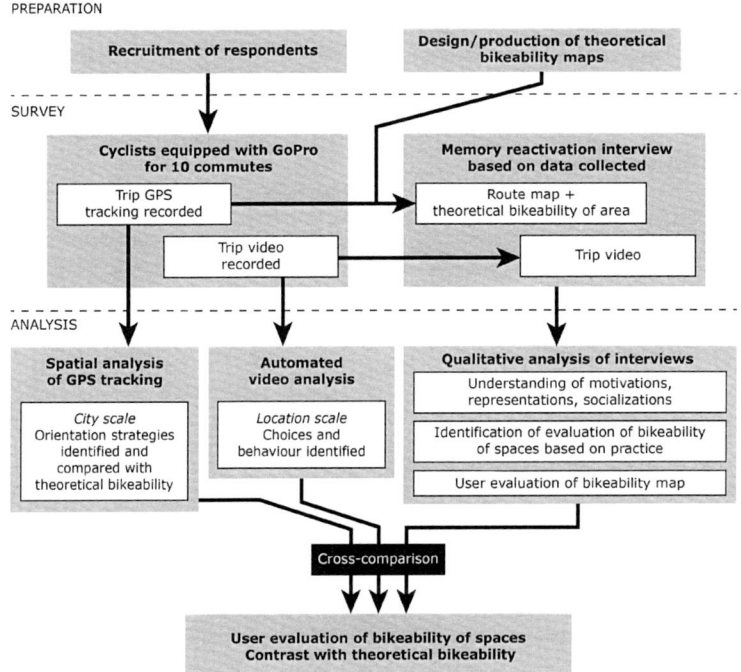

Figure 2.2: Methodological and analytical set-up.

method is designed to inquire into cyclists' practices, their (self) representations, the material conditions of the practice and lastly the relation between conditions and practices. The aim is to explain how relations between the city, the bike and urban cycling are formed with respect to both situation and the social trajectory of participants.

Methodological Development, Participant Involvement and Difficulties
From GPS Capture to Video Follow-Up
Initially we planned only GPS tracking of trips. GPS video, combining tracking and images enhanced the method and avoided recognized problems:

- GPS accuracy in urban settings varies from a few metres to more than 10m, depending on the surroundings. Elements we initially hypothesized as influential in enabling cyclists to be "at ease" in any given situation (taking a cycle lane or not, or riding on the pavement, lane position), require a more precise location. Video enables us to observe these elements and question participants about the reasons for their choice.
- GPS data (speed, acceleration, position) cannot help us to determine the elements involved in certain behavioural traits we wish to question cyclists about. (For example, slowing at an intersection does not tell us the colour of the traffic light.) Video supplements such data.

The principle of elicitation prompts in the memory reactivation interviews is to jog people's memories after the actions have been performed and to provide sources of discussion. In principle, the main medium should be the map. However, the ability to read maps and to engage in discussion based on them varies greatly among individuals. The use of video excerpts to jog memory increases the potential for gaining valuable feedback during interviews (Figure 2.2).

A Methodological Protocol That Involves Participants Closely
Cameras closely involve the cyclists. Unlike a tracking application working in the background, using a camera requires frequent manipulation: removing it, fitting it to the handlebars, recharging it. This prompted us to limit data collection time to just 10 trips (in theory one week of commuting both ways). Commercial digital GPS cameras (GoProHero 5 black) were used for the reasons above. In practice the research was conducted as follows (compare Figure 2.2):

- Participants were equipped with a camera mounted on the handlebars (Figure 2.3) to record 10, otherwise normal, commuting journeys.
- Map and video data were processed.

Conducting Interviews with Maps and Videos

Figure 2.3: Cameras on a private bike (left) and a Vélo'v (right) (Matthieu Adam, 2018).

- A memory reactivation interview was conducted based on two maps (the route only and the route superimposed on the cyclability map) and on the video of the trip.

Collection of the paired GPS tracking/video data had multiple effects on the survey: change in the panel, longer collection time, better quality of data collected (cf. B.1) and on the participants' potential behaviour and the course of the interviews. Many of them said that they worried that filming themselves (and therefore knowing their behaviour was being recorded and thus was observable with the potential for judgement by outside observers) might influence their practice. Even if such influence is difficult to measure, this concern seemed unfounded after a few trips. For this reason, the trip discussed in the reactivation interview was never among the first recorded.

> *I forgot all about it. Well, no, on the first trips I thought: "Oh, yes, I've got a camera, I'd better watch out." And afterwards I thought: "No, just the opposite, I have to do as I normally do." And there were even times when I forgot the camera was there. I was oblivious to it. When I talked with those guys ... I completely forget the camera was there. I think besides I found out later it was one of the trips filmed. (Daniel, Villeurbanne)*

Replacing GPS tracking by GPS/video influenced certain stages in the survey. Most of the extra work relates to algorithmic processing of the videos and the time to prepare data and extract GPS tracking from the video file metadata. That could have disrupted the surveys or influenced responses because participants could use the waiting time to think about their practices.

> Well I didn't find it intrusive because you never see me. It's just bike rides. No, the camera, tops. No trouble, it motivates you in fact because it's not often we're asked our opinion, and the idea was to promote cycling after all. (…) And afterwards, I had time to get ready for the survey. I've been thinking about all these questions for a while now. And that forces you to think about what you do. (Nathan, Saint-Étienne)

Lastly, this close involvement was accepted overall and viewed positively by the participants who often saw it as a form of "useful" or even militant contribution to developing city cycling.

Fieldwork Was More Complicated and Time-Consuming Than Expected

The first participants were provided with cameras in June 2018. This required a short demonstration and instructions for use, a form about taking part in the project and for collecting personal data. Participants were told to get in touch once they had recorded 10 commuting trips.

In theory, the commute trips could have been filmed in five days (one return trip per day). It was hoped that participants would take about two weeks to complete the recordings. This forecast proved to be very optimistic.

First, none of the participants actually filmed 10 trips. Some filmed more, up to 15, most others filmed fewer, sometimes just five or six, and often filming only their outward commute. These disparities meant the data available for each individual were not balanced and limited the scope for analysis of variations and recurrences based on GPS tracking and videos.

> I might have forgotten it one time. Or I wanted to take it but when putting it on I realized the battery was flat or something of the sort. I knew we'd

Conducting Interviews with Maps and Videos

Figure 2.4: Shots filmed by our participants (Véléval Project, 2018).

> said two weeks and I'd overrun a bit, actually two, three trips more, so there'd be the right number of trips. I don't remember what we'd said. (Samantha, Lyon)

Second, the time between entrusting the camera to the participants and recovering it invariably exceeded one month. This was affected in part by the first phase of the survey being conducted in summer, because most participants were on holiday for some of the time. However, this contextual point is not the main reason for the "time excursions". The following problems emerged when viewing the videos and in discussions on the camera's return:

- Forgetting or not having enough time to recharge the camera. This is the leading cause of delays. The camera could film without recharging for about 90 minutes and so most participants had to recharge it several times over the course of the experiment. They did not always have time for this (about two hours for a full recharge) or simply forgot, delaying the next recording session. Failure to recharge was also commonplace because participants had to remember to take a cable, possibly a charger as well, and to remove the camera from its support.

> The only damper I would say is the life of the battery, it was nothing special, you had to recharge it quite often, I seem to remember. (Antonin, Saint-Étienne)

> The thing is that I really concentrated on starting it at first, on leaving home, and when leaving work too. And so it was fairly easy for me to start it in the

> *mornings. But on leaving in the evenings, because I had shopping to do or stuff on coming out of work, it was then that it was a bit more complicated. (Benjamin, Lyon)*

- Forgetting the camera altogether. The camera is easy to overlook, especially when strong time pressures are at work (for example for those on shift work or having a train journey as part of their commute).
- The inconvenience of fitting the camera. The black plastic handlebar support fitting is not highly visible and could be left on private bikes without risk of theft. This was not true of the camera itself which had to be removed whenever it was left unguarded. Users of shared use bikes faced a further hurdle to fit and remove both camera and support for each trip, making their involvement more demanding/time-consuming.

> *My one dread was that I would forget it. I mean ... Because it's not my bike, and I park it where it's not guarded, I thought to myself ... Because I've already forgotten one or two umbrellas, I've already forgotten ... It's a bit of a problem with Vélo'v [shared use bikes] when you have things you just leave and then, quick, you're in a hurry, and then crap. So then, that stressed me out, but other than that, no, there were no other worries. (Ambre, Lyon)*

- Forgetting to switch the camera off. Almost every participant forgot to switch off and remove the camera at the end of a journey at least once. The camera continued filming, usually a bike garage wall, some corner of the workplace, a stairway, sometimes a street. This drained the battery and filled the camera SD card with useless information. In turn, this further delayed subsequent recordings, or prevented any further recording if the available memory was saturated. Similarly, the camera could be lost: one Vélo'v user forgot the camera on its bracket for five minutes on a shared use bike, which was long enough for a passer-by to take it, together with the videos and GPS tracking already recorded.

Conducting Interviews with Maps and Videos

And then in the end I think it was full. But several times it stopped on the way and I think it was because I hadn't … I thought it was full, but I don't know how to check whether it's full or not. (Bénédicte, Lyon)

Me, I forgot the camera several times, left it, left it running and sometimes I gave myself a scare because I fasten my bike up in the stairs which are open and one night I left it there, all night long … (Johan, Lyon)

- Other use of the camera. Participants and their friends sometimes used the cameras for personal fun and games. While this had no direct influence on the survey it did contribute to discharging the batteries and saturating the SD card. Sometimes such uses meant participants altered the camera settings, which could prove troublesome for obtaining good quality uniform data. More rarely, operating problems with the cameras delayed data collection. Frequent use at the maximum of their capacities of SD cards and batteries resulted in charging difficulties. Straightforward formatting of the SD card solved the problem but this meant recovering it, which was time-consuming and made relations with participants, for whom the survey was already demanding, more complex.

Documenting Feelings, Skills and Know-How
Panel Recruitment and Implicating Method: Two-Fold Complexity
These observations call for discussion of the characteristics and timing of the survey. First, we underestimated the involvement required in using the camera and the complexity in handling it. More than any other aspect of the instructions, the technical device itself influences the survey dynamics and extends the initially planned completion time. The use of cameras equipped with GPS underscores one of the difficulties in implementing a multi-disciplinary approach. The data collected are richer than they would have been with a more classical and more familiar method (GPS monitoring without interviews, straightforward semi-directive interviews). Data processing was more time-consuming, data collection more difficult and complementarity between methods

involved making constant adjustments. Forgetting the camera on the handlebars at the end of the journey shows that while the set-up is very involving it is not very intrusive once in operation. However, the consequences in terms of the length of the survey and possible loss of equipment are not negligible.

Second, this time-consuming aspect is the result of a choice independent of the technical device: that of investigating just the commuting trip. This provides the possibility of analysing recurrent journeys and looking into the construction of a cycling routine. In addition, it is the only journey for which substantial statistical surveys are to be found (Insee, EMD) that allow the study to be set in a wider context. But this choice makes it difficult for participants to follow our instructions over a short period. The daily commute is very much constrained (Aguilera et al., 2010) in terms of family, work, costs, space and time. In this context, being equipped with a camera, making sure it is charged, and actually starting and stopping recording may quickly seem like additional constraints, associated only with the moral commitment made to investigators to film trips. It is not surprising, then, that the action is regularly forgotten or disregarded. In addition, the focus on the daily commute implies that participants recharge the camera either at work during the day or at home overnight. Work is not always the best place for recharging and other demands may mean it is easily overlooked. Upon returning home, participants also have other calls on their time – household, family, leisure that come before recharging the battery. These various factors lead us to consider that the choice of the commuting journey is one of the main factors that makes our method more complex.

From Cyclability as Experienced to the Cyclists' "Tricks of the Trade"
The difficulties with the method have an upside: the data collected is particularly rich and detailed and will make it possible to produce new knowledge about the practice of city cycling. Since this chapter

Conducting Interviews with Maps and Videos

has focused on method, we list only the first insights here. Presenting the participants with an objectified view of certain aspects of their practice makes explicit certain behaviours, choices or strategies that they would not necessarily have mentioned spontaneously. The video recording and the map give rise to discourse justifying practices while they also bring an awareness of actions performed or choices made by participant cyclists by force of habit or reflex and which they had not necessarily thought about before the interview. Compared with a classical interview, the methodological set-up therefore provides access to a precise evaluation of cyclability as experienced but also makes it possible to highlight skills and understanding gained from experience of city cycling and from the detailed knowledge of the area that it affords. Compared with the video and maps alone, the memory reactivation survey makes it possible to call on the reflexivity of actors so as to characterize the data collected more finely.

> *There, on that bit, you have to watch out, because you've got the give way, there it's one way, so cars come from here, you have to watch out there's no-one coming. And at the next one it's the other way round. (Béatrice, Lyon)*

Encouraging cyclists to talk about an external vision of their behaviour first provides access to a finely grained characterization of their evaluation of space, which theoretical cyclability mapping or GPS tracking analysis does not allow. As a result, it is possible to map cyclability as experienced, pointing out the pros and cons of certain streets, certain intersections, and more specifically, to discuss the relevance of indicators depending on the (micro)geographical context.

The interview data collected supplements the results provided by the quantitative method. For example, it can shed light on drivers' actual behaviour, which may be far removed from that suggested by the geographical information, whether indicated by the cyclability map as a danger or not. Speeds and traffic volumes may conversely prove lower than might be expected for the class of road.

> That stretch there is not great because the people behind they get onto the campus saying "That's it now", they're going to be able to drive at 80[km/hr]. But now they've put in speed bumps all along, so … […]. And then there are fewer and fewer cars on this campus. They're closing it, there, like. I mean … Einstein, there … More and more. So that means it's getting easier and easier for bikes. Oh, a heavy contraption … Well now he's going right against the direction of traffic. Yeah, so you see, it's quiet all the same … There's no-one about. (Ambre, Lyon)

The increase also occurs the other way around. The media employed enhance the interview data collected compared with, for example, a more classical semi-directive interview. In this way, reactions elicited by the media highlighted behaviour that cyclists had not mentally processed. This is shown by expressions such as "Hey, I did that!?" or questions of the "What the heck am I doing?" kind. Videos and maps together mean that points can be discussed that would have escaped notice in the context of a "classical" semi-directive interview.

Far from merely describing the journey shown in the video or traced on the map, participants' comments contain points about the variations along the route, whether it has changed since the time of recording or whether it varies regularly depending on the weather, the time they have available, or their mood. In the same way that a photograph may contain fuzziness or noise, the memory reactivation media reveal time variations. In addition to regular or sporadic variations, comments made about the video or map also prompt cyclists to reveal their "tricks of the trade", that is, their scripts (Moliner, 1996), which cyclists acquire through experience. Scripts are the structures of cognitions directly intended to guide ordinary conduct. They organize cognition into coherent sequences of "events expected by individuals and involving them as participants and observers" (Moliner, 1996, p. 57). They

Conducting Interviews with Maps and Videos

give structure to certain cognitions (in the case in point sporadic actions) by breaking them down into a chronological sequence of events. What determines conduct, then, is less the content of a request than the way it matches a known structure, in our case both a geographical and social structure (other road users' behaviour). These scripts mean cyclists can behave "automatically" for greater safety, comfort, speed or pleasure, but they can also adapt to the bike they are riding, the weather or motor traffic.

> *There, you see, I always come towards the gate too because the cars can't see me and that way I can work up some momentum a bit to the side. There, and so that means cars that want to overtake me overtake me (Albane, Lyon)*

In the end, the complexity and time-consuming character of the method did bring its rewards. With a little patience, it is possible to gain insight into cyclists' feelings as, unlike an in situ method where the investigator accompanies the cyclist and discusses with him or her the experiences during the ride, the camera has little influence on behaviour.

Conclusion

The time-consuming nature of the method led us to shift from a logic of two stages of video recording, one in summer 2018 and one in spring 2019, to continuous capture from spring 2018 to winter 2019, which was compatible with the length of capture and the planned end of financing for the project. Institutional time and technical requirements (Adam, 2015) ultimately won out over purely academic objectives in determining the timing of the survey.

The first consequence was that it meant weather and light (day/night) variations had more influence than we would have wished, necessarily affecting "being at ease on a bike" but also our ability to find participants. Urban cyclists are to be found in greater numbers in fine weather, whereas the daily commute is often made in the hours of darkness in winter. This made our analyses more complex, adding differences in the trips recorded. The interviews revealed that this change has a minor influence on discourse but that it can enhance our observation material and bring out the diversity of factors that affect the material circumstances of cycling. The research method presented in this paper has become an important issue for the Véléval Project. This chapter provides feedback on that project.

Once the difficulties were identified and survey times reassessed, the memory reactivation set-up allowed the harvesting of rich material. Although discourse analysis and its comparison with theoretical cyclability of the spaces covered remains to be finalized, the method does enable the collection of a wealth of data on "cyclability as experienced" and its contributory factors. Having videos and maps during the interview means that cyclists can be asked about their practice in situ, with the result that responses are formulated spontaneously without systematic prompting from the investigator. In this sense, this memory reactivation can be viewed as an effective process for bringing out participants' reflexivity and for gaining insight into their feelings, their evaluation of the environment, the quality of infrastructures and their various socialization processes.

Apart from the recurrent references to the times of construction and changes in route that punctuate the data collected, the time spent between recording the videos and conducting the interviews (several months) sometimes provided participants with the opportunity to change their daily route or to change their way through a key intersection. This led to discussion about these changes that illuminated both changes in geographical areas (new facilities, temporary road works) and changes in cyclists themselves (improving skills, better knowledge of the area, combination of the commute with another reason for making regular trips). These points fit in with those emerging from the personal narratives (first part of our interviews) to cast light on socialization and expertise in city cycling. Finally, methodological triangulation makes it possible to highlight the skills and expertise that cyclists deploy in their daily journeys.

Conducting Interviews with Maps and Videos

For all these reasons, and making allowance for inherent difficulties and timing, the method set out here is reproducible in other areas, adaptable to other modes than cycling and to other reasons for travel than commuting. Comparing and contrasting findings from such future studies with those yielded in the context of Véléval will open up a new stage in consolidating the academic value of memory reactivation.

Note: Sections of this work have been adapted from M. Adam, N. Ortar, L. Merchez, G.-H. Laffont, & H. Rivano. (2020). *Susciter la parole des cyclistes : Traces GPS et vidéos au service de l'entretien*. EspacesTemps.net. [French only].

References

Adam, M. (2015). L'éternel retard. Réflexion sur le moment d'observation des objets dynamiques : L'exemple des projets urbains et des représentations de la ville. *Nouvelles Perspectives en Sciences Sociales*, *10*(2), 273–303.

Adam, M. (2017). Caractéristiques des 1,9% de cyclistes utilitaires français. *Cyclops.hypotheses.org*. https://cyclops.hypotheses.org/82

Aguilera, A., Massot, M.-H., & Proulhac, L. (2010). Travailler et se déplacer au quotidien dans une métropole. Contraintes, ressources et arbitrages des actifs franciliens. *Societes contemporaines*, *80*(4), 29–45.

Augé, M. (2010). *Éloge de la bicyclette*. Payot.

Bailleul, H., & Feildel, B. (2011). Le sens des mobilités à l'épreuve des identités spatiales : Un éclairage par le récit de vie spatialisé et l'herméneutique cartographique. In S. Depeau & T. Ramadier (Éds.), *Se déplacer pour se situer. Places en jeux, enjeux de classes* (pp. 25–55). Presses Universitaires de Rennes.

Carré, J.-R. (2001). *Recherche et expérimentation sur les stratégies des cyclistes dans leurs déplacements urbains*. INRETS.

Chalas, Y. (2000). *L'invention de la ville*. Economica Anthropos.

Chamoux, M.-N. (2010). La transmission des savoir-faire : Un objet pour l'ethnologie des techniques ? *Techniques & Culture. Revue semestrielle d'anthropologie des techniques*, *54–55*, 139–161. https://doi.org/10.4000/tc.4995

Cook, M., & Edensor, T. (2014, December). Cycling through dark space: Apprehending landscape otherwise. *Mobilities*, 1–19.

Cox, P. (2019). *Cycling: A sociology of velomobility*. Routledge.

Delbos, G., & Jorion, P. (2019). La transmission des savoirs. In *La transmission des savoirs*. Éditions de la Maison des sciences de l'homme. http://books.openedition.org/editionsmsh/13647

Drevon, G., Klein, O., & Gwiazdzinski, L. (2017). Identifier les barrières au déplacement à partir de la vidéo géo-référencée. In G. Drevon, L. Gwiazdzinski, & O. Klein (Éds.), *Chronotopies, lecture et écriture des mondes en mouvement* (pp. 148–159). Elya Éditions.

Freudendal-Pedersen, M. (2015a). Cyclists as part of the city's organism: Structural stories on cycling in Copenhagen. *City & Society, 27*(1). https://doi.org/10.1111/ciso.12051

Freudendal-Pedersen, M. (2015b). Whose commons are mobilities spaces? —The case of Copenhagen's cyclists. *ACME: An International Journal for Critical Geographies, 14*(2), 598–621.

Füssl, E., & Haupt, J. (2016). Understanding cyclist identity and related interaction strategies. A novel approach to traffic research. *Transportation Research Part F: Traffic Psychology and Behaviour*. https://doi.org/10.1016/j.trf.2016.08.003

Hartanto, K., Grigolon, A. B., Maarseveen, M. F. A. M., & Brussel, M. (2017). *Developing a cyclability index in the context of transit-oriented development (TOD)*. 15th International Conference on Computers in Urban Planning and Urban Management, 11 July 2017, Adelaide, Australia.

Jensen, O. B., & Lanng, D. B. (2016). *Mobilities design: Urban designs for mobile situations*. Routledge.

Kaufmann, V. (2011). *Rethinking the city: Urban dynamics and motility*. Routledge.

Kaufmann, V., Bergman, M. M., & Joye, D. (2004). Motility: Mobility as capital. *International Journal of Urban and Regional Research, 28*(4), 745–756. https://doi.org/10.1111/j.0309-1317.2004.00549.x

Kellstedt, D. K., Spengler, J. O., Foster, M., Lee, C., & Maddock, J. E. (2020). A scoping review of cyclability assessment methods. *Journal of Community Health*. https://doi.org/10.1007/s10900-020-00846-4

Conducting Interviews with Maps and Videos

Krenn, P., Oja, P., & Titze, S. (2015). Development of a cyclability index to assess the bicycle-friendliness of urban environments. *Open Journal of Civil Engineering, 5*, 451–459. https://doi.org/10.4236/ojce.2015.54045

La Branche, S. (2012). La schizophrénie écologique : Le cas des déplacements quotidiens à Lyon. *VertigO, Hors-série 11*. https://doi.org/10.4000/vertigo.11754

Larsen, J. (2014). (Auto)ethnography and cycling. *International Journal of Social Research Methodology, 17*(1), 59–71. https://doi.org/10.1080/13645579.2014.854015

Larsen, J. (2016, 6 December). The making of a pro-cycling city: Social practices and bicycle mobilities. *Environment and Planning A*. https://doi.org/10.1177/0308518X16682732

Larsen, J. (2018). Commuting, exercise and sport: An ethnography of long-distance bike commuting. *Social & Cultural Geography, 19*(1), 39–58. https://doi.org/10.1080/14649365.2016.1249399

Lawson, A. R., Pakrashi, V., Ghosh, B., & Szeto, W. Y. (2013). Perception of safety of cyclists in Dublin City. *Accident Analysis & Prevention, 50*, 499–511. https://doi.org/10.1016/j.aap.2012.05.029

Lugo, A. E. (2013). CicLAvia and human infrastructure in Los Angeles: Ethnographic experiments in equitable bike planning. *Journal of Transport Geography, 30*, 202–207. https://doi.org/10.1016/j.jtrangeo.2013.04.010

Lusk, A. C., Wen, X., & Zhou, L. (2014). Gender and used/preferred differences of bicycle routes, parking, intersection signals, and bicycle type: Professional middle class preferences in Hangzhou, China. *Journal of Transport & Health, 1*(2), 124–133. https://doi.org/10.1016/j.jth.2014.04.001

Madsen, T. K. O., & Lahrmann, H. (2016). Comparison of five bicycle facility designs in signalized intersections using traffic conflict studies. *Transportation Research Part F: Traffic Psychology and Behaviour*. https://doi.org/10.1016/j.trf.2016.05.008

Moliner, P. (1996). *Images et représentations sociales. De la théorie des représentations à l'étude des images sociales*. Presses Universitaires de Grenoble.

Nello-Deakin, S., & Nikolaeva, A. (2020). The human infrastructure of a cycling city: Amsterdam through the eyes of international newcomers. *Urban Geography, 42*(3), 1–23. https://doi.org/10.1080/02723638.2019.1709757

Nielsen, T. A. S., & Skov-Petersen, H. (2018). Cyclability—Urban structures supporting cycling. Effects of local, urban and regional scale urban form factors on cycling from home and workplace locations in Denmark. *Journal of Transport Geography*, *69*, 36–44. https://doi.org/10.1016/j.jtrangeo.2018.04.015

Noël, N. (2003). *Formes urbaines, aménagements routiers et usage de la bicyclette* [Thèse de Doctorat]. Université Laval.

Ortar, N. (2019). What the e-bike tells us about the anthropology of energy. In S. Abram, B. R. Winthereik, & T. Yarrow (Eds.), *Electrifying anthropology. Exploring electrical practices and infrastructures* (pp. 83–99). Bloomsbury.

Papon, F., Belton Chevallier, L., Abours, S., Come, E., Midenet, S., Soulas, C., Beauvais, J. M., & Polombo, N. (2015). *Rapport final du projet VERT. Le vélo évalué en rabattement dans les territoires. Volume 1* (p. 103) [Research Report]. IFSTTAR—Institut Français des Sciences et Technologies des Transports, de l'Aménagement et des Réseaux. https://hal.archives-ouvertes.fr/hal-01239828

Pink, S. (2011). From embodiment to emplacement: Re-thinking competing bodies, senses and spatialities. *Sport, Education and Society*, *16*(3), 343–355. https://doi.org/10.1080/13573322.2011.565965

Pritchard, R. (2018). Revealed preference methods for sudying bicycle route choice—a systematic review. *International Journal of Environmental Research and Public Health*, *15*(3). https://doi.org/10.3390/ijerph15030470

Raulin, F., Lord, S., & Negron-Poblete, P. (2016). Évaluation de la marchabilité de trois environnements urbains de la région métropolitaine montréalaise à partir de l'outil MAPPA. *VertigO—la revue électronique en sciences de l'environnement*, *16*(2). https://doi.org/10.4000/vertigo.17774

Reckwitz, A. (2002). Toward a theory of social practices: A development in culturalist theorizing. *European Journal of Social Theory*, *5*(2), 243–263. https://doi.org/10.1177/13684310222225432

Shove, E., Pantzar, M., & Watson, M. (2012). *The dynamics of social practice: Everyday life and how it changes*. Sage.

Soulas, C., & Papon, F. (2003, Novembre). Les conditions d'une mobilité alternative à l'automobile individuelle. *Annales des Mines*, 84–93.

Conducting Interviews with Maps and Videos

Spinney, J. (2011). A chance to catch a breath: Using mobile video relationships between corporeal and digital mobilities. *Mobilities*, 2(6), 161–182.

Vogel, M., Hamon, R., Lozenguez, G., Merchez, L., Abry, P., Barnier, J., Borgnat, P., Flandrin, P., Mallon, I., & Robardet, C. (2014). From bicycle sharing system movements to users: A typology of Vélo'v cyclists in Lyon based on large-scale behavioural dataset. *Journal of Transport Geography*, 41, 280–291. https://doi.org/10.1016/j.jtrangeo.2014.07.005

Wang, K., & Akar, G. (2018). The perceptions of bicycling intersection safety by four types of bicyclists. *Transportation Research Part F: Traffic Psychology and Behaviour*, 59, 67–80. https://doi.org/10.1016/j.trf.2018.08.014

Williams, D. G., Spotswood, F., Parkhurst, G., & Chatterton, T. (2019). Practice ecology of sustainable travel: The importance of institutional policy-making processes beyond the traveller. *Transportation Research. Part F, Traffic Psychology and Behaviour*, 62, 740–756. https://doi.org/10.1016/j.trf.2019.02.018

Winters, M., Brauer, M., Setton, E. M., & Teschke, K. (2013). Mapping cyclability: A spatial tool to support sustainable travel. *Environment and Planning B: Planning and Design*, 40(5), 865–883. https://doi.org/10.1068/b38185

Winters, M. L. (2011). *Improving public health through active transportation: Understanding the influence of the built environment on decisions to travel by bicycle* [University of British Columbia]. https://doi.org/10.14288/1.0071676

Winters, M., Teschke, K., Brauer, M., & Fuller, D. (2016). Bike Score®: Associations between urban cyclability and cycling behavior in 24 cities. *International Journal of Behavioral Nutrition and Physical Activity*, 13(1), 18. https://doi.org/10.1186/s12966-016-0339-0

Wood, J. M., Lacherez, P. F., Marszalek, R. P., & King, M. J. (2009). Drivers' and cyclists' experiences of sharing the road: Incidents, attitudes and perceptions of visibility. *Accident Analysis & Prevention*, 41(4), 772–776. https://doi.org/10.1016/j.aap.2009.03.014

CHAPTER 3
KEY EVENTS, MOTIVATIONS AND PRIOR EXPERIENCE IN E-BIKE ADOPTION

Dimitri Marincek

Introduction: E-bikes and Urban Cycling
Urban cycling has much potential as a sustainable mode of transport to replace journeys by car and public transport and increase population health. Electrically assisted bicycles (e-bikes) provide assistance while pedalling, which makes cycling less physically challenging, and enables a broader spectrum of people to cycle in a wider range of conditions, such as trips that involve carrying loads, or long or hilly journeys (Behrendt, 2017; Rose, 2012). E-bike users include people who had stopped cycling and wish to return to it, as well as existing cyclists who would otherwise have stopped cycling (Marincek & Rérat, 2020). In recent years, e-bike sales have grown significantly and now represent a third of bicycles sold annually in Switzerland (Velosuisse, 2020). There are two categories of e-bike in Switzerland. E-bikes that offer assistance up to 25km/h, classed as pedelecs (86% of sales in 2018), and those providing assistance up to 45km/h, speed-pedelecs (14% of sales in 2018). Categorizations and the requirements attached to different classes vary between legislatures; speed-pedelecs in the EU, for example, have more restrictive regulations than in Switzerland. However, in general, understanding why and when people adopt e-bikes (and which categories they use) may be helpful for cycling policies.

Traditional research on cycling considers the effect of determinants in the decision to cycle: the built environment (density), the natural environment (topography, weather), socio-economic variables (age, gender, income and education level), psychological factors (attitudes), and aspects related to cost, time, effort and safety (Handy et al., 2014; Heinen et al., 2010; Rérat, 2019). However, cross-sectional data collected at a specific time point

Key Events, Motivations and Prior Experience

may only show a correlation between factors, but cannot establish causality for why people cycle (Janke & Handy, 2019). To gain a deeper understanding of how travel behaviour changes across time, mobility biographies research (MBR) adopts a longitudinal view of mobility, which sees current behaviour as the result of a life course trajectory (or "mobility biography") influenced over time by "key events" such as residential relocations or childbirth (Lanzendorf, 2003; Scheiner, 2007). Recently, cycling research has started to take advantage of a biographical approach to understand how cycling varies over the course of a person's life, and why and when people start or stop cycling (Bonham & Wilson, 2012; Chatterjee et al., 2013).

Contributors to this book give various clues as to how people become or stay urban cyclists throughout their lives. Sometimes, the impetus for getting into cycling can come from unexpected events, such as the Covid-19 pandemic, which acted as a trigger for cycling in many cities (Cox, this volume). Planned interventions such cycling promotion campaigns (Rérat, this volume) may also provide an opportunity to try out new habits. Maintaining and developing cycling over time also requires learning certain skills, such as knowledge of a given spatial context and its "cyclability" (Adam & Ortar, this volume), or bicycle repair and maintenance skills (Abord de Chatillon, this volume). However, cycling habits can also be fragile, especially for adult beginner cyclists who are vulnerable to interrupting cycling (Buhler, this volume) and weakened by social pressure, as for young women in low-cycling contexts (Sayagh, Dusong & Papon, this volume) or second-generation immigrants (Welsch, this volume).

This chapter aims to explore the adoption of e-bikes as one way of "becoming urban cyclists". We argue that e-bike adoption offers an interesting case study for understanding the processes and key events involved in taking up or continuing to cycle. Our research question is simple: What makes people adopt an e-bike? To answer it, we first offer a theoretical framework for biographical approaches to cycling and e-bike use. We then present our method, case study, and data, which is based on retrospective, biographical interviews with e-bike users in Lausanne, Switzerland (N = 24). Later, we present and discuss our results in relation to existing literature, before suggesting implications for future research and policy.

Theoretical Framework: Biographical Approaches to Cycling
Mobility Biographies Research and Key Events as Turning Points
Mobility biographies research has its roots in life course studies (Elder et al., 2003). The mobility biography refers to an individual's life course trajectory in the domain of mobility (Lanzendorf, 2003), where present behaviour is seen as the cumulative outcome of past behaviour. It assumes that mobility is influenced by events happening in other domains of life—lifestyle and accessibility for Lanzendorf (2003), employment, household and residence for Scheiner (2007).

Most research on travel behaviour has focused specifically on the role of key events (also called life events or turning points) as triggers for changing behaviour. Since most travel behaviour is understood as habitual, it is hypothesized that key events break routines and act as a "window of opportunity" for reconsidering travel behaviour (Klöckner, 2004; Verplanken et al., 2008). In their review of papers on the subject, Müggenburg et al. (2015) make a distinction between "life events" that fall outside of transport, such as relationships or childbirth, "long-term mobility decisions" including vehicle ownership and use as well as residential relocations, "exogenous interventions" such as road closures (Marsden & Docherty, 2013) and "long-term processes" of socialization (Döring et al., 2014; Tully & Baier, 2011). Life events can be private or professional. An example of a private life event is the birth of a child, which affects professional activity and leads to changes in travel, especially for women (Lanzendorf, 2010). An example of a professional event is a change in employment, such as a move from full- to part-time work, which is most likely to occur between the ages of 20 and 35 years (Beige & Axhausen, 2008); another example is retirement.

Key Events, Motivations and Prior Experience

Long-term mobility decisions such as residential relocations and changes in vehicle ownership (Clark et al., 2016) imply a substantial cost and long-lasting implications. We choose to consider them as key events, although they may also be considered as adaptations to life events (Müggenburg et al., 2015).

Research on key events has been criticized by some authors for its narrow focus on specific events, leaving out long-term changes in the cultural meanings of transport (Sattlegger & Rau, 2016). While some key events have a limited effect on travel behaviour, others, such as getting a driver's licence, have been called "mobility milestones" (Rau & Manton, 2016) because they act as rites of passage and have lasting effects over the life course. In some cases, it may be difficult to distinguish between specific key events and longer-term processes, such as retirement or entry into adult working life (Müggenburg et al., 2015). Scheiner (2017) also argues that the social aspects of mobility biographies have been under-researched. Notably, the influence of peers and family (also called "linked lives" in life course research—Elder, 1994) plays an important role in travel socialization among children and youth for the development of individual travel behaviour (Baslington, 2008; Döring et al., 2014; Tully & Baier, 2011). Lastly, on a larger scale, individuals should be considered as evolving within a specific social and spatial context or "mobility culture", which influences generations of individuals over time (Deffner et al., 2006; Klinger et al., 2013).

Key Events and Cycling Trajectories
Although most research on cycling is still cross-sectional (Handy et al., 2014), a few studies have adopted a biographical perspective on the variation of cycling throughout the life course. According to a British study (Chatterjee et al., 2013), changes in the frequency of cycling are mostly triggered by one or more life events in the domain of education and employment, relationships, residential location, children's development, physical health, or leisure and fitness interests. Transport-related events (linked to car and bicycle

availability) or changes to the cycling environment are less likely to have an effect. In The Netherlands, Oakil et al. (2016) identified residential relocations and job changes as the key events most frequently linked to taking up bicycle commuting, particularly when those changes resulted in shorter commuting distances. Meanwhile, in the United States, Janke and Handy (2019) found changes in cycling at various stages of life to be triggered in particular by residential relocation and meeting a partner, while women mentioned parenthood as both a reason to decrease or increase cycling. Another contribution to this book by Sayagh, Dusong and Papon finds women in France reduce cycling due to social pressure during their teenage years, and later in life, due to pregnancy and childcare duties.

Going beyond key events, a few studies have used retrospective qualitative data to analyse whole life course trajectories of cycling, or "cycling trajectories". In Australia, Bonham and Wilson (2012) showed that women often returned to cycling despite frequent interruptions due to their changing life circumstances and family roles, challenging linear visions of mobility as a progression from cycling to car use. A series of studies by H. Jones (H. Jones, 2013; H. Jones et al., 2014, 2015) analysed individual walking and cycling trajectories over the whole life course, and categorized them as either "restorative" (increasing), "diminishing" (decreasing), or "resilient" (stable).

Few studies have sought to understand the theoretical role of key events in cycling. Chatterjee et al. (2012) put forward a conceptual model which sees changes (or "turning points") in cycling as the result of a deliberation triggered by a life course event, a change to the external environment, or a transport-related event, with mediating factors such as personal motivations, facilitating conditions, and personal history (Chatterjee et al., 2012, 2013). This model sees an individual's current cycling practice as the result of a cycling trajectory over their life course which includes "a person's thoughts, feelings, capabilities and actions related to cycling [...]

Key Events, Motivations and Prior Experience

developed over the course of their lives and shaped by transitions (or life-change events) that they have made and the contexts that they encounter" (Chatterjee et al. 2012, p. 5). More recently, Janke and Handy (2019) theorized about the influence of key events on cycling through four processes, namely (1) forcing a reconsideration of travel behaviour, (2) involving changes to the social environment and the norms around cycling, (3) unleashing a latent demand for cycling, or (4) triggering new destinations and interest in cycling (Janke & Handy, 2019).

Our conceptual framework (Figure 3.1) draws from Chatterjee et al. (2012) and Jones et al. (2015). We consider the e-bike within a lifelong cycling trajectory which also includes conventional cycling. Although the adoption of the e-bike constitutes by itself a "transport-related event" in the cycling trajectory (Chatterjee et al., 2013), we assume that it is also influenced by key events which may happen

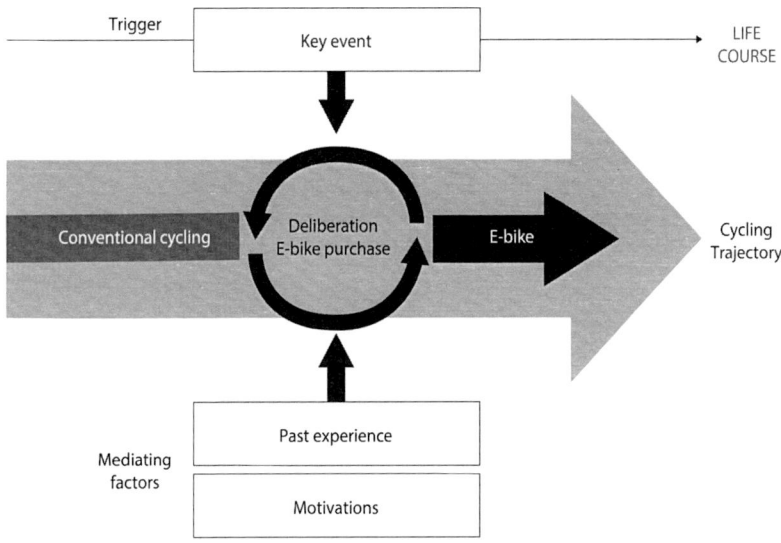

Figure 3.1: Conceptual model of the adoption of the e-bike — adapted from Chatterjee et al. (2012); Jones et al. (2015).

in other spheres of life. We view the deliberation process leading to the adoption of an e-bike as influenced by mediating factors such as intrinsic motivations and past experiences related to conventional cycling (the cycling trajectory).

E-bike Adoption
Research on the e-bike is still quite recent (Bourne et al., 2020; Fishman & Cherry, 2016). Since the first studies in 2006 (Weinert et al., 2006), there have been significant developments in e-bike technology, increasing availability and concomitant market penetration, yet consistent data on e-bike users remains scarce. There are large differences between studies in terms of geographical origin, sample size and method of recruitment. In this section, we will present existing research on the profile of e-bike users and their motivations for adopting the e-bike.

E-bikes offer an electric assistance that reduces physical effort when pedalling. This means that they may broaden cycling to people who would not consider conventional bicycles, and for trips which may have been considered too difficult (Behrendt, 2017; Rose, 2012). E-bikes were initially marketed to mature and near-retired people between the ages of 50 and 65 years old, who are over-represented among e-bike users in most studies (see Fishman & Cherry, 2016). The gender make up of e-bike users follows that of conventional cyclists: women are more represented in cycle-friendly contexts like Denmark (Haustein & Møller, 2016), but not in the United States or Australia (Johnson & Rose, 2013; MacArthur et al., 2014).

The main motivation for acquiring an e-bike is the reduced effort it requires compared to a conventional bicycle, which presents an advantage over longer distances or hilly terrain. The reduced effort required may also motivate people with reduced strength or physical disabilities (due to age or illness) to continue to cycle (T. Jones et al., 2016; MacArthur et al., 2014; Popovich et al., 2014). E-bikes have health benefits because they provide a low-intensity physical activity that meets recommended health guidelines (Bourne et al., 2018; Gojanovic et al., 2011; Van Cauwenberg et al., 2018). A further motivation is the replacement of car trips reported in car-centred contexts in North America or Australia, for practicality as well as environmental concerns (Dill & Rose, 2012; Johnson & Rose, 2013; MacArthur et al., 2014; Popovich et al., 2014).

Few studies have explicitly considered the role of key events in the adoption of the e-bike. In terms of cycling experience, e-bike users seem to fall into two main categories: existing cyclists, on the one hand, and non-cyclists (or interrupted cyclists) on the other. Le Bris (2016) finds e-bike users to have a pre-existing cycling practice, with the e-bike having the objective of either conserving, reactivating, or facilitating cycling. In terms of trip purpose, Haustein and Møller (2016) distinguish "enthusiastic" users wishing to increase their cycling, "utilitarian" users already cycling, and "recreational" users cycling less regularly for leisure.

Existing research gives some clues as to which key events may trigger e-bike adoption. Among older users, these include health problems or loss of strength which make cycling more difficult (Leger et al., 2018), or "a personal sense of decline in health" (T. Jones et al., 2016). For parents, the need to carry young children can also be a trigger for adopting the e-bike, as the additional weight makes conventional cycling difficult (Le Bris, 2016). Another category of triggers is changes in the physical environment, such as the shortening of distances to work or residence, which may lead to switching from the car or public transport to the e-bike (Plazier et al., 2017). Moving to a new city or neighbourhood and the resulting change in social and cycling environment may also trigger the adoption of the e-bike, by forcing a reconsideration of existing travel patterns, or especially in relation to environmental concerns (Le Bris, 2016). Lastly, external interventions such as subsidies or the opportunity to do a test-ride (see also chapter 3 by Rérat, this volume) may also encourage individuals to purchase an e-bike (Le Bris, 2016).

Method: A Biographical Approach to Cycling
E-bike Users in Lausanne

Lausanne is the fourth largest city in Switzerland with a population of 140,000 (Canton of Vaud, 2018) and 415,000 in the urban area in 2017 (Federal Statistical Office — FSO, 2018). It is notoriously hilly and has the lowest modal share of cycling among large cities in Switzerland, with only 1.6% of trips made by bicycle in 2015 (Federal Statistical Office — FSO & Federal Office for Spatial Development — FOSD, 2017). Switzerland is one of the foremost countries in the world in terms of e-bike adoption. In the 2015 Swiss micro-census, 7% of households owned an e-bike, of which 5.9% owned a pedelec (assistance up to 25km/h) and 1.2% owned an s-pedelec (assistance up to 45km/h). In cities such as Lausanne, where only 2.4% of households owned an e-bike in 2015 (FSOD, 2017), e-bike ownership is generally lower than in suburban or rural areas due to smaller household sizes.

Since the year 2000, the municipality of Lausanne has offered a subsidy for the purchase of an e-bike. At the time of the study, the subsidy for an e-bike purchase had a value of 15% of the price, to a maximum of 500 Swiss francs. A smaller subsidy was also available for the purchase of an e-bike battery (100 Swiss francs). With the city's approval, we sent out an online and postal survey to beneficiaries of the e-bike subsidy and received 1,466 responses. Out of those who had agreed to be contacted for interviews ($N = 717$), 20 users were chosen randomly. Additional users were recruited through exploratory interviews organized with staff and students of the University of Lausanne ($n = 4$), for a total of 24 in-depth interviews.

Due to our small sample size, we aimed to include a diversity of users in terms of age, gender and e-bike use, rather than seeking to be representative of the general population of e-bike users. Our sample of participants (see Table 3.1 on p. 55) is slightly skewed, with 14 men and 10 women, as men were more willing to participate in the interviews. This contrasts with the quantitative

Key Events, Motivations and Prior Experience

survey, where 53% of participants were women. Ages ranged from 20 to 81 years at the time of the interview, with participants evenly spread between age groups under 40 years old, 40–59, and over 60. A high proportion of users (16 out of 24) had a university degree, and the same proportion was professionally active, which reflects results from our quantitative survey. Only half of the users interviewed (12) had access to a car in their household, slightly less than the 53.7% of households who own a car in the municipality of Lausanne (Federal Statistical Office—FSO & Federal Office for Spatial Development—FOSD, 2017). Compared to e-bike users in Lausanne, our interviewees included more long-time users who had bought their e-bike more than four years previously (12 out of 24), whereas most e-bike users responding to the survey had bought an e-bike in the previous two years.

Retrospective Biographical Interviews
It has been argued that the complexity of influences arising as a result of key events is more suited to qualitative than quantitative analysis (Lanzendorf, 2003; Müggenburg et al., 2015). We chose a qualitative retrospective approach, using semi-structured interviews rather than life course calendars, in line with narrative approaches to mobility biographies (Sattlegger & Rau, 2016); this enabled a more inductive data collection. Retrospective data has been shown to be effective for recalling travel changes associated with key events (Behrens & Mistro, 2010; Beige & Axhausen, 2008; Lanzendorf, 2003; Oakil et al., 2016). The time of purchase of the e-bike was generally recalled well by most of our interviewees, as it had taken place only a few years prior. However, experienced users who had owned multiple e-bikes had more difficulty in recollecting events leading to the purchase of the e-bike, as they were prone to confusing memories of initial adoption of the e-bike with their most recent e-bike purchase.

Each in-depth interview lasted about one hour and covered both the individual's long-term relationship with cycling over their life course, and the short-term period around the purchase of the e-bike. The resulting transcripts were coded with the software "Atlas.Ti" and used to build individual cycling trajectories. These consisted of a timeline of periods of bicycle and e-bike use, as well as dates of specific biographical events. The trajectories were then classified on the basis of the presence of a significant period of interruption in cycling practice in the years before the purchase of the e-bike, the perceived frequency of cycling and the type of cycling (utilitarian or leisure), both before the purchase of the e-bike and throughout the life course.

The next section presents our results, starting with the influence of key events on e-bike adoption, and then looking at the role of motivations and prior experiences of cycling.

Results: Understanding the Adoption of the E-bike
Key Events as Triggers for Adoption

As this chapter aims to study the influence of key events on the adoption of the e-bike, we limit our focus to the first purchase of an e-bike, even though there may be a second or third e-bike whose purchase may have been influenced by other occurrences (e.g. accidents, theft, mechanical issues). In line with mobility biographies research, we chose to focus on larger key events in the life course, excluding smaller triggers like the municipal subsidy (available to all users), discounted prices or test rides, although these may play a role in precipitating the purchase of an e-bike (Le Bris, 2016).

For 14 e-bike users out of 24, a key event played a role in the purchase of their first e-bike. We found six types of key events to trigger the adoption of the e-bike: residential changes ($n = 4$), workplace changes ($n = 4$), day care/schooling changes ($n = 2$), childbirth ($n = 3$), health events ($n = 3$), partner-related events ($n = 3$). Ten users did not mention any key event whatsoever linked to the adoption of the e-bike, while three users mentioned more than one. We will now describe each of these types of events in detail.

Table 3.1: Interviewee characteristics (opposite).

Key Events, Motivations and Prior Experience

User number	Name (fictional)	Age	Employment status	E-bikes owned	Bicycles owned	Cars in household
1	Pascal	51	Employed full-time	2 or more	2 or more	1
2	Philippe	55	Employed full-time	1	1	None
3	Marie	36	Employed full-time	1	None	None
4	Sébastien	29	Employed full-time	1	2 or more	None
5	Nicole	42	Employed part-time	1	1	1
6	David	25	Student	1	2 or more	None
7	Hélène	36	Employed full-time	2 or more	None	1
8	Pierre	43	Employed full-time	1	2 or more	1
9	Denis	52	Employed full-time	1	2 or more	1
10	Laure	52	Employed full-time	1	1	None
11	Paul	30	Employed full-time	1	1	None
12	Claudine	50	Employed full-time	1	None	None
13	Sarah	33	Employed part-time	1	1	None
14	Daniel	34	Employed full-time	2 or more	None	None
15	Stéphanie	38	Employed part-time	2 or more	1	None
16	Lucas	40	Unemployed	1	None	None
17	Jacques	61	Employed full-time	2 or more	2 or more	2 or more
18	Christine	65	Retired	2 or more	1	1
19	Céline	69	Retired	1	None	1
20	Michèle	76	Retired	2 or more	1	2 or more
21	Robert	79	Retired	2 or more	1	None
22	Jean	69	Retired	1	1	2 or more
23	Hubert	80	Retired	1	1	1
24	Michel	70	Retired	1	1	1

Becoming Urban Cyclists

Workplace changes lead to a change in spatial context. This can trigger a reconsideration of existing travel habits, which in turn may lead to the purchase of an e-bike. On the one hand, the e-bike can be adopted in order to cope with a location that is difficult to reach, for example because of a steep gradient which would have made conventional cycling difficult, as in the case of Laure (52). On the other hand, starting a job in a location closer to one's residence or to the city centre can also be used as an opportunity to change commuting habits. Daniel (34) mentions how a restriction on car parking at his new job and a discount on public transport passes acted as triggers to sell his car and switch to an e-bike.

> Laure, 52: I used to work in another city and left my bike at the train station. I moved around Lausanne by bike. Then two years ago I changed job and started working in the upper part of the city. The problem is that it's uphill and I carry a heavy bag, so I was sweating when I arrived. So I thought I should buy an e-bike [...] I wanted to wait for Christmas [to buy it] but couldn't because with my old bike there was just too much of a gradient.

> Daniel, 34: After I left my previous job [...] I was living in the city centre and working in the urban area, I had a stable job, so no need for my car. I added up the price of the car and the time lost in traffic, and realized that [...] the best mode of transport for me was an e-bike, combined with public transport. So, I sold my car and bought two e-bikes, one for my wife and one for myself.

Like workplace changes, ***residential changes*** have an impact on the spatial context and often go together with another event, like a new job, the birth of a child, or moving in with a partner, and these events act together to change travel circumstances. In the case of Paul (30), deciding to move to a suburban neighbourhood served as a trigger to buy an e-bike in anticipation, in order to keep cycling and to compensate for the increase in distance and lack of public transport at his new location. Residential moves also change the social context and norms around cycling. For Hélène (36), moving to the city triggered a change in her travel behaviour and she started

Key Events, Motivations and Prior Experience

travelling by bicycle instead of by car (using a conventional bike at first, and then an e-bike a few months later).

> Paul, 30: I recently moved to [a suburban neighbourhood] and left Lausanne. That's when I bought the e-bike, to keep my freedom of movement. I don't have to check the public transport schedule and can travel on my own when I want to, by day or night.

> Hélène, 36: I arrived in Lausanne in August 2015. My partner used to live in [a central neighbourhood] and I had a normal bicycle which I had begun to use. [...] Since we live in the city centre, we don't want to use the car as our daily mode of transport, and we didn't want the bicycle to be just for exercise but for transport. [...] That's why we switched to the e-bike.

Planning for *childbirth* leads future parents to start thinking about how to travel with their children. For some users, the e-bike was a solution to carry children more easily than a conventional bicycle, thanks to its electrical assistance, and was often bought together with a trailer or child seat. For Stéphanie (38), who wanted to keep cycling, it was also a way of avoiding having to use a car to transport children, groceries or other things.

> Stéphanie, 38: Since I became pregnant, I knew I wouldn't be able to carry a child seat on a non-electric bicycle, [...] my body wouldn't have held up [with the effort required].

> Daniel, 34: At around the same time [as I changed my job], I became a father [...] and my son was born. That made us ask ourselves how we should carry him, how we should travel with him.

Day care and schooling changes can affect the space-time constraints imposed upon young, working parents. Faced with car traffic in the city, the e-bike can provide a simple way to carry children without a car. For Denis (52), buying an e-bike with a trailer was intended as a way to transport his two children to school and avoid using the car in the city, while also getting some exercise. Meanwhile, for Nicole (42), the e-bike seemed to be the only way to bring her child to a day care centre before work hours.

Becoming Urban Cyclists

> Denis, 52: I bought [my e-bike] in 2013. I used to go down to the school and continue on to the day care centre, where I left my daughter. But doing the school run by car was complicated with traffic, going to the day care and not knowing where to park, and then taking my son to the school [...] I'm convinced that if I hadn't had children, I wouldn't have bought an e-bike.

> Nicole, 42: Two years ago, my daughter changed day care. Before, she came with me and I could drop her off before work. Once she was older, she wasn't allowed to go there any more so we put her in [another day care centre]. Since I had to be [at work] either at 6:45 or 7:15 and the day care opened at 6:45, it was impossible to get to work on time. It was really difficult because the day care centre is 20 minutes away from home and 20 minutes from the metro. [...] The only solution I found was an e-bike. By carrying her by e-bike and then taking the metro, I saved a huge amount of time.

Experiencing a serious **health event** like heart disease or an injury can also lead to the adoption of the e-bike. When regular cycling becomes too difficult, turning to an e-bike can be a way to avoid giving up cycling and to keep exercising. For Pascal (51), who had experienced an injury, the e-bike offered a form of rehabilitation by enabling a moderate effort, when a conventional bicycle would have been too intense.

> Pascal, 51: I went from a [gasoline-powered] scooter to the electric bicycle during my rehabilitation following a knee accident. [...] With a broken knee, it was a bit too hard to cycle. The e-bike was the right solution.

The interrelation between people in the same household or social circle is called "linked lives" in mobility biographies research (Holz-Rau & Scheiner, 2015). These **partner-related events** (Lanzendorf, 2010) can also have an indirect effect on the decision to adopt an e-bike. Often, the purchase of an e-bike is discussed among couples, and some of them purchase two e-bikes at the same time. An example of this is Jacques (61), for whom the decision to buy an

Key Events, Motivations and Prior Experience

e-bike was made to be able to keep up with his partner, who had already bought one previously.

> Jacques, 61: I talked about it with my partner because during our bike trips I was having trouble. She also had some knee pain, so she bought hers first. We noticed we were not performing the same, and that's what decided us. After that we visited a trade fair, and she bought her e-bike, and I followed soon after, because I saw her so at ease that I was becoming jealous.

The above examples show that key events can act as triggers for the decision to adopt an e-bike. These events can be summed up in three main categories. First are contextual changes (workplace, residence, day care), which change the spatial context of everyday mobility through the location and schedule of activities, as well as changing the social context and social norms associated with cycling (i.e. a positive image of cycling), prompting users to consider the e-bike as an alternative to the car and public transport. Second are biographical changes (childbirth and health events), which lead to a change in the conditions for cycling and the individual's physical capacity, or trigger a reconsideration of travel behaviour, leading to the adoption of the e-bike as a way to keep cycling or return to cycling. Third, partner-related events, which may include their purchase of an e-bike, influence the individual indirectly through socialization effects (such as the desire not to be left behind when cycling together for leisure).

However, for 10 users out of 24, the adoption of the e-bike was not found to be linked to a specific key event. This is probably because most users who did not mention a key event were near or past retirement age, and the majority of key events tend to happen before the age of 40 (Beige & Axhausen, 2012). In these cases, longer processes that fall outside the scope of key events, such as ageing or the transition to retirement may be related to the adoption of the e-bike, although they do not trigger it directly. Indeed, we found many older users had bought their e-bike while they were still working in order to get back in shape or keep cycling despite reduced physical capacity. After retirement, reducing their daily trips had given them more free time and the opportunity to take up cycling as a regular form of leisure, often practised as a couple.

Motivations and Prior Experiences of Cycling as Mediating Factors
In addition to key events, both motivations for adopting an e-bike and prior experience of cycling can play a mediating role in the decision to adopt an e-bike. We identified six main motivations for buying an e-bike, namely (1) avoiding using the car or public transport, (2) taking up a physical exercise, (3) cycling for leisure, (4) cycling in hilly terrain, (5) continuing to cycle in winter, and (6) carrying children or heavy goods. These can be classified into two main groups. A first group of motivations is often linked to biographical changes such as the birth of a child, or day care changes, which may lead to the purchase of an e-bike in order to be able to transport children. Adopting an e-bike to avoid using the car or public transport, or to cycle in hilly terrain, is often linked to spatial changes in workplace or residential location. A second group of motivations is more associated with long-term processes such as ageing. This is often the case when physical exercise is the motivation for adopting an e-bike, as a way of preserving one's physical capacity and mobility.

The degree of prior experience of conventional cycling, or the individual's "cycling trajectory" (Jones, 2013), is an important factor in the adoption of the e-bike, but greatly varies between e-bike users. Inspired by the categorization of Jones et al. (2015), we identify two main categories, depending on whether or not cycling was practised before adopting the e-bike: (1) restorative trajectories and (2) resilient trajectories. The restorative trajectory (Figure 3.2) includes people who either did not cycle previously, or had stopped cycling for multiple years before adopting the e-bike. For e-bike users with a restorative trajectory, the e-bike had the effect of either beginning to cycle, or restoring their cycling practice to its former level (for those who had previously been regular cyclists). The

Key Events, Motivations and Prior Experience

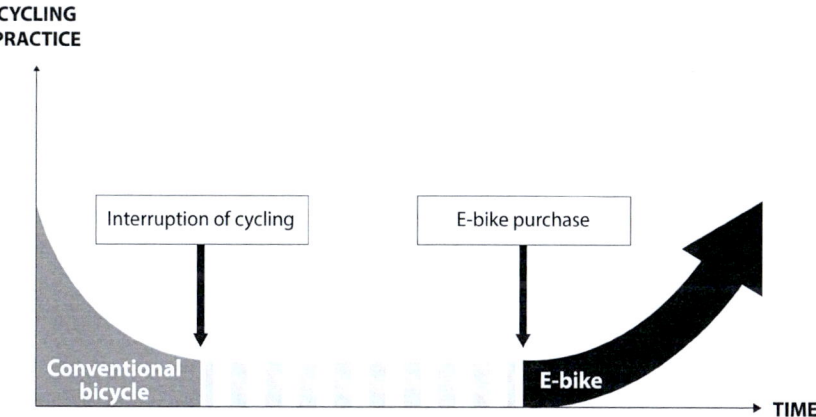

Figure 3.2: Restorative cycling trajectory.

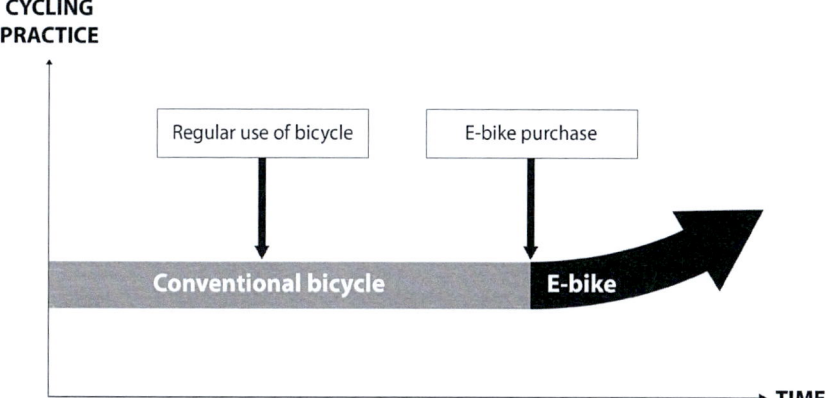

Figure 3.3: Resilient cycling trajectory.

resilient trajectory (Figure 3.3) includes people for whom conventional cycling was a regular activity that had not been interrupted by key events, and often constituted their main mode of transport, as many did not own a car. For them, the adoption of the e-bike was a way to maintain this continuous or "resilient" cycling practice.

Cycling trajectories change the role that key events can play in the adoption of the e-bike. For restorative trajectories (new or returning cyclists), key events such as health issues or contextual changes serve as opportunities to start cycling or get back into cycling. This rediscovery of cycling is motivated by the wish to engage in physical exercise or leisure, or to switch to a different mode of transport in the city. For resilient trajectories (regular cyclists), switching from conventional cycling to the e-bike is mostly linked to either a contextual change (in the workplace or place of residence) or a biographical change (e.g. childbirth) which poses a threat to conventional cycling and prompts the adoption of an e-bike. An increase in distance or declivity, the need to transport children, or the effect of age, were all mentioned as making the use of a conventional bicycle too difficult. This desire to continue cycling despite difficult circumstances can be explained by the high value this practice has within these individuals' lifestyle, and the freedom and independence associated with cycling.

Discussion

The goal of the present chapter was to investigate the adoption of the e-bike. We conducted retrospective biographical interviews to consider the role of key events, motivations and prior experiences of cycling in this process.

Just over half of all interviewed e-bike users (14 out of 24) adopted an e-bike following a key event or a combination of events, either a workplace change, residential change, the birth of a child, a day care or schooling change, a health event, or a partner-related event. These events can be broadly categorized as either contextual changes (workplace, residential or day care changes), which change the spatial and also the social context for cycling; biographical changes (childbirth, health events), which lead to changes in the conditions for cycling and in the individual's physical capacity; or

Key Events, Motivations and Prior Experience

partner-related events, which influence the individual's decision to adopt the e-bike.

We found that residential and workplace relocations linked to shorter distances triggered a shift towards the e-bike, confirming results for conventional cycling (Bonham & Wilson, 2012; Oakil et al., 2016). Moving to a new spatial and social context in the city also acted as a trigger for starting to use an e-bike, confirming findings on residential relocation to a bike-friendly city (Janke & Handy, 2019). However, while research on conventional cycling links an increase in commuting distance to a shift away from cycling, we found that increased distances were mentioned in this case as a reason for switching from conventional cycling to the e-bike. Thus, adopting the e-bike may be a way to adjust to a new cycling environment, steeper gradients, or longer distances, while avoiding giving up cycling.

Childbirth was mentioned as a trigger for adopting an e-bike in order to be able to continue cycling despite the additional weight of carrying children (on a bicycle seat) and despite an increased number of trips. This contrasts with conventional cycling literature, which shows that the birth of a child tends to interrupt cycling (Oakil et al., 2016), suggesting that e-bikes could help maintain a person's cycling practice throughout the phase of children's development. We also found that the birth of a child could trigger a reconsideration of travel behaviour, which led to restarting cycling with an e-bike. This confirms findings on the importance of parenthood as a potential opportunity to restart an interrupted cycling practice (Bonham & Wilson, 2012; Janke & Handy, 2019).

Our results show that health events may act as triggers for adopting the e-bike as a form of moderate exercise or as a way of continuing cycling despite reduced physical capacity. Conversely, in cycling literature, health events are generally linked with a decrease in conventional cycling, although the desire to stay healthy has also been found to be a reason for restarting cycling (Chatterjee et al., 2013). This confirms studies that have shown that e-bikes can act as a mobility aid for people with limited abilities or of older age (T. Jones et al., 2016).

As for partner-related events, we found that the e-bike was a topic of discussion within couples, with the purchase of a first e-bike often followed by a second one. This shows the importance of considering cycling not only as an individual choice but as a social activity, and the role partners may play in the decision to restart cycling (Bonham & Wilson, 2012; Janke & Handy, 2019). E-bikes may be especially useful as an "equalizer" (Popovich et al., 2014) between different levels of physical ability, also helping to extend cycling as a social activity into later life.

In addition to key events, we found that motivations and prior experiences of conventional cycling played a mediating role in adopting the e-bike. Adopting the e-bike to avoid car or public transport use, and being able to cycle uphill, was often related to contextual changes (changes in residence or workplace), while adopting the e-bike to take up physical exercise and cycle for leisure was related to ageing and health preoccupations.

Based on H. Jones et al. (2015), we distinguished two different kinds of cycling trajectories depending on an individual's past experience of cycling. First, restorative trajectories (new or returning cyclists) adopted the e-bike as an opportunity to get into (or return to) cycling, for leisure or physical exercise, or to reduce car use. In this trajectory, motivations for returning to cycling play an important role, while key events act as opportunities to put these plans into action by "unleashing a latent demand for cycling" (Janke & Handy, 2019). Meanwhile, resilient trajectories (continuing cyclists) adopted the e-bike in order to continue cycling despite a contextual change or health event. For these users, childbirth, ageing, or moving to a new home or job act as threats to their cycling practice, leading to a switch to an e-bike as a way to continue cycling. This confirms findings on the role of the e-bike as a form of "adaptive" change for cyclists (Jones et al., 2015).

Key Events, Motivations and Prior Experience

Nonetheless, our results are not without a few limitations. Compared to other studies, a smaller proportion of users than expected (14 out of 24) mentioned a key event as a trigger for adopting an e-bike. First, this may be because our study only considers what Chatterjee et al. (2013) call "life events", and not transport-related events (such as changes in car possession) or changes to the external environment (such as a new cycling infrastructure). Second, another explanation may be related to the limited time frame we considered. This included just the period of adoption of the first e-bike, not its subsequent use. Nor did we count the purchase of the e-bike itself as a key event, nor the subsidy received for it, in contrast with other studies (Janke & Handy, 2019; Plazier et al., 2017). Third, the use of qualitative rather than quantitative data limits the number of key events to those voluntarily reported by users, although we argue that it presents a more realistic account of the causality of these events on e-bike adoption. In fact, the actual number of key events mentioned by e-bike users as linked to their e-bike adoption was quite restricted.

Future research could go further than the adoption of the e-bike by investigating the effects of key events on e-bike use over time. This includes the purchase of other vehicles (whether additional e-bikes, different e-bike types, or other modes of transport), and variations in the frequency of e-bike use. More generally, with increasing numbers of e-bikes and data on e-bike users, more opportunities for the field of e-bike research should become available.

Conclusion

E-bikes hold much potential for increasing urban cycling. By removing physical barriers to cycling, they may give some people the confidence to become urban cyclists or the means to continue cycling despite challenging circumstances. This includes categories less represented among cyclists, such as mature or retired people, those with limited physical abilities, and parents of young children. Our research has shown that the adoption of the e-bike can be triggered by key events—contextual changes, biographical events, or partner-related events—happening over the life course. Because conventional cycling is vulnerable to changing spatial and biographical circumstances that make it more difficult, e-bikes may be a solution to help recruit new cyclists, but also re-engage lapsed cyclists and retain regular cyclists over time. It follows that to promote urban cycling, e-bikes should be targeted not just to non-cyclists, but also to conventional cyclists who could benefit from switching to electrically assisted cycling. Public policies could also address existing and returning cyclists differently. New or returning cyclists may respond to interventions limiting car use such as mobility schemes (e.g. restricting car parking) and to e-bike trials at the workplace, while existing cyclists could be attracted to switch from conventional bicycles to e-bikes after residential relocation or childbirth through encouragements such as financial subsidies for e-bikes or cargo bicycles. In conclusion, a biographical approach to cycling has helped us to understand the adoption of the e-bike better. A greater understanding of the role of cycling over the life course could help to develop more effective policies to serve the diversity of cyclists, both present and future.

References
Baslington, H. (2008). Travel socialization: A social theory of travel mode behavior. *International Journal of Sustainable Transportation*, 2(2), 91–114.
Behrendt, F. (2017). Why cycling matters for electric mobility: Towards diverse, active and sustainable e-mobilities. *Mobilities*, 13(1), 1–17.
Behrens, R., & Mistro, R. D. (2010). Shocking habits: Methodological issues in analyzing changing personal travel behavior over time. *International Journal of Sustainable Transportation*, 4(5), 253–271.
Beige, S., & Axhausen, K. W. (2008). Long-term and mid-term mobility decisions during the life course: Experiences with a retrospective survey. *IATSS Research*, 32(2), 16–33.
Beige, S., & Axhausen, K. W. (2012). Interdependencies between turning points in life and long-term mobility decisions. *Transportation*, 39(4), 857–872.

Key Events, Motivations and Prior Experience

Bonham, J., & Wilson, A. (2012). Bicycling and the life course: The start-stop-start experiences of women cycling. *International Journal of Sustainable Transportation*, *6*(4), 195–213.

Bourne, J. E., Cooper, A. R., Kelly, P., Kinnear, F. J., England, C., Leary, S., & Page, A. (2020). The impact of e-cycling on travel behaviour: A scoping review. *Journal of Transport & Health*, *19*, 100910. https://doi.org/10.1016/j.jth.2020.100910

Bourne, J. E., Sauchelli, S., Perry, R., Page, A., Leary, S., England, C., & Cooper, A. R. (2018). Health benefits of electrically-assisted cycling: A systematic review. *International Journal of Behavioral Nutrition and Physical Activity*, *15*(1), 116. https://doi.org/10.1186/s12966-018-0751-8

Canton of Vaud. (2018). *Statistique Vaud – Chiffres-clés annuels de la population, 1981–2018* [Annual key population figures]. http://www.scris.vd.ch/Default.aspx?DocID=6808

Chatterjee, K., Sherwin, H., & Jain, J. (2013). Triggers for changes in cycling: The role of life events and modifications to the external environment. *Journal of Transport Geography*, *30*, 183–193.

Chatterjee, K., Sherwin, H., Jain, J., Christensen, J., & Marsh, S. (2012). Conceptual model to explain turning points in travel behavior: Application to bicycle use. *Transportation Research Record: Journal of the Transportation Research Board*, *2322*, 82–90.

Clark, B., Chatterjee, K., & Melia, S. (2016). Changes in level of household car ownership: The role of life events and spatial context. *Transportation*, *43*(4), 565–599.

Deffner, J., Götz, K., Schubert, S., Potting, C., Stete, G., Tschann, A., & Loose, W. (2006). *Schlussbericht zu dem Projekt „Nachhaltige Mobilitätskultur". Entwicklung eines Integrierten Konzepts der Planung, Kommunikation und Implementierung einer nachhaltigen, multioptionalen Mobilitätskultur.* Institüt für sozial-ökologische Forschung (ISOE) GmbH. http://isoe-publikationen.de/fileadmin/redaktion/Downloads/Mobilitaet/mobilitaetskultur-bericht-2006.pdf

Dill, J., & Rose, G. (2012). Electric bikes and transportation policy: Insights from early adopters. *Transportation Research Record: Journal of the Transportation Research Board*, *2314*, 1–6.

Döring, L., Albrecht, J., Scheiner, J., & Holz-Rau, C. (2014). Mobility biographies in three generations — socialization effects on commute mode choice. *Transportation Research Procedia*, *1*(1), 165–176.

Elder, G. H. (1994). Time, human agency, and social change: Perspectives on the life course. *Social Psychology Quarterly*, 57(1), 4–15.

Elder, G. H., Johnson, M. K., & Crosnoe, R. (2003). The emergence and development of life course theory. In *Handbook of the life course* (pp. 3–19). Springer.

Federal Statistical Office—FSO. (2018). Portraits City Statistics 2018: Agglomerations. https://www.bfs.admin.ch/bfs/fr/home/statistiken/ querschnittsthemen/city-statistics/agglomerationsportraets/lausanne. html

Federal Statistical Office—FSO, & Federal Office for Spatial Development —FOSD. (2017). *Comportement de la population en matière de transports – Résultats du microrecensement mobilité et transports 2015* [Swiss microcensus on mobility and transport 2015]. https://www.bfs.admin.ch/ bfsstatic/dam/assets/1840478/master

Fishman, E., & Cherry, C. (2016). E-bikes in the mainstream: Reviewing a Decade of Research. *Transport Reviews*, 36(1), 72–91. https://doi.org/ 10.1080/01441647.2015.1069907

Gojanovic, B., Welker, J., Iglesias, K., Daucourt, C., & Gremion, G. (2011). Electric bicycles as a new active transportation modality to promote health. *Medicine & Science in Sports & Exercise*, 43(11), 2204–2010.

Handy, S., van Wee, B., & Kroesen, M. (2014). Promoting cycling for transport: Research needs and challenges. *Transport Reviews*, 34(1), 4–24. https://doi.org/10.1080/01441647.2013.860204

Haustein, S., & Møller, M. (2016). Age and attitude: Changes in cycling patterns of different e-bike user segments. *International Journal of Sustainable Transportation*, 10(9), 836–846.

Heinen, E., van Wee, B., & Maat, K. (2010). Commuting by bicycle: An overview of the literature. *Transport Reviews*, 30(1), 59–96.

Holz-Rau, C., & Scheiner, J. (2015). Mobilitätsbiografien und Mobilitätssozialisation: Neue Zugänge zu einem alten Thema. In J. Scheiner & C. Holz-Rau (Eds.), *Räumliche Mobilität und Lebenslauf* (pp. 3–22). Springer.

Janke, J., & Handy, S. (2019). How life course events trigger changes in bicycling attitudes and behavior: Insights into causality. *Travel Behaviour and Society*, 16, 31–41. https://doi.org/10.1016/j.tbs.2019.03.004

Key Events, Motivations and Prior Experience

Johnson, M., & Rose, G. (2013). Electric bikes—cycling in the New World City: An investigation of Australian electric bicycle owners and the decision making process for purchase. *Proceedings of the 2013 Australasian Transport Research Forum*, 13. https://www.australasiantransportresearchforum.org.au/sites/default/files/2013_johnson_rose.pdf

Jones, H. (2013). *Understanding walking and cycling using a life course perspective* [Doctoral dissertation]. University of the West of England.

Jones, H., Chatterjee, K., & Gray, S. (2014). A biographical approach to studying individual change and continuity in walking and cycling over the life course. *Journal of Transport & Health, 1*(3), 182–189.

Jones, H., Chatterjee, K., & Gray, S. (2015). Understanding change and continuity in walking and cycling over the life course: A first look at gender and cohort differences. In J. Scheiner & C. Holz-Rau (Eds.), *Mobility biographies and mobility socialisation* (pp. 115–132). Springer. https://doi.org/10.1007/978-3-658-07546-0_7

Jones, T., Harms, L., & Heinen, E. (2016). Motives, perceptions and experiences of electric bicycle owners and implications for health, wellbeing and mobility. *Journal of Transport Geography, 53*, 41–49.

Klinger, T., Kenworthy, J. R., & Lanzendorf, M. (2013). Dimensions of urban mobility cultures—a comparison of German cities. *Journal of Transport Geography, 31*, 18–29. https://doi.org/10.1016/j.jtrangeo.2013.05.002

Klöckner, C. (2004). How single events change travel mode choice: A life span perspective. *3rd International Conference on Traffic and Transportation Psychology: Papers of the ICTTP 2004, IAAP division 13: Traffic and Transport Psychology, 2004*.

Lanzendorf, M. (2003, 10 August). *Mobility biographies. A new perspective for understanding travel behaviour* (pp. 10, 15). [Paper presentation]. 10th International Conference on Travel Behaviour Research. Lucerne, Switzerland.

Lanzendorf, M. (2010). Key events and their effect on mobility biographies: The case of childbirth. *International Journal of Sustainable Transportation, 4*(5), 272–292.

Le Bris, J. (2016). *Die individuelle Mobilitätspraxis und Mobilitätskarrieren von Pedelec-Besitzern: Adoption und Appropriation von Elektrofahrrädern*. [Doctoral dissertation]. Eberhard Karls Universität Tübingen.

Leger, S. J., Dean, J. L., Edge, S., & Casello, J. M. (2018). "If I had a regular bicycle, I wouldn't be out riding anymore": Perspectives on the potential of e-bikes to support active living and independent mobility among older adults in Waterloo, Canada. *Transportation Research Part A: Policy and Practice*. https://doi.org/10.1016/j.tra.2018.10.009

MacArthur, J., Dill, J., & Person, M. (2014). Electric bikes in North America: Results of an online survey. *Transportation Research Record: Journal of the Transportation Research Board*, 2468, 123–130.

Marincek, D., & Rérat, P. (2020). From conventional to electrically-assisted cycling. A biographical approach to the adoption of the e-bike. *International Journal of Sustainable Transportation*, 15(10), 768–777. https://doi.org/10.1080/15568318.2020.1799119

Marsden, G., & Docherty, I. (2013). Insights on disruptions as opportunities for transport policy change. *Transportation Research Part A: Policy and Practice*, 51, 46–55.

Müggenburg, H., Busch-Geertsema, A., & Lanzendorf, M. (2015). Mobility biographies: A review of achievements and challenges of the mobility biographies approach and a framework for further research. *Journal of Transport Geography*, 46, 151–163.

Oakil, A. T. M., Ettema, D., Arentze, T., & Timmermans, H. (2016). Bicycle commuting in the Netherlands: An analysis of modal shift and its dependence on life cycle and mobility events. *International Journal of Sustainable Transportation*, 10(4), 376–384.

Plazier, P. A., Weitkamp, G., & van den Berg, A. E. (2017). "Cycling was never so easy!" An analysis of e-bike commuters' motives, travel behaviour and experiences using GPS-tracking and interviews. *Journal of Transport Geography*, 65, 25–34. https://doi.org/10.1016/j.jtrangeo.2017.09.017

Popovich, N., Gordon, E., Shao, Z., Xing, Y., Wang, Y., & Handy, S. (2014). Experiences of electric bicycle users in the Sacramento, California area. *Travel Behaviour and Society*, 1(2), 37–44. https://doi.org/10.1016/j.tbs.2013.10.006

Rau, H., & Manton, R. (2016). Life events and mobility milestones: Advances in mobility biography theory and research. *Journal of Transport Geography*, 52, 51–60. https://doi.org/10.1016/j.jtrangeo.2016.02.010

Rérat, P. (2019). Cycling to work: Meanings and experiences of a sustainable practice. *Transportation Research Part A: Policy and Practice*, 123, 91–104.

Key Events, Motivations and Prior Experience

Rose, G. (2012). E-bikes and urban transportation: Emerging issues and unresolved questions. *Transportation, 39*(1), 81–96.

Sattlegger, L., & Rau, H. (2016). Carlessness in a car-centric world: A reconstructive approach to qualitative mobility biographies research. *Journal of Transport Geography, 53*, 22–31.

Scheiner, J. (2007, April–June). Mobility biographies: Elements of a biographical theory of travel demand. *Erdkunde*, 161–173.

Scheiner, J. (2017). Mobility biographies and mobility socialisation — New approaches to an old research field. In J. Zhang (Ed.), *Life-oriented behavioral research for urban policy* (pp. 385–401). Springer.

Tully, C. J., & Baier, D. (2011). Mobilitätssozialisation. In *Verkehrspolitik* (pp. 195–211). Springer.

Van Cauwenberg, J., de Geus, B., & Deforche, B. (2018). Cycling for transport among older adults: Health benefits, prevalence, determinants, injuries and the potential of e-bikes. In A. Curl & C. Musselwhite (Eds.), *Geographies of Transport and Ageing* (pp. 133–151). Springer.

Velosuisse. (2020). Marché suisse de la bicyclette 2019 [Swiss market for bicycles 2019]. http://www.velosuisse.ch/files/Veloverkaufsstatistik_Schweizer_Markt_2019.pdf

Verplanken, B., Walker, I., Davis, A., & Jurasek, M. (2008). Context change and travel mode choice: Combining the habit discontinuity and self-activation hypotheses. *Journal of Environmental Psychology, 28*(2), 121–127.

Weinert, J. X., Ma, C., & Yang, X. (2006). The transition to electric bikes in China and its effect on travel behavior, transit use, and safety. *Institute of Transportation Studies.* http://escholarship.org/uc/item/38b3q3jg.pdf

CHAPTER 4
THE EFFECTS OF A PROMOTIONAL CAMPAIGN ON THE PRACTICE OF UTILITY CYCLING: BIKE-TO-WORK IN SWITZERLAND

Patrick Rérat

Introduction

Each year, thousands of employees take part in the bike-to-work action in Switzerland. This campaign is based on teams of usually four employees who commit to cycling to work as much as possible in May and/or June. While many participants are already regular cyclists, others use it as an opportunity to try it out.

The bike-to-work initiative aims to encourage some commuters to try utility cycling (cycling as a means of transport rather than for leisure or sport), with the hope that this temporary change will have a long-term effect. This can be seen as a "nudge in the right direction", a way of influencing people's behaviour without the need for prohibitions or imposed changes (Thaler & Sunstein, 2009). Giving people the opportunity to change is a way to facilitate a change in practice that would otherwise be difficult, given that most travel behaviour is highly habitual and generally occurs in stable contexts (Moser et al., 2018; Scheiner & Holz-Rau, 2013). Without such opportunities, the inertia of habitual mobility practice can prevent any modal shift.

The positive impacts of cycling are well documented in terms of public health, ecological footprint reduction, and traffic regulation and a growing number of cities are taking measures to promote cycling. While there is an important body of literature on the factors that may increase the modal share of cycling (such as dedicated and segregated infrastructures, and reduction in the speed and volume of motorized traffic), less is known regarding how cycling may be adopted again after the initial learning phase in childhood, and

The Effects of a Promotional Campaign

how it evolves over the life course (Marincek & Rérat, 2020; see also Sayagh, Dusong & Papon, as well as Buhler, this volume).

Bike-to-work schemes exist in several countries, but they are usually quite short (e.g. a day) (Lee, 2015; Piatkowski et al., 2015; Rose & Marfurt, 2007). Lasting one or two months, the duration of the Swiss campaign makes it an interesting case to analyse how participants develop a variety of skills and a set of knowledge, and how they experience bike commuting. Switzerland occupies an intermediate position in Europe in terms of the modal share of cycling. According to the 2015 *Microcensus Mobility and Transport*, 7% of all journeys are made by bike. This is higher than in most Latin and English-speaking countries, but lower than in Northern Europe, where several countries have a more mature cycling culture (Pucher & Buehler, 2012).

The aim of this chapter is to explore the effects of the bike-to-work action on the practice of utility cycling. In the following sections, the theoretical framework and the methods are presented. The empirical material shows that the effects of such a promotion campaign are manifold and are observed in terms of uses of the bike (motivational effect), individuals' cycling potential (learning effect), and the cyclability of the context (legitimating effect).

Analysing the Effects of Cycling Promotion Campaigns
Campaigns promoting cycling take a great variety of forms. Some diffuse information to the general public or to a specific target group (e.g. within a company); some others, which are of interest here, encourage participants to try cycling for a certain duration (from one day to several weeks), for certain motives (utility, leisure or sport), or certain purposes (environment, health, etc.) (e.g. de Kruijf et al., 2018; Lee, 2015; Piatkowski et al., 2015).

The Various Dimensions of Event-Based Behaviour Changes
Existing research usually addresses event-based behaviour changes through interviews and surveys before, during and after the

experience, sometimes in comparison to a control group (Yang et al., 2010). Core questions usually centre around who participates in these actions, why they participate, and what impact participation has on mobility behaviour. While Piatkowski et al. (2015) find no evidence to suggest that the bike-to-work day in Denver, USA, caused significant change with regard to cycling frequency, other research studying longer events that are more focused on a particular kind of user (e.g. car owners to whom an e-bike is lent) or that imply various incentives (e.g. prizes) shows positive impacts, albeit to varying extents (Bowles et al., 2006; Moser et al., 2018; Pucher et al., 2010; Rose & Marfurt, 2007; Yang et al., 2010).

Some studies go more into detail regarding the practice of cycling, analysing self-reported skills and confidence (Bowles et al., 2006; Telfer et al., 2006), satisfaction with travel (de Kruijf et al., 2018), or health indicators (Rissel & Watkins, 2014). The impact of cycling events may go beyond bike use, to have an influence on self-confidence, sense of belonging and empowerment, as shown in the case of cycling lessons attended by women migrants (Mundler & Rérat, 2018; see also Buhler, this volume).

Another approach centres on psychology-based individualist models such as Ajzen's theory of planned behaviour, which looks at how behaviours are formed and linked with intentions (e.g. Nkurunziza et al., 2012). Types of (potential) cyclists are also distinguished on the basis of Prochaska's transtheoretical model and on the various stages of change: precontemplation (unaware of problems, no intention to change), contemplation (aware of problems, thinking about change), prepared for action (intention to change in the next six months), action (action being taken), and maintenance (has maintained action for six months or more) (e.g. Gatersleben & Appleton, 2007). In this perspective, modal shift is a slow process and each stage requires specific strategies, including those that help individuals to maintain new mobility practices.

This chapter takes a different view and starts with the concept of velomobility. Based on a questionnaire survey and interviews

The Effects of a Promotional Campaign

with participants, it highlights the variety of effects an event like bike-to-work may have on both an individual and a contextual level.

The System of Velomobility

The theoretical framework I propose in this chapter draws on the work by Kaufmann (2011). I adapt his conceptualization of mobility to cycling, based on three interlinked dimensions: movement in physical space (the use of the bike), the aptitude of movement or motility (the individual's cycling potential), and the field of possibilities of a context, or its hosting potential for cycling (its cyclability) (Figure 4.1). Together, these dimensions form the system of velomobility (Behrendt, 2018). This framework can be used at a macro level to analyse the system of velomobility in a city or a country (Rérat, 2021; Rérat et al., 2019). It is applied here in a dynamic way to address the changes that participation in bike-to-work may imply.

The first dimension of the theoretical framework—the use of the bike—covers factual elements that transportation studies traditionally address: the characteristics of the trips (frequency,

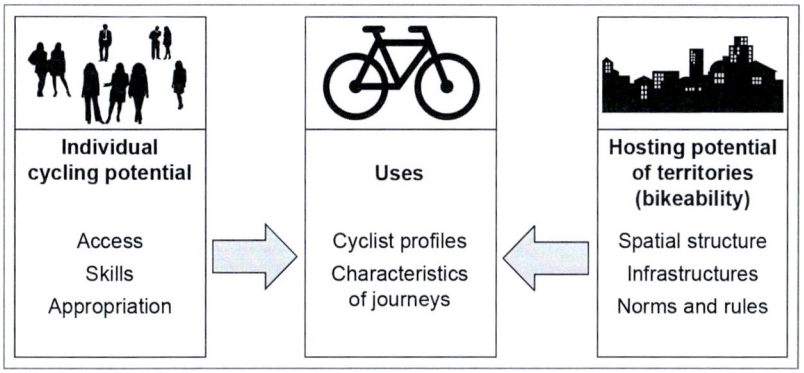

Figure 4.1: The System of Velomobility (Rérat, 2021; images from pixabay.com).

length, origin/destination, motives, etc.) and the profile of users (socio-economic status, gender, age, etc.). The level of use of the bike can be regarded as resulting from the confluence of two potentials: the individual's cycling potential and the territories' hosting potential (cyclability). Applied to bike-to-work, an increase in the practice of cycling may be explained by changes in these two dimensions.

The individual's cycling potential is the set of characteristics enabling an individual to use a bike. Individuals are characterized by their aptitude for movement in a given physical, economic and social context (Kaufmann, 2011, p. 37). This aptitude, or cycling potential, comprises three dimensions: access ("can"), skills ("know"), and appropriation ("want") (Kaufmann, 2011, p. 37).

Access covers the options for mobility, that is, "all the instrumental resources which individuals get the right to use" (Flamm & Kaufmann, 2006, p. 171). This applies, for example, to vehicles (different kinds of bikes, etc.), public transport passes, and subscriptions to bike-sharing schemes.

Riding a bike involves skills in five fields in addition to keeping balance while pedalling (Flamm, 2004): physical condition; experience of concrete traffic situations; knowledge of the spatial context (in order to find a convenient route or to avoid disruptions in the urban fabric); ability to estimate the duration of trips; and organizational knowledge (for example, the ability to orient oneself, to plan activities, or to do repairs; for repair and maintenance, see Abord de Chatillon, this volume). These skills develop with experience ("learning by doing" and training). Skills can involve the adoption of tactics (de Certeau & Giard, 2010) in order to cycle in a social and spatial context dominated by automobility (Urry, 2004). Choosing a route involves several of the required skills (Flamm, 2014), as there is often a "substantial investment in route determination" (trial-and-error selection, taking secondary and residential roads, taking exhaust-free off-road paths, timing the commute to avoid rush hours, etc.) (Bonham & Koth, 2010, p. 100).

The Effects of a Promotional Campaign

Appropriation defines the way individuals perceive and select mobility options according to their plans, aspirations and habits. The actual use of a transportation mode depends, among other things, on individuals' perceptions of the various modes.

The hosting potential of a context is how receptive or suitable it is for a practice. A context offers a specific field of possibilities (Kaufmann, 2011) and favours some modes of transportation to the detriment of others. I define the hosting potential of a territory for cycling as its cyclability, which has three dimensions: spatial context, infrastructure, and norms and rules.

The spatial context includes topography and weather conditions but also—and perhaps more importantly—the urban form. Density, compactness, functional diversity, the attractiveness of the landscape, and the built environment along cycling routes are all factors that favour (or not) the practice of cycling (Handy et al., 2014; Heinen et al., 2010).

Infrastructure and material artefacts refer to cycling urbanism. Cities and regions experiencing a cycling renaissance have implemented policies to increase their cyclability through traffic calming measures and cycling infrastructures, such as networks of integrated bikeways and the provision of bicycle parking (e.g. Buehler & Dill, 2016; Héran, 2014; Pucher & Buehler, 2012).

A territory's cyclability also has immaterial and symbolic dimensions, such as the rules of the road, and social norms. The car has informally privatized public space so that other users do not feel legitimate anymore, and the road has become a dangerous place for them (Lee, 2015). Where the bike is widespread, it is accepted; where it is rare, it is less tolerated and is the target of negative attitudes, as the minority practice of cycling may be perceived as a critique to the dominant system of automobility (Prati et al., 2017; see also Caimotto, this volume). Social norms regarding cycling may also differ between social groups as shown by Welsch (this volume) in an analysis of the differences in cycling behaviours and socialization between people from immigrant and non-immigrant backgrounds.

Becoming Urban Cyclists

The modal share of cycling can be interpreted as the meeting point between individual cycling potential and the hosting potential of a context for cycling. It is important to note that these are interrelated. Geller, a planner in Portland, proposed a typology of transportation cyclists: "The Strong and the Fearless", "The Enthused and the Confident", "The Interested but Concerned", and, finally, the "No Way No How" group of non-riders (for a discussion and empirical survey, see Dill & McNeil, 2013). This typology is based on people's relationships to bicycle transportation and highlights the differing needs of different types of cyclist in terms of bikeways and other infrastructure. In other words, a weak level of cyclability will restrict cycling to a specific part of the population (as risk awareness differs between ages and genders), while a high level of cyclability widens the profile of cyclists (Garrard et al., 2012; Pucher & Buehler, 2012). Indeed, skills for utility cycling do not only refer to individual characteristics. They are highly dependent on what the hosting potential of a space requires or its bikeability (see below and Adam et al., this volume).

Method

Organized by PRO VELO, the national bicycle advocacy association, the Swiss bike-to-work campaign has been in place since 2005. Similar schemes exist in many countries, with some differences, particularly in terms of duration. In the Swiss case, participation is open to any company, in exchange for a small financial contribution. It is usually based on teams of four employees, who commit to cycling to work as much as possible in May and/or June. The participants fill in a diary (number of trips, distances, etc.), and take part in a contest to win prizes. The objectives of the campaign are to make utility cycling more visible, and to convince employees to try bicycle commuting in the hope that they will consider adopting this practice.

An online survey was sent to the participants in September 2016. A total of 44,726 emails were sent, and 13,744 questionnaires were filled in (response rate: 31%). The survey addressed the dimensions of the system of velomobility discussed above. In addition to closed questions, several spaces throughout the questionnaire gave participants the opportunity to write spontaneous comments (11,000 were collected). Thirty semi-structured interviews were also carried out with students and members of staff at the University of Lausanne who participated in the campaign.

The goal of the research project was not primarily to assess the impact of the bike-to-work event. This would have implied tracking changes among participants through surveys or interviews before, during and after the campaign. However, several questions addressed the uses of the bike before and after the action, the motivations to participate in bike-to-work and its impact on their perception of bicycle commuting. In addition to quantitative data, we gathered qualitative material through comments left in the questionnaire and interviews. The many comments mentioning the bike-to-work action were used to identify its multiple potential effects and to look at how commuters can become urban cyclists. This explorative study paves the way for future research on the impacts of cycling promotion campaigns.

In the sample, women are slightly under-represented in comparison to the labour force (42% vs 46.6%), which may be explained by a higher likelihood of women working part-time and by the over-representation of men among sports cyclists (some of whom may join bike-to-work). On the national scale, the shares of men and women commuting by bike are actually similar and both account for 7% (OFS, 2018). Two age groups are over-represented in comparison to the working population: the 25–39 year-olds (35.6% vs 32.2%) and the 40–54 year-olds (46% vs 35.3%), whilst the younger and older age groups are under-represented. People with a higher education level feature more prominently (54% vs 41.2%). Finally, although it is open to students (1.7% of the sample), bike-to-work targets the working population and excludes children, teenagers or seniors, for whom other campaigns exist.

Becoming Urban Cyclists

The empirical sections of this chapter analyse the three main effects of the bike-to-work campaign: the motivational effect (recruiting new bike commuters), the learning effect (developing the individuals' cycling potential) and the legitimating effect (normalizing a minority practice).

Motivational Effect: Recruiting New Bike Commuters
For a third of participants, this was the first time they had taken part in bike-to-work. For half of them, it was at least their third participation. Most participants were used to bicycle commuting: three-quarters cycled to work regularly, defined as at least every other time (17.2%) or most of the time (56.2%) before bike-to-work. 18.4% claimed that they cycled for less than half of their commuting journeys, and 8.2% did not cycle to work previously. Even though those who did not previously cycle to work represent a minority of participants, their number accounts for several thousand each year and highlights the potential of the campaign to extend the practice of cycling.

This diversity of cyclists is also found in the motivations for participating in bike-to-work (Figure 4.2), which include both extrinsic motivations ("to do something in order to attain some external goal" (Hennessey et al., 2015)) and intrinsic motivations ("doing something because it is inherently interesting or enjoyable" (Ryan & Deci, 2000)).

The most frequently mentioned motivation, quoted by more than six participants, was intrinsic: the opportunity to get some exercise. The other intrinsic (micro) motivations are seen as less important: the possibility of winning a prize, the opportunity to try cycling or to increase their cycling practice. Ranking second and fourth in importance are two extrinsic (macro) motivations: the opportunity to do something for the environment and a desire to reassert the importance of the bike. As bike-to-work is a group activity, two (meso) factors related to the team are found: participation in order to encourage colleagues to cycle or in response

The Effects of a Promotional Campaign

to an invitation. Thus, the team aspect of bike-to-work provides a context, although for a limited time, that supports behavioural changes.

Comparing the weight given to these motivations with the number of participations shows a relative stability for exercise, being with friends and winning a prize. Three factors increase in importance with the number of participations: doing something for the environment, motivating colleagues and reasserting the importance of the bike. For those who participated for the first time, trying cycling or responding to the enthusiasm of colleagues is logically given more weight.

The formation of teams creates a motivational effect that concerns three kinds of participants. The first category gathers commuters who did not cycle to work previously. Three months

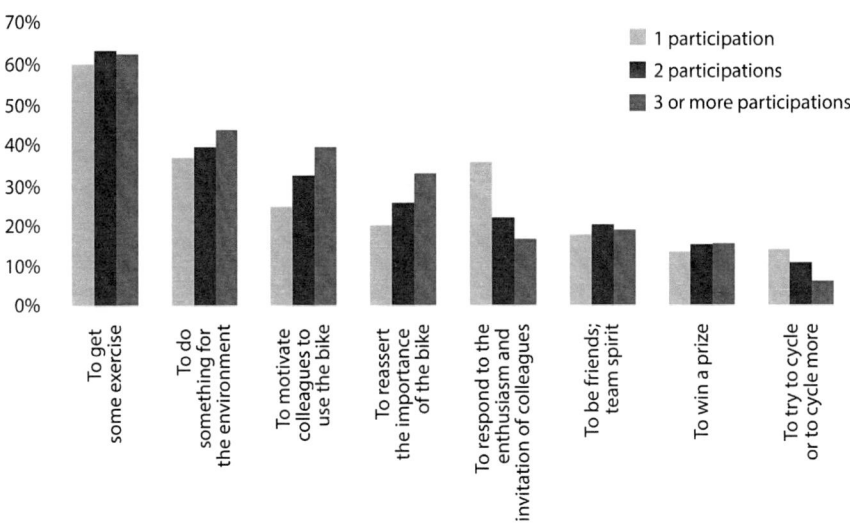

Figure 4.2: Motivations to participate in bike-to-work according to the number of years of participation (maximum of three answers per participant).

after bike-to-work, 65% of those who did not cycle before stated that they were now cycling more (this includes 50% who did so but on an irregular basis). The initiative may restore a practice of cycling after a period of abandonment for various reasons (e.g. preference for motorized vehicles, new residential or work location, etc.). It provides a "trigger" or "kick start" and gives "a new impetus" to start cycling again and to maintain the practice:

> It has motivated me to cycle more again. When I lived in the city, the bike was MY means of transportation. I did not need a car. In the countryside this habit changed. Participation in bike-to-work has given me new momentum. [Male, 53]

> Bike-to-work was the momentum I needed to start cycling again. [Male, 46]

> Bike-to-work was the trigger. The idea, the intention to commute by bike, had already been there for a long time. [Male, 44]

Comments in the questionnaire show that the effect is not always immediate and may require more than one participation:

> It is mid-September and I am still cycling. After my first participation last year, no lasting effect was visible yet and I got straight back into the car. [Female, 51]

A second group assembles people with a seasonal cycling practice or a practice more oriented toward leisure and sport. Bike-to-work motivates them "to get their bikes out", "to get the season started", "to overcome their cycling inertia":

> Bike-to-work motivates me every year in spring to get my bike back into working order. Then I've got it at my disposal again and I use it more, all summer and autumn. [Female, 38]

> Bike-to-work gives me the kick-start to use my bike most of the time till the end of the year. [Male, 44]

These two groups are mobilized by the bike-to-work action. A third category of regular bike commuters is motivated to increase their

The Effects of a Promotional Campaign

cycling practice even further. The setting up of teams creates a "group dynamic" and the opportunity to "share experiences", and facilitates a team spirit between colleagues around "a common hobby", encouraging them to be "proud" of cycling. Some interviewees are spurred on by the team aspect of the contest and by counting the kilometres they do:

> During bike-to-work, we set challenges between colleagues and we went by bike every day, even in heavy rain, which I usually do not do. With the right equipment, it does not pose any problem. [...] We pushed the limits and added additional kilometres to lengthen the trip. We were proud! Generally, I felt great and happy when I arrived in the morning and I looked forward to cycling again in the evening. [Female, 39]

> Participation in bike-to-work increased my ambition because we compared who rode the most in my team. [Female, 36]

This effect, however, may be experienced in a negative way and can be felt as peer pressure:

> The fact of "having to" commute by bike for a whole month was not positive for me. I forced myself to come by bike for my teammates and colleagues. At the end of the "required" month, I did not touch my bike again to come to work. [Male, 35]

Learning Effect: Developing the Individuals' Cycling Potential
Bike-to-work is a crucial period for which, or during which, some commuters develop their cycling potential. This may be as a result of improved access to equipment (e.g. through repairing one's bike or buying one that is more adapted to one's needs) and accessories (waterproof clothing, bike lock, etc.), skills (knowledge of the trip, physical condition, behaviour in traffic, organization of everyday life), and/or appropriation (feasibility and attractiveness of trips made by bike).

Getting Access to Suitable Equipment
Participating in bike-to-work relies on access to a bike. Only 0.1%

used mainly bike sharing to commute (due to the limited size of bike-sharing schemes), and a similar proportion stated that they had borrowed a bike (e.g. from a colleague). Access to a functioning bike is therefore widespread among the participants. It is worth noting, however, that the lack of a bike may prevent other employees from giving cycling a try.

In terms of equipment, bike-to-work has more impact before it actually takes place. Some participants stated that it had prompted them to repair their bike or to buy one suitable for commuting:

> It gave me the impetus to repair my bike. That's why I used it more again afterwards. [Male, 28]

For others, bike-to-work was an opportunity to try various kinds of bike and to choose one that was adapted to their needs and that would make their journey more enjoyable. This is specifically the case for e-bikes:

> I bought an e-bike to be able to meet my commitment to bike-to-work, because I do not have the physical condition for a "normal" bike. [Female, 47]

> The first year I had a standard bike. I told myself that I would never participate again. My trip was too long (35–40 minutes). The second and third years I used an e-bike with a 25km/h assistance. It was OK, without real pleasure. I therefore did it only in June and then absolutely not the rest of the year. The fourth and fifth years I used an e-bike with a 45km/h assistance. The trip really became a pleasure. Without bike-to-work, I wouldn't have taken the step. [Male, 53]

> I bought an e-bike after having participated in bike-to-work, and I use it every day now, because I can ride the steep hill on my way back and I do not have to fall back on public transport. [Male, 47]

Other impacts mentioned are equipment, such as waterproof clothing, helmets, bike locks, etc. Some purchases are made in anticipation of the bike-to-work action; others in hindsight:

The Effects of a Promotional Campaign

> Because of bike-to-work I bought a helmet and a bike lock. I restored my old bike to good condition with a full service. My experience showed me that it was completely possible to commute by bike. [Female, 52]

Developing Skills and Confidence

Both the participation in the event and the creation of teams represent a way to gain or exchange experiences between colleagues that are crucial for neophyte cyclists, since commuting by bike requires skills and tactics to cope with the traffic and the level of infrastructure.

Bike-to-work gives novice cyclists the opportunity to gain skills and to become accustomed to cycling. Participants who did not cycle to work before bike-to-work were asked to evaluate the impact of the experience. Globally, the participation had a positive impact. As mentioned above, two-thirds of them stated that, three months after the end of bike-to-work, they were cycling to work more often than they had used to. This result is explained by several positive effects on perceptions of the commuting trip (Table 4.1 overleaf). Among the participants who did not cycle to work previously, 44.5% feel that the trip requires less effort than expected, 35.5% that it is more enjoyable, and 31.8% that it takes less time:

> Before bike-to-work, I had always thought that my place of work was located too far away from my home. [Female, 35]

> The more we ride, the fitter we are, and the less tiring it is! [Female, 22]

> I am just more trained and quicker, and therefore it is less tiring and I find the trip shorter. [Female, 46]

> My pleasure at being in nature has increased and I have a more vivid experience of the seasons. [Male, 54]

A feeling of increased ease is mentioned by 15.5% of the neophyte cyclists, and 7.7% find the trip to be safer than they thought:

> I use the bike more. I feel safer and I am more motivated. I always had the feeling that all this was so hard, but the reality has changed. [Female, 33]

Table 4.1: Impact of participation in bike-to-work on perceptions of the commuting trip among people who did not previously cycle to work.

	Less than before	As much as before	More than before
It seems to me that the trip requires physical effort	44.5%	42.2%	13.3%
It seems to me that the trip is enjoyable	4.0%	60.5%	35.5%
It seems to me that the trip is safe	11.1%	81.2%	7.7%
It seems to me that the trip takes less time	31.8%	56.0%	12.2%
I feel at ease in traffic	8.4%	76.1%	15.5%

> There was a time when I was afraid of cycling. This has changed with this team event, in the sense that at the beginning we often rode together, and that safety came with the exercise. I still feel more at ease on countryside paths than on the road, but this has much improved and I am not afraid anymore. But still, I always have rushes of adrenaline! ;-). [Female, 44]

However, the feeling of safety is the only one for which the negative answers are more numerous (11.1%) than the positive evaluations. Experience may lead to a greater awareness of the dangers:

> Gaining confidence in traffic is not necessarily positive. We take more risks! And car drivers are really aggressive with cyclists. I have been insulted several times! [Male, 38]

> I have noticed more dangerous points, and I have had a bump with a car/a distracted driver at a roundabout. [Female, 54]

> The more I cycle across Geneva, the less confidence I have! The risk taken is proportional to the number of journeys!!! [Male, 42]

Participation in bike-to-work enabled neophytes to gain knowledge of the local area and of the realities on the ground, and to identify situations that are potentially problematic:

The Effects of a Promotional Campaign

> My awareness of "black spots" of traffic has increased so much that I could map them! [Female, 56]
>
> I have realized how many times my rights are denied. For example, failure to give way by car drivers, etc. [Female, 50]

It can also help participants to grasp the point of view of other road users. This is specifically the case of motorists who, through taking part in bike-to-work, now have a better understanding of the needs and behaviours of cyclists, and recognize their legitimacy on the road:

> I now understand the problems in traffic from the point of view of the cyclist but also of the car driver, and I try to behave the best way from both perspectives. [Female, 59]
>
> I have become more sensitive to other road users across the board. [Female, 47]
>
> With participation in bike-to-work, we have become more aware of the dangers that are on the way to work. We drive in a more respectful way with regard to cyclists. [Male, 52]

The low score for safety is explained by the fact that safety depends on not only the participants' skills and level of ease but also, and especially, on the existing infrastructure and on co-existence with motorized traffic. This partly explains why one-third of the neophytes do not continue cycling long-term. This highlights the limits of an event that promotes cycling by focusing on behaviour and not on the material conditions:

> I see the biggest problem for cyclists in Switzerland is the deficient infrastructure. There are almost no cycle tracks separated from the road in the regions of Basel and Zurich. A cycle lane painted on the road unfortunately does not provide enough safety. If we want to motivate people to cycle, we should invest in this kind of infrastructure. Bike-to-work is unfortunately not enough. [Male, 39]
>
> For me, bike-to-work was a very motivating factor to travel by bike. Unfortunately, conditions are not very favourable. There should be

more cycle tracks separated from the road. It would require significant changes, but would make it possible to increase the modal share of bikes. Some cities have taken it up, but unfortunately not Lausanne and its region. [Female, 44]

It is motivating to be made aware of the bike in spring. But safety on my way to work does not improve, nevertheless. That's why I've not been using my bike to commute since the bike-to-work campaign. But in my free time I am motivated to find nice rides in nature and on paths that are quieter and less frequented. [Female, 48]

Some comments identified additional effects of bike-to-work: some individuals not only bought equipment for riding in the rain, as mentioned above, but also they have become used to cycling in inclement weather or have adopted strategies (e.g. leaving earlier or later to avoid a storm, using weather forecast apps, etc.).

Finally, choosing a mode of transport is part of an individual's daily organization. Mobility brings together the different facets of their lifestyle by connecting the places where their activities take place. Changing mode of transport therefore frequently involves adjustments to their daily life and organizational skills:

Using a bicycle requires me to think more about my organisation, in order to focus my need for a motor vehicle on a single day, and do everything on that day. [Female, 49]

Thanks to bike-to-work I have learned to organise myself better in terms of the things I take with me or leave behind, in terms of the time I take to change. This makes the exercise easier and less tedious. The weight of your bag is still an issue when you have to carry your laptop. [Female, 42]

Finding a Suitable Route
Interviews and comments highlighted the importance of a specific skill: the ability to choose the commuting route. A low level of ease would imply the choice of a safe route away from car traffic. Yet research carried out in Geneva, Switzerland, showed that the importance of habit in the choice of routes is underestimated in the

The Effects of a Promotional Campaign

promotion of cycling (Flamm, 2014). Indeed, when people first start to cycle, they often choose the routes they are used to taking by car or by bus, although these may not be the most suitable.

Choosing a route may require an investment of time. It involves trial and error, consulting paper or online maps, and testing various options, such as moving away from the busiest roads and from certain junctions during rush hours:

> Thanks to bike-to-work, I discovered a safer route from my home to my workplace. These paths are inaccessible to cars and parallel to the road, and I didn't know they were there before. [Female, 39]

> Bike-to-work had me "visit" my city via different routes. And to find the least frequented ones ... . [Female, 33]

> With practice we optimize the trip to gain time and/or safety and/or pleasure. As for me, I have found several alternative routes for my commuting trip. [Male, 44]

The learning process may have a collective dimension: neophyte cyclists make inquiries of more experienced colleagues. The following discussion took place on a social network among students at the University of Lausanne. It summarizes the necessary skills and the interest in developing exchanges of experience between cyclists of different levels:

> Person 1: Would it be possible to do "accompanied" or "guided" journeys from UNIL? I would like to do my journeys by bicycle, but I don't know how to behave (with a two-wheeler) on the road. The big roundabout at [...] is the main reason why I come by bus and not by bicycle. In any case, I'm not sure it's a "good route" for a cyclist ...

> Person 2: There may be cycle tracks and underpasses that would enable you to avoid cycling via the [...] roundabout.

> Person 3: I don't know exactly where you come in from but one possibility, [...] is to take the [...] cycle paths. It does take you on a detour, but there's hardly anyone on this route. On the other hand, if you want to go to [...], you have to weave along UNIL's cycle paths.

I don't know if that is of help to you, if not, let me know! [A section of a map illustrating the route is included here]

Person 1: It's already clearer ;-). [...] There are lots of us who "don't know how to ride a bicycle on the road". It's a skill that can't just be taken for granted, even if you have a driving licence. I think that offering to accompany people could be a great way of promoting it [...] and would encourage cycling [...].

Person 4: Totally! We'll have to put it in place. If you cycle regularly, there are a few "keys" to understanding motorists and putting yourself in as little danger as possible. But the first thing is to make sure you can be seen (lights, etc.), to pay attention (watch cars carefully and anticipate their movements) and, above all, signal your own changes of direction, etc. And it's also true that the more your journey involves car-free routes, the lower the risk ;-) In any case, let us know your route, so that a regular cyclist [...] can go with you and show you the best paths.

Cohabiting with Motorized Traffic

An additional challenge for utility cyclists is frequent co-existence with motorized traffic due to a lack of separated cycling infrastructure. Cyclists adopt various tactics in order to cope with the dominance of motorized traffic. On the basis of the 30 interviews carried out at the University of Lausanne (Schmassmann, 2018), a gradient could be identified from the cautious cyclist to the self-confident cyclist. These two ideal types refer to different strategies in motorized traffic—keeping out of the way, or forging a way—and trade-offs between safety and speed.

Cautious cyclists tend to keep out of the way in traffic, to keep a low profile, to take up as little space as possible, and to ride as near as possible to the right side of the road in order to avoid disturbing other road users:

If the routes I have to use are not designed for bikes, it is true that I quickly get frightened [...]. I try to ride as far to the right as possible, to not be in the traffic too much. So I don't really take my place as a vehicle. Either I am on the pavement because I feel really protected there, or I am really on the edge. [Female, 26]

Their feeling of safety is low, and this influences their choice of route. They prioritize safety over speed and directness, try to avoid motorized traffic as much as possible, and are quick to make detours. For this category, cycling infrastructure and separation from cars are crucial. It is worth noting that this behaviour refers to subjective, but not objective, safety. What is seen as a cautious way of riding may actually lead to dangerous situations (e.g. riding too close to the edge of the road makes the cyclists vulnerable to potholes, car-dooring, etc.).

As level of ease increases, cyclists tend not to necessarily keep away from traffic but to adapt their behaviour according to the traffic conditions. In their choice of route, speed becomes more important, and they tend to find safe routes without too much of a detour:

> My commuting trip is on an 80km/h road without a cycle lane. In the morning it is not a problem, as there is little traffic. But in the evening, I always make a detour. [Male, 32]

> It depends a lot on the traffic. Bicycle lanes are not really protected, they are often on major roads [...]. In the morning, it's OK as motorists are calm. In the evening, they are excited ... At that point, frankly, we don't feel safe when they accelerate. [Male, 34]

Confident cyclists are less afraid of the traffic. They tend to be younger, fitter and more experienced. They do not hesitate to take their place and to claim their legitimacy as road users. They are confident in their bike, in their riding, in their ability to anticipate the rhythm of the traffic. These cyclists use their bike more intensively (during rush hours, bad weather, etc.). Most important in their choice of route are speed and efficiency. For them, a route should be, as far as possible, linear, and without detour, as they feel more capable of facing various situations by forging a way through the traffic:

> For me the commuting trip is fine. [...] I don't mind being a cyclist in the car lane. If I need to take my place, I take it. I don't worry! [Female, 35]

The level of ease is linked to experience and regularity of cycling, but also depends on other factors (e.g. gender, age, personality, physical condition, equipment). It is worth noting, however, that skills and context are closely linked. Suitable infrastructure is likely to make cycling accessible and attractive to a large part of the population independently of their skills and level of ease.

Legitimating Effect: "Normalizing" a Minority Practice
As stated above, a promotion event over the short term does not address problems that exist due to inadequate infrastructure. However, some discourses refer to the context and its cyclability on a symbolic level. It is indeed worth remembering that only a small minority (7%) of the Swiss working population use the bike as their main means of transport to commute. According to the survey, one-third of the participants do not feel respected by other road users, and this proportion is much higher in regions with a low modal share (Rérat, 2021).

For some participants, bike-to-work represents an opportunity to legitimate the bike as a fully fledged mode of transportation, to make a minority practice visible. It is also a way to create a sense of belonging to a larger group, to "be part of something", and to "cast a vote for cycling":

> It was fun. And I noticed that we weren't the only bike freaks! [Female, 39]

> It has some positive influence. We speak more about bikes at work. [Female, 57]

> I am and I was a bike freak. I take part to underline the importance of the bike as a means of transportation. [Female, 48]

> I feel linked to my colleagues who took part in bike-to-work as well. I feel less isolated in road traffic. [Male, 58]

The Effects of a Promotional Campaign

> Bike-to-work is a way to give [cycling] more visibility. It may also motivate new people to cycle. [...] It is a way to cast a vote for the bike. [Female, 35]

Some institutions organize events to highlight the importance of the bike. The University of Lausanne and the Federal Institute of Technology Lausanne, who share the same campus, organize parades inspired by events such as critical masses in which cyclists meet at a given place and time to ride together in a city. At the end of bike-to-work, a parade gathers cyclists who ride in the surrounding roads, stopping the motorized traffic for a while (with the permission of the police in that case) (Figures 4.3 and 4.4 overleaf). An event T-shirt reinforces the group effect, as well as an aperitif organized afterwards. Other institutions use teams of personalities—e.g. members of a city council—to communicate the importance of the bike. The organizers of bike-to-work also take the opportunity to cite information about the number of participants, which gives visibility to utility cycling in the national media.

Conclusion

Bike-to-work is an event organized each year in Switzerland that gathers thousands of teams of around four employees who commit to cycling to work as much as possible over one or two months. Several questions from a survey sent to participants, as well as information given as comments in interviews, were used in an explorative way to identify three effects of the bike-to-work action. First, a motivational effect (a group dynamic to recruit utility cyclists), second, a learning effect (to increase the cycling potential of individuals through the gaining and exchanging of experience), and third, a legitimating effect (to normalize a minority practice) (Table 4.2 overleaf). While many studies focus on the issue of modal shift—which may be the ultimate goal—these results highlight some of the mechanisms that are necessary to recruit new utility cyclists and to convince commuters to change their habits.

Table 4.2: Effects of the bike-to-work event on cycling practice.

Motivational effect (group dynamic)	Recruitment (new utility cyclists) Reminder (leisure, sport, seasonal cyclists) Extension (distances, time)
Learning effect (gaining and exchanging experience)	Access to suitable bikes and equipment Skills (physical condition, choice of route, co-existence with motorists, etc.) Appropriation (feasibility of the commuting trip, etc.)
Legitimating effect (recognition of minority practice)	Sense of belonging A way to "cast a vote" for cycling

Figure 4.3: Parade at the end of bike-to-work 2017 at the Federal Institute of Technology and the University of Lausanne (source: EPFL, 2017).

The Effects of a Promotional Campaign

The motivational effect stems from the group dynamic induced by bike-to-work. It is a tool of recruitment as it encourages several kinds of people to try and adopt cycling. According to the survey, 8.2% of the participants did not cycle to work before. Among them, two-thirds claim to have taken up bicycle commuting three months later (this represents several thousand people each year). The survey here is limited due to its methodology: the frequency of cycling to work is not known precisely, nor is it known whether the practice is continued over the longer term (including winter). Moreover, as stated by some participants, the adoption of cycling may take more than a single participation in bike-to-work.

The motivational effect creates a period during which the practice of cycling is encouraged. It may lead some car drivers or public transport users to question their habits, kick-starting a

Figure 4.4: Parade at the end of bike-to-work 2018 at the Federal Institute of Technology and the University of Lausanne (source: EPFL, 2018).

change to another means of transport that may see them becoming utility cyclists. The motivational effect also concerns additional categories of commuters: leisure or sport cyclists may widen their practice (temporarily or not) to utility cycling. This is important, as cycling can actually be divided into several different practices (utility, leisure, sport) that are somewhat separate, at least in the case of Switzerland. Bike-to-work may also be a reminder for seasonal cyclists to start cycling again. Finally, during the competition, some regular utility cyclists deliberately travel further than they otherwise would.

The learning effect leads to an increase in cycling potential for neophyte and irregular cyclists. Skills and knowledge are often underestimated in transport studies (Kaufmann, 2011), but our results highlight their crucial importance in the adoption of utility cycling. Even though these skills may appear mundane or self-evident, they require a certain period of learning. This is made possible by the length of time that the Swiss campaign lasts (one to two months, while many others are much shorter) and by the exchanges between regular cyclists and neophytes. The increased individual cycling potential may result from (a) improved access to equipment (through getting their bike back into working order, or buying a bike that is better adapted to their needs, for example) and accessories (waterproof clothing, bike locks, etc.); (b) improved skills (knowledge of the trip, physical fitness, knowing how to cycle in traffic); and/or (c) appropriation (feasibility and attractiveness of bicycle commuting).

The legitimating effect makes utility cycling more visible, and generates an image of critical mass. It helps to normalize and legitimate cycling, which is still a minority practice, particularly in the professional world, where the car is often strongly embedded. Bike-to-work contributes to a sense of belonging and a sense of community. This kind of argument gradually gains in importance with the number of participations in bike-to-work.

The Effects of a Promotional Campaign

For the newcomers, the impacts of bike-to-work are usually positive on the perception of the commuting trip (in terms of physical effort, length, duration and enjoyability). However, the effect is much less positive as far as safety is concerned, due to the lack of dedicated infrastructure in Switzerland. Many participants left comments in the survey about the problems they face on an everyday basis in a context dominated by the car and where cycling is a minority practice. One-third of all participants state that they do not feel respected by other road users on their commute. This proportion is much higher in regions with a low cycling culture (defined in terms of modal share, dedicated infrastructures, or general image), and it is more difficult for neophytes to take up cycling in these contexts. This assessment highlights the limits of promotional campaigns such as bike-to-work, as well as initiatives that focus on improving individual skills: they do not influence the material dimensions and cyclability of territories. In other words, although bike-to-work represents a favourable moment for the practice of cycling, it encounters restrictions due to the spatial context. It is therefore important to focus not only on individuals but also to question current planning and transport policies, and to implement cycling urbanism, making the practice of cycling attractive, efficient and safe for all.

The goal of the research project on which this chapter is based was not to evaluate precisely the impacts of bike-to-work. This would have required other methods, such as interviews or surveys before, during and after the action. However, the empirical material found that the initiative had three types of effect (motivational, learning and legitimating). These effects, although sometimes difficult to measure, go far beyond the potential of modal shift usually addressed in the literature. They also show that utility cycling has a dynamic dimension and this could be addressed in further research.

Moreover, various elements of cycling trajectories are to be considered while promoting cycling: the continuation of the practice, its abandonment (e.g. after a residential move, a new job, or the birth of a child), and the decision to start again after events like bike-to-work. In other words, it is crucial to understand not only why some people adopt cycling but how they can maintain the practice or why they gave it up at some point in their life course.

On the whole, the identification of the motivational, learning and legitimating effects not only calls for further research (in terms of quantification, among others), but could also inform policies. Indeed, these effects refer to various dimensions—access to equipment, skills, appropriation, legitimacy and image—that could be more explicitly integrated into the design of promotional campaigns and activities.

Acknowledgements

The author would like to thank Gianluigi Giacomel, Antonio Martin and Aurélie Schmassmann for their work on collecting and analysing the data; PRO VELO Switzerland and the organizers of bike-to-work for sending the survey to the participants; and the University of Lausanne, the Canton of Vaud, and Romande Energie for funding the project as a part of the Volteface programme.

References

Behrendt, F. (2018). Why cycling matters for electric mobility: Towards diverse, active and sustainable e-mobilities. *Mobilities*, *13*(1), 64–80. https://doi.org/10.1080/17450101.2017.1335463

Bonham, J., & Koth, B. (2010). Universities and the cycling culture. *Transportation Research Part D: Transport and Environment*, *15*(2), 94–102. https://doi.org/10.1016/j.trd.2009.09.006

Bowles, H. R., Rissel, C., & Bauman, A. (2006). Mass community cycling events: Who participates and is their behaviour influenced by participation? *International Journal of Behavioral Nutrition and Physical Activity*, *3*(1), 39. https://doi.org/10.1186/1479-5868-3-39

Buehler, R., & Dill, J. (2016). Bikeway networks: A review of effects on cycling. *Transport Reviews*, *36*(1), 9–27. https://doi.org/10.1080/01441647.2015.1069908

Cox, P. (Ed.). (2015). *Cycling cultures*. University of Chester Press.

The Effects of a Promotional Campaign

de Certeau, M., & Giard, L. M. (2010). *Arts de faire* (New ed.). Gallimard.
de Kruijf, J., Ettema, D., Kamphuis, C. B. M., & Dijst, M. (2018). Evaluation of an incentive program to stimulate the shift from car commuting to e-cycling in the Netherlands. *Journal of Transport & Health, 10*, 74–83. https://doi.org/10.1016/j.jth.2018.06.003
Dill, J., & McNeil, N. (2013). Four types of cyclists?: Examination of typology for better understanding of bicycling behavior and potential. *Transportation Research Record: Journal of the Transportation Research Board, 2387*, 129–138. https://doi.org/10.3141/2387-15
Flamm, M. (2004). La mobilité quotidienne dans la perspective de la conduite de vie. In B. Montulet & V. Kaufmann (Éds.), *Mobilités, fluidités... Libertés?* (pp. 71–94). Publication des Facultés Universitaires St-Louis.
Flamm, M. (2014). *Etude sur les choix d'itinéraires des cyclistes à Genève*. Etat de Genève & MICODA.
Flamm, M., & Kaufmann, V. (2006). Operationalising the concept of motility: A qualitative study. *Mobilities, 1*(2), 167–189.
Garrard, J., Handy, S., & Dill, J. (2012). Women and cycling. In J. Pucher & R. Buehler (Eds.), *City cycling* (p. 211–234). MIT Press.
Gatersleben, B., & Appleton, K. M. (2007). Contemplating cycling to work: Attitudes and perceptions in different stages of change. *Transportation Research Part A: Policy and Practice, 41*(4), 302–312. https://doi.org/10.1016/j.tra.2006.09.002
Handy, S., van Wee, B., & Kroesen, M. (2014). Promoting cycling for transport: Research needs and challenges. *Transport Reviews, 34*(1), 4–24. https://doi.org/10.1080/01441647.2013.860204
Heinen, E., van Wee, B., & Maat, K. (2010). Commuting by bicycle: An overview of the literature. *Transport Reviews, 30*(1), 59–96. https://doi.org/10.1080/01441640903187001
Hennessey, B., Moran, S., Altringer, B., & Amabile, T. M. (2015). Extrinsic and intrinsic motivation. In *Wiley Encyclopedia of Management*. Wiley. https://doi.org/10.1002/9781118785317.weom110098
Héran, F. (2014). *Le retour de la bicyclette : Une histoire des déplacements urbains en Europe, de 1817 à 2050*. La Découverte.
Kaufmann, V. (2011). *Rethinking the city: Urban dynamics and motility*. Routledge.

Lee, D. J. (2015). Embodied bicycle commuters in a car world. *Social & Cultural Geography*, *17*(3), 402–420. https://doi.org/10.1080/14649365.2015.1077265

Marincek, D., & Rérat, P. (2020). From conventional to electrically-assisted cycling. A biographical approach to the adoption of the e-bike. *International Journal of Sustainable Transportation*, *15*(10), 768–777. https://doi.org/10.1080/15568318.2020.1799119

Moser, C., Blumer, Y., & Hille, S. L. (2018). E-bike trials' potential to promote sustained changes in car owners' mobility habits. *Environmental Research Letters*, *13*(4), 044025. https://doi.org/10.1088/1748-9326/aaad73

Mundler, M., & Rérat, P. (2018). Le vélo comme outil d'empowerment. Les impacts des cours de vélo pour adultes sur les pratiques socio-spatiales. *Les cahiers scientifiques du transport*, *73*, 139–160.

Nkurunziza, A., Zuidgeest, M., Brussel, M., & Van Maarseveen, M. (2012). Examining the potential for modal change: Motivators and barriers for bicycle commuting in Dar-es-Salaam. *Transport Policy*, *24*, 249–259. https://doi.org/10.1016/j.tranpol.2012.09.002

OFS—Office fédéral de la statistique. (2018). *La pendularité en Suisse 2016*. Office fédéral de la statistique. https://www.bfs.admin.ch/bfs/fr/home/statistiques/mobilite-transports/transport-personnes/pendularite.assetdetail.5827317.html

OFS—Office fédéral de la statistique & ARE—Office fédéral du développement territorial. (2017). *Comportement de la population en matière de transports : Résultats de microrecensement mobilité et transports 2015* (Office fédéral de la statistique et Office fédéral du développement territorial). OFS.

Piatkowski, D., Bronson, R., Marshall, W., & Krizek, K. J. (2015). Measuring the impacts of bike-to-work day events and identifying barriers to increased commuter cycling. *Journal of Urban Planning and Development*, *141*(4), 04014034. https://doi.org/10.1061/(ASCE)UP.1943-5444.0000239

Prati, G., Marín Puchades, V., & Pietrantoni, L. (2017). Cyclists as a minority group? *Transportation Research Part F: Traffic Psychology and Behaviour*, *47*, 34–41. https://doi.org/10.1016/j.trf.2017.04.008

Pucher, J., Dill, J., & Handy, S. (2010). Infrastructure, programs, and policies to increase bicycling: An international review. *Preventive Medicine, 50*, S106–S125. https://doi.org/10.1016/j.ypmed.2009.07.028

Pucher, J. R., & Buehler, R. (Éds.). (2012). *City cycling*. MIT Press.

Rérat, P. (2021). *Cycling to work. An analysis of the practice of utility cycling*. Springer Nature.

Rérat, P., Giacomel, G., & Martin, A. (2019). *Au travail à vélo… La pratique utilitaire de la bicyclette en Suisse*. Editions Alphil–Presses universitaires suisses.

Rissel, C., & Watkins, G. (2014). Impact on cycling behavior and weight loss of a national cycling skills program (AustCycle) in Australia 2010-2013. *Journal of Transport & Health, 1*(2), 134–140. https://doi.org/10.1016/j.jth.2014.01.002

Rose, G., & Marfurt, H. (2007). Travel behaviour change impacts of a major ride to work day event. *Transportation Research Part A: Policy and Practice, 41*(4), 351–364. https://doi.org/10.1016/j.tra.2006.10.001

Ryan, R. M., & Deci, E. L. (2000). Intrinsic and extrinsic motivations: Classic definitions and new directions. *Contemporary Educational Psychology, 25*(1), 54–67. https://doi.org/10.1006/ceps.1999.1020

Scheiner, J., & Holz-Rau, C. (2013). A comprehensive study of life course, cohort, and period effects on changes in travel mode use. *Transportation Research Part A: Policy and Practice, 47*, 167–181. https://doi.org/10.1016/j.tra.2012.10.019

Schmassmann, A. (2018). *Vers un environnement cyclable de qualité : Un diagnostic du campus de l'Université de Lausanne*. Institut de géographie et durabilité.

Spotswood, F., Chatterton, T., Tapp, A., & Williams, D. (2015). Analysing cycling as a social practice: An empirical grounding for behaviour change. *Transportation Research Part F: Traffic Psychology and Behaviour, 29*, 22–33. https://doi.org/10.1016/j.trf.2014.12.001

Telfer, B., Rissel, C., Bindon, J., & Bosch, T. (2006). Encouraging cycling through a pilot cycling proficiency training program among adults in central Sydney. *Journal of Science and Medicine in Sport, 9*(1–2), 151–156. https://doi.org/10.1016/j.jsams.2005.06.001

Thaler, R. H., & Sunstein, C. R. (2009). *Nudge: Improving decisions about health, wealth, and happiness*. Penguin Books.

Urry, J. (2004). The "system" of automobility. *Theory, Culture & Society, 21*(4/5), 25–39.

Yang, L., Sahlqvist, S., McMinn, A., Griffin, S., & Ogilvie, D. (2010, 18 October). Interventions to promote cycling: Systematic review. *BMJ, 341*(2), c5293–c5293. https://doi.org/10.1136/bmj.c5293

CHAPTER 5
PROMOTING URBAN CYCLING: AN ECOLINGUISTIC AND DISCURSIVE APPROACH

M. Cristina Caimotto

Introduction

Environmentalist movements experienced unprecedented popularity and attention throughout 2019. Across the world, the vast participation in the Fridays for Future strikes, the non-violent disobedience of Extinction Rebellion, the unexpected success of the environmentalist coalition in the European elections all testified to a new level of attention directed at ecological issues. This was reflected in the media, which started dedicating more space and heightened attention to the language employed to discuss the topics (CCNow, 2019; *The Guardian*, 2019). The following year, 2020, brought a halt to that debate as well as to a huge number of everyday activities, including some that contributed to the anthropogenic origin of the climate crisis. The Covid-19 pandemic introduced a sudden threat that forced entire countries to suspend everyday life.

The toll taken by the pandemic in terms of lives, mental health and incomes is impossible to calculate at the time of writing. But after the first shock, some of the people who had been involved in environmentally friendly activities of any kind started wondering what would become of the attempts to slow down global warming in time. While experts from different disciplinary areas have pointed out the connection between the climate crisis and the pandemic (EHN, 2020; Ventura, 2020; WWF, 2020 to name but a few), many have wondered why the scale of actions to respond to Covid-19 is starkly different from the scale of actions to reverse climate change, even though both kill a large number of people. This question deserves detailed answers that go beyond the scope of this paper, but in general we can affirm that climate change is not perceived as imminent and as closely menacing our everyday life and that of the people we love.

Lakoff (2010) points out that, when trying to convey the urgency and importance of taking action on tackling climate change, communication is lost on what he describes as "tragic environmental hypocognition". Because we lack words to truly express the concepts with which we are dealing, we fail to communicate. Writing in the wake of the 2008 economic crisis, Lakoff explains that most of us lack the frames that we need in order to understand that:

> *the economic and ecological meltdowns* have the same cause, namely, the unregulated free market with the idea that greed is good and that the natural world is a resource for short-term private enrichment. The result has been deadly: toxic assets and a toxic atmosphere. (2010, p. 77, emphasis in the original)

Nature is mostly envisaged as something separate from us humans and the economy as something separate and in conflict with the protection of the environment.

The Covid-19 pandemic caused a sudden temporary turn in this narrative as the protection of the economy became secondary to the protection of life, this time not life on planet Earth in general but, more specifically and closely, the lives of local citizens, our own lives. The new narrative has the potential to emerge from the pandemic and is a narrative that "could work better in the conditions of the world we face" (Stibbe, 2014a, p. 217), but the dichotomy needs to be abandoned in favour of a more holistic vision focusing on the well-being of people, a vision that encompasses both aspects rather than seeing them as in conflict. This chapter employs an ecolinguistic approach to observe recent documents promoting cycling, with the aim of retrieving "discourses, frames, metaphors and in general, clusters of linguistic features that come together to convey particular worldviews" (Stibbe, 2014a, p. 217).

Discourses of Cycling, Road Users and Sustainability

As Stibbe (2014b, p. 585) explains, ecolinguistics

> is a discipline that arises out of erasure—the perception that mainstream linguistics has forgotten, or overlooked, the embedding of humans in the larger systems that support life. It analyses discourses such as consumerism which are destructive in encouraging people to consume too much, destroy resources and produce waste. It analyses discourses such as those of environmentalism which attempt to deal with the ecological destruction but often contain hidden assumptions which may reduce their effectiveness. And it seeks alternative ways of thinking and talking about the world that are useful in addressing the overarching issues that humans face as the ecological systems which support life are damaged and become less able to do so.

One of the tenets of a Critical Discourse Analysis approach—whether focusing on revealing destructive discourse strategies or observing the effectiveness and potential of positive discourses (Martin, 2004)—is that the researcher's motivation lies in an interest in how a social or political issue is played out in language, rather than in language for its own sake. This motivation is explicitly defined and defended (van Dijk, 2001, p. 96), rather than implied. Thus, the aim of my research is to reveal hidden discourses that may hinder the effectiveness of the promotion of cycling and observe discursive strategies that are more likely to facilitate becoming urban cyclists, increasing the number of people cycling and the frequency with which old and new cyclists choose to move around by bicycle.

In *Discourses of Cycling, Road Users and Sustainability* (Caimotto, 2020), I investigated various cycling-related discourses from an ecolinguistic perspective. I analysed a range of documents including British newspaper articles concerning the fatal collision between Kim Briggs and Charlie Alliston, the institutional documents published by the Mayor of London and Transport for London in 2018, various institutional documents addressing a European readership and, finally, transcriptions of spoken discourse, retrieved from the interviews which Aldred and her team carried out as part of the Cycling Cultures in a Mass Motorised Society project (see Aldred, 2012, 2015). These analyses revealed, respectively, the framing in newspapers of cyclists and cyclist advocates as enemies, the presence of the hegemonic ideology of growthism embedded in the languages we speak (Halliday, 2001), the downsides of an economy-focused promotion of cycling (Spinney, 2021, see also Cox, this volume). The investigation of spoken discourse revealed, on the one hand, the existing frames that hinder increases in cycling numbers while, on the other hand, offered frames and viewpoints of people who cycle that can be employed to construct new effective ways of promoting cycling.

Overall, strategies of reframing are presented in Caimotto (2020) with the aim of contributing to the creation of ways of promoting cycling that may improve people's awareness of the importance of life and the need to cherish it. The centrality of "celebrating, respecting and valuing the life of all living beings" — while granting the ability to live with well-being to both present and future generations (Stibbe, 2015, p. 14) — are pivotal when promoting everyday cycling and when nurturing narratives that will enable us humans to find a better balance within the ecological systems of which we are part. Within the analytical framework employed both in Caimotto (2020) and in this chapter, everyday cycling is thus envisaged as a goal — by improving the strategies employed to promote an increase in people using bicycles — and, at the same time, as a key starting point. People who cycle are likely to be more inclined than average to appreciate life and the need to protect it, to enjoy the natural environment, to notice the improvement in personal well-being generated by better health, less pollution and less stress.

While an increase in cycling would obviously generate the positive effect of reducing local emissions due to the excessive use of cars in urban areas, the approach employed in my research is also based on the assumption that, if more people cycle as part of their everyday routine, more people are likely to be more receptive to narratives celebrating life and effectively tackling climate change. Being more in contact than average with one's local surroundings, being more aware of life through the bodily experience of moving and the reawakening of bodily senses (see Popan, 2019, p. 138) is likely to foster in people's minds the frames that are required to listen to and accept discourses of environmentalism. Cycling is seen here both as an everyday activity that can help to improve the well-being of people in many ways (breathing cleaner air, exercising and thus improving one's physical and mental health, reducing the probabilities of being involved in a collision as a consequence of the effect known as "Safety in Numbers" see Jacobsen, 2003) and, at the same time, as a contained and well-defined topic, the dynamics of which reflect—on a smaller scale—the kind of challenges posed by the communication of climate change.

In the following sections, we shall introduce Mautner's notion of marketization in discourse (2010a), showing how the hegemonic, neoliberal, market mentality is deeply linked to the dominance of automobility and how the effective promotion of a better urban mobility—shifting away from excessive car dependence—requires the removal of marketization in language as well. Next, we observe how the Covid-19 pandemic introduced—at least temporarily—an alternative to the dominant narrative and hypothesize how this could be exploited discursively when constructing new paradigms. The "Climate Safe Streets" report from the London Cycling Campaign (LCC, 2020b) is then analysed from an ecolinguistic perspective in order to observe positive discourse strategies that can be employed to promote cycling effectively. This text was chosen because linguistic analysis reveals that its authors paid as much attention to discursive choices as to the accuracy of their data. Moreover, from a historical perspective, it will be one of the few cycling advocacy documents exploiting the heightened attention to the climate crisis—the official recognition of a climate emergency and the Mayor's ambition to make London carbon neutral by

2030 — while not yet mentioning the effects of the pandemic. In the concluding thoughts, some advice from the improvement of cycling promotion discourse is discussed.

Marketization and Automentality

The notion of marketization employed here is drawn from the work of Mautner (2010a, 2010b, 2014). She explains that the marketization of language is increasingly spreading to other social domains that should not be driven by a market logic. She shows (2010a, 2010b) the examples of public sector administration, higher education, religion and the personal sphere, observing how the language employed within these spheres is increasingly influenced by the language, and the logic, of the market. "We have moved from a market economy to a market society", she explains (2014, p. 462). Her diagram illustrates the process of "interdiscursive alignment", showing how the most powerful subsystems in language are able to influence the less powerful ones by eroding their borders. The dominant system of business is taken as the model and accommodative acts can be observed. The accommodation is oriented towards the source of power with the aim of appearing more legitimate, of obtaining approval and of being more intelligible (Figure 5.1).

Why is this relevant to cycling promotion? Because this tendency to imitate business speech is often visible in advocacy documents and, in general, documents promoting an increase in cycling by presenting the economic advantages as the most relevant ones. The analysis of the "Mayor's Transport Strategy" for London (Mayor of London, 2018) reveals the prominence of the notion of "growth" framed as an unquestionably positive effect (see Caimotto, 2020, pp. 75-98). What follows is an example of marketized language in cycling promotion, drawn from London's *Cycling Action Plan* (TfL, 2018, p. 14; emphasis added):

> Enabling more Londoners to cycle is not just about helping people get around the Capital quickly and easily. It also assists in *creating the conditions for London's economy to thrive* by keeping the city moving.

Promoting Urban Cycling

> Cycling helps our streets move more people at the busiest times, *making the city function more efficiently for businesses.*

Similar strategies are found in the *EU Cycling Strategy* published by the European Cyclists' Federation (ECF, 2017):

> Another economic benefit of cycling comes with the physical and mental health benefits of regular commuting by bike to work, namely diminished work absenteeism, hence providing significant benefits for businesses and employers. (p. 13)

> A healthy lifestyle is urgently needed in view of the huge costs of a lack of physical activity to Europe's health care systems. (p. 31)

What we observe here is the promotion of cycling as something important from an economic perspective. The implications generated by this way of framing the issue are that the money-related aspects are the most relevant and that cycling is important because it also

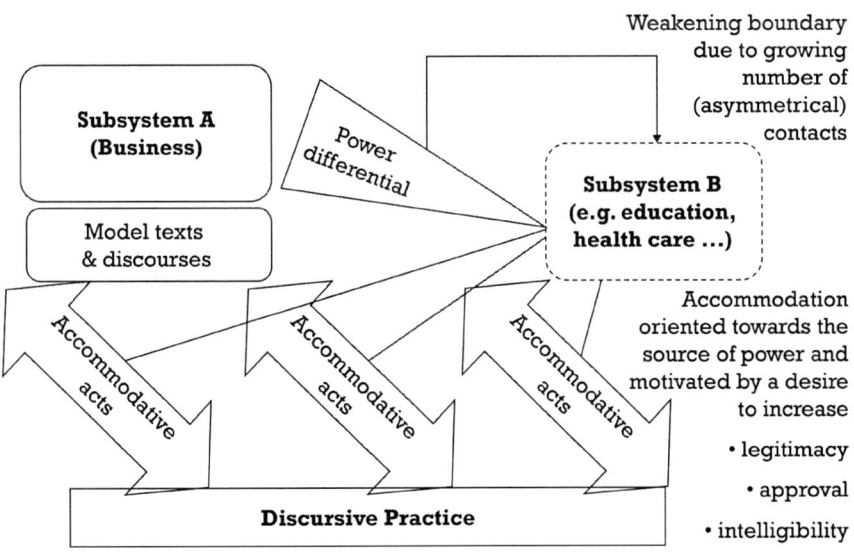

Figure 5.1: Interdiscursive alignment adapted from Mautner (2010a).

affects the economy. Thus, the real important reasons that should guide the choice of increasing cycling and reducing car dependency (better quality of life, better health, less collision-induced deaths, to name but a few) become secondary and the promotion of cycling is compared to the status quo mainly in terms of money saving, shifting the whole debate on grounds that do not favour cycling as the other life-related arguments would. This happens because the importance attributed to money in our society is overwhelmingly higher than the importance attributed to any other aspect.

As explained by Meadows (2008), when approaching problems observed within complex systems, a very common mistake is to get the hierarchy of different systems wrong, envisaging a subsystem (the economy in this case) as the overarching system encompassing everything else. The economy cannot exist without resources, thus the biosphere system is the one within which any other system is embedded. The most blatant example of this mistake is the fact that Gross National Product (GNP) is employed to measure a nation's performance. Meadows (2008, p. 140) explains:

> If you define the goal of a society as GNP, that society will do its best to produce GNP. It will not produce welfare, equity, justice, or efficiency unless you define a goal and regularly measure and report the state of welfare, equity, justice, or efficiency. The world would be a different place if instead of competing to have the highest per capita GNP, nations competed to have the highest per capita stocks of wealth with the lowest throughput, or the lowest infant mortality, or the greatest political freedom, or the cleanest environment, or the smallest gap between the rich and the poor.

From an ecolinguistic perspective, we observe the effects of the approach described by Meadows in the marketization of language, the overwhelming presence of the language of market ideology where it should not be. The effects of marketization are a widespread problem unlikely to be stopped easily. If people have to use "marketized" language at all, Mautner explains, they should at least be as aware as possible and should be helped to do so self-reflexively, critically and — hopefully — more sparingly. "Selling out to market ideology is bad enough; but worse is to sleepwalk into it" (2014, p. 462). If this is a problem concerning all kinds of aspects of our lives, it is particularly relevant when it comes to promoting an increase in cycling. According to Walks, "the values promoted by contemporary automobility, including freedom, autonomy, individualism, self-reliance, self-responsibility, and unfettered mobility, are among the core ideals of liberalism" (2015, p. 205). Thus, when we promote an increase in cycling by drawing upon a marketized discourse not only are we reinforcing those narratives that are detrimental to our well-being and the survival of life as we know it, but we are also reinforcing the very "pro-car neoliberal automentality" that we are trying to fight. That mentality, Walks explains, has been internalized as part of people's natural rights and is employed to challenge any limitations to driving. The examples shown above (ECF, 2017; TfL, 2018) show how marketized discourse surfaces in texts that are trying to promote cycling while exploiting neoliberal mentality. As reported by Oosterhuis (2019, p. 95) after having carried out an extensive meta-analysis on more than 200 published and unpublished research papers and several policy documents,

> policies during the last two decades have largely failed to generate significant increases in everyday cycling in countries with low to average pedalling levels, whereas in countries with relatively high cycling volumes, such policies have contributed to a consolidation of its existing, relatively high level, rather than to further growth

If cycling numbers are to be increased, the presence of marketized language in documents promoting cycling needs to be reduced as much as possible, because it promotes a mentality which cherishes neoliberal values that are in contrast with the values that would promote urban cycling effectively. In the following section, we observe how the narratives that have emerged during the pandemic can be exploited to work towards a more effective promotion of cycling.

Cycling Advocacy and the Covid-19 Pandemic
From the perspective of cycling advocacy, two themes emerged in the first weeks of the lockdown in March–April 2020. One was the immediate attempt to promote cycling as a form of transport and physical activity that allows physical distancing. In the UK, public health and transport researchers called on government to enable safe walking and cycling during the pandemic (Aldred et al., 2020). The other theme focused on the return to "normal" once the crisis would be over. For example, some wondered how the collateral effects of lockdowns — e.g. a reduction in air pollution, an increase of remote working allowing a reduction in commuting — could be maintained after their being raised. Many city administrations took road space previously reserved to motorized traffic and created temporary spaces dedicated to active mobility (Laker, 2020). At the same time, activists worried about the necessity to make sure all previous work (e.g. limitations to private car use in inner cities) would not be lost in the name of the need to restart economic activities and overcome the financial crisis.

Thus, the narrative of a new normality was required, fostering the new awareness generated by the Covid-19 crisis, which, Stibbe (2020) observed, "for all its tragic consequences, has caused many people to slow down, notice the natural world around them and find some kind of enchantment or well-being from connecting with it. Hopefully this is a turning point in our society where we re-evaluate what is important and start to notice, protect and preserve the ecosystems that support our well-being and all life on the planet." In order to contribute to the creation of a new paradigm, the promotion of everyday cycling should avoid the pitfalls of hypocognition, envisaging the economy as opposed to, and in conflict with, environmental conservation. The Covid-19 crisis is bound to generate a deep economic recession, and the way out is through the promotion of well-being economics, one that envisages the well-being of persons as more important than GDP growth (see Dalziel et al., 2018; Raworth, 2017; Jackson, 2017).

When we observe communication about the climate crisis and communication about the Covid-19 crisis, we notice that both can be reduced to the same dichotomy, envisaging the protection of life as opposed to the protection of the economy. Environmentalists know well how the argument of the need to protect the economy, "the right to development"—as worded in the 2015 Paris Agreement—has often been employed to maintain the levels of production and consumption, to maintain a highly consuming lifestyle by simply transforming the economy in a "greener" version of itself, a process also known as "greenwashing". The novelty brought upon by the Covid-19 crisis is that the narrative of protecting the economy as more important than the protection of life was temporarily overturned, and the protection of life became prominent. The life being protected from immediate, tangible and approaching danger, this time, was not perceived as that of plants or exotic animals, but as our own which, of course, shifted the perception of urgency.

Still, if the recovery from the crisis keeps being framed as protecting life vs protecting the economy, as witnessed in many of the debates concerning the best times and modalities to raise the lockdowns, the effects of Lakoff's tragic hypocognition will not leave us. Once the contagion becomes more controllable, climate change issues and effects are likely to strike even harder in the context of the ensuing economic crisis. Of course, changing this frame is easier said than done. Lakoff (2010) repeatedly underlines that reframing is a complex process that requires time and that cannot be solved by a few nice-sounding slogans. But in order to work towards effective reframing, it is important to carry out positive discourse analysis (Martin, 2004; Stibbe, 2018). In the following section, we observe positive discourse strategies employed by cycling activists to frame the promotion of cycling as a pivotal part of the creation of a new, more balanced, lifestyle.

Becoming Urban Cyclists

The "Climate Safe Streets" Report

In this section, we observe discourse strategies from the words of cycling advocates by analysing the London Cycling Campaign's (LCC) "Climate Safe Streets" report. The London Cycling Campaign is a registered charity founded in 1978 to promote cycling and help to grow cycling across Greater London. It has nearly 12,000 members (LCC, 2020a). Its report was launched on 19 March 2020, four days before the UK went into lockdown on 23 March. The report was produced to lay out the specific decisions that need to be taken by the next Mayor of London in order to decarbonize the capital's roads in the next 10 years. It was produced before the Covid-19 crisis caused the postponement of the London mayoral election by 12 months. On the webpage accompanying the launch of the report, LCC stated:

> right now we face a global health crisis that risks derailing action to rapidly decarbonise our transport systems, which is an absolute necessity if we're to avoid an even more terrifying future and even larger global crises. However, the same current pandemic also represents an opportunity to reimagine how London works, shift away from our most unsustainable habits and reshape the capital to be healthier and more sustainable going forward. (LCC 2020b)

This shows the historical value of this document, which was prepared for one purpose, the mayoral elections, and proved relevant for a different purpose, which had just emerged when it was published. The first aspect that deserves attention is the use of metaphors. We analyse metaphors by observing the source domain—the image or idea used to describe what we are actually talking about—and mapping its characteristics onto the target domain—i.e. what we are actually talking about. Metaphors are often employed to describe something abstract and difficult to grasp by comparing it to something that the recipient will perceive as easier to understand, more familiar and less abstract. They are a very powerful discursive strategy as they enable us to turn something that is remote and difficult into a clear, actual image that is easier to grasp. But at the same time, they can be employed to hide responsibility, to distort perceptions, to alter the emotions associated to a phenomenon. For example, when politicians arguing against immigration talk of "waves" or "a flood" of immigrants, they remove the perception of desperate persons seeking a better life and heighten the perception of danger (see Lakoff & Johnson, 2003; Charteris-Black, 2014). After mentioning the failure of the Paris Agreement in curbing global emissions, the introduction states:

> We shouldn't be gambling with the lives of future generations in this way. Nor should we put our faith in the false god that is the notion we can adapt our way out of this.
>
> We can and must take a more revolutionary approach.

In this passage, we can observe three metaphors. The first metaphor "gambling" evokes a strongly negative moral judgement. The source domain, gambling, is a risky and pointless activity, induced by dependency. We normally gamble money and we usually lose most of it. It is thus highly immoral to gamble something that does not belong to us. What is being gambled in this metaphor is the lives of future generations, thus it is not money but life, something that, once lost, cannot be recovered elsewhere. And not our own life, but that of innocents unable to defend themselves from our irresponsible actions. The second metaphor, "faith in a false god", employs religion to talk about the implied notions of "sustainable growth and resilience to climate change". The source domain, faith in a false god, is once again morally despicable, as it requires abandoning real faith. Most of the time, individuals promoting false gods do so for personal monetary gain. Thus, this metaphor implicitly evokes strong criticism against those who argue that it is possible for humans to adapt to the effects of the climate crisis, implying that they are doing it exclusively for their own interests — they will probably be dead by the time the lives of future generations will have to suffer the consequences.

These very negative images are contrasted with a "revolutionary approach". "Revolutionary" is metaphorical, as it evokes political revolutions and rebellions, it could evoke violence and coups, but in this context, it takes a very positive connotation in contrast to the previous negative metaphors. Interestingly, Poli (2011, pp. 164–166) employs the same expression to label the only approach to traffic policy that he deems effective. He envisages three approaches, "traditional", "moderate reform" and "revolution". In the traditional approach, "if roads are filled with cars, it means that we have to build more roads to respond to the demand" (p. 164). This is the model of the market, in which supply responds to demands. The approach of the "moderate reform" matches the notion of sustainable development, as "in the attempt to involve traditional industry in environmental projects, the sustainable growth environmentalists have become lost in convenient negotiations and have forgotten the real goals" (p. 166). It consists in changing part of the mobility choices and shifts a percentage of travellers from using cars to using public transport. He compares his "revolutionary approach" to the solutions that have been envisaged to solve the problem of waste management by addressing excessive packaging, i.e. the origin of the problem (p. 168). By analogy, we should question our mobility needs and introduce strategies to reduce them.

This view is consistent with Urry's (2004) who argued that we will never go back to a 19th-century public mobility dominated by buses, trains, coaches and ships, because of the need of individualized, fragmented and instantaneous mobility generated by the car system (2004, p. 36). Urry envisaged a new "post-car" system that would arise at the reaching of some tipping point in the 21st century after which the car would be seen as a dinosaur, like fax machines, immobile phones or early freestanding PCs. This new system would see "a mixed flow of slow-moving semi-public micro-cars, bikes, many hybrid vehicles, pedestrians and mass transport integrated into a mobility of physical and virtual access" (2004, p. 35). Thus, according to Poli, what he labels the "traditional approach" is clearly destructive, the "moderate reform" doomed to fail just like the promotion of "sustainable development" has not yet shown significant results in reducing the worsening effects of the climate crisis. A reduction in travel, Poli argues, is the only actual, feasible and constructive solution.

The next discourse strategy worthy of attention is that employed in the section titled "London in 2030". In a total of 336 words, it describes a busy morning in London as idyllic and the following is a selection of sentences:

> of a spring morning, someone takes a seat under the shade of a tree, coffee and pastry in hand, and watches the world go by. A few years ago, the view was mostly parked cars, but it's people that draw the attention now, especially people on the move. [...] There are other sights to take in: the trees, the flowers and the little green spaces where people sit and play; the electric van driver trolleying his load to the greengrocer's before the morning delivery window closes; [...] Despite the busyness, the atmosphere is energising, not enervating. It feels good. It looks good. It sounds good. It even smells and tastes good, and that's not just the coffee. It's because it's clean and there's nothing to choke on—unless a bit of pastry goes down the wrong way. (LCC 2020b, p. 18)

In terms of discursive strategies, what makes this text particularly effective is, of course, the use of the present tense to talk about events that have not happened yet and the past tense to talk about what is the actual present for the readers. A similar strategy is employed by Popan (2019) in his prologue. This consists in texts written by himself in 2050 that mix real facts and real publications before 2020 with imaginary ones belonging to 2021-2050 and leave the reader with a feeling of heightened feasibility compared to what could be achieved by referring to the future as we would usually do. In the passage above, we also notice the relevance given to one's senses, and how all of them are involved in perceiving the present. Popan (2019, p. 89) argues in favour of slow cycling, as it is more natural for the human body and it reawakens bodily senses that are otherwise numbed inside automobiles. It allows appreciation of the urban environment and "enables playful interactions with other cyclists, conversations, as well as the transformations of the utilitarian space of the road into a more socially open space". He adds (pp. 172–186) that slow cycling can be a form of reappropriation of time-space, in contrast with the compression that characterizes our postmodern, growth-oriented societies (Harvey, 1989). Because, in certain cases, the development of the bicycle contributes to prolonging the current form of urbanization, oriented towards the most fluid circulation of capital possible, slow cycling represents a form or reappropriation and the element of slowness is fundamental in the process of reintroducing what really matters (well-being, health) in contrast with the values promoted by neoliberalism and automentality.

In line with what was also observed (Caimotto, 2020, pp. 75–98) in the "Mayor's Transport Strategy" (Mayor of London, 2018), the "Climate Safe Streets" report avoids the reification of people into categories of road users, but uses "Londoners" (26 occurrences) to refer to the citizens who would benefit from the policies proposed. It only uses the words "pedestrians and cyclists" once, and the word "driver(s)" 13 times, of which only four refer to drivers as a broad category. These latter uses are not detrimental, they do not aim to criticize their choice of using a car, but rather describe the expected reactions of people who drive to specific policies. For example: "But if we do not also then close through motor traffic routes (also known as 'ratruns' on residential and other non-distributor roads, drivers will simply redirect journeys to more and more inappropriate routes)." As in the "Mayor's Transport Strategy", the phrase "car dependency" is employed to frame people who drive as victims of poor planning, victims who deserve to be freed from this dependency. For example: "Planning policy has a vital role to play in enabling the use of sustainable travel modes, and in ensuring that residents and other occupiers of new developments are not locked into car dependency."

Promoting Urban Cycling

The following passage exemplifies these strategies, highlighting what is wrong with the current mobility choices without implying that car owners are stupid and egoistic, but rather as the victims of a destructive induced need:

> Making streets Climate Safe will enable almost everyone to be able to live decently without having to own or drive a car. This may sound radical and, to some, far-fetched, but it's also appealing. Because Londoners deserve better than to sit in traffic, than to breathe toxic air, than to feel unsafe while walking or cycling, than to suffer a poor public transport experience, than to feel unable to turn the school run into a stroll, than to think they have no option but to spend so much money on owning and running cars that sit idle for more than 23 hours out of every 24. (LCC, 2020b, p. 63)

The clause "Londoners deserve better" is worth mentioning, as it is clearly part of a discursive strategy. In the text the verb "deserve" is always used to talk about what Londoners deserve and the clause almost works as a slogan. The following Table 5.1 shows the occurrences of "deserve" in context. These are retrieved by using a software for the analysis of language data (Brezina et al., 2018). The node word, "deserve" in this case, is shown in context and sentences are cut, showing a number of words before and after (seven in our case), notwithstanding sentence boundaries.

Overall, the "Climate Safe Streets" report frames radical changes in everyday mobility as part of changes that are vital in order to save human civilization from total collapse and transform everyday life, making it happier and healthier. In the introduction, it specifies "this isn't about saving the planet" (LCC, 2020b, p. 8). The sense of urgency and the moral imperative to act are accompanied by the attractive promise of a high quality of life. This is in line with the ecosophy proposed by Stibbe, who underlines that measures to address ecological issues must also grant high well-being because any measure that harms human interests is not going to be adopted (2015, p. 14). In the following section we shall summarize some of

Becoming Urban Cyclists

Table 5.1: The occurrences of "deserve" in context in the Mayor's Transport Strategy (Mayor of London, 2018) giving the preceding or succeeding seven words in the report.

Corpus: LCC| Search Term: deserve| Occurrences: 14 (6.44)| Texts: 1|

Left	Node	Right
9.8 Enable car-free planning 60 10 Londoners	deserve	better 62 11 Endnotes 64 12 Acknowledgements
simply, the Climate Emergency demands, and Londoners	deserve,	much better transport options. They deserve better
Londoners deserve, much better transport options. They	deserve	better than to sit in traffic, making
idle 95% of the time. Londoners also	deserve	to be better engaged in the process
knowhow to do this is available. Londoners	Deserve	Climate Safe Streets
will be the better streets that Londoners	deserve.	Decarbonising motor transport would reduce pollution and
access to car travel for most trips	deserve	better alternatives than they currently have. Improving
very low or eliminated altogether. 61 LONDONERS	DESERVE	BETTER: THEY DESERVE CLIMATE SAFE STREETS 10.
eliminated altogether. 61 LONDONERS DESERVE BETTER: THEY	DESERVE	CLIMATE SAFE STREETS 10. In the face
change. The climate emergency demands, and Londoners	deserve,	much better alternatives to private car travel.
rather than choose it, is false. Londoners	deserve	to be better engaged in the process
far-fetched, but it's also appealing. Because Londoners	deserve	better than to sit in traffic, than
23 hours out of every 24. They	deserve	a zero-carbon transport system that is universal,
all in this together. Londoners don't just	deserve	Climate Safe Streets, we need them within

the ideas and effective strategies that can be employed to reframe the promotion of cycling.

Concluding Thoughts on Reframing Cycling Promotion

When attempting reframing, it is good to bear in mind Lakoff's general advice: "go on offense, never defense": do not accept the frames you are trying to counter, do not negate them, do not repeat them, do not structure your arguments to counter them. Frames cannot be avoided and they are linked to emotions. All we can do is choose the right frames to activate. Any of the mistakes he warns against will activate the wrong frames and reinforce the frames we are trying to fight. It is important to tell stories that exemplify the values, rouse emotions, and find general themes or narratives that incorporate the points we are making. As framing is complex, it is important to address everyday concerns, to be aware of the context, the visuals, the messenger, the body language. To use words that people can understand (Lakoff, 2010, pp. 79–80).

The lockdown imposed a drastic change in lifestyle on the majority of people on the planet, creating the conditions for a huge involuntary and unexpected experiment. According to a study by the RSA (The Royal Society for Arts, Manufactures and Commerce) think tank carried out in the first lockdown weeks found that only 9% of people wanted a total return to "normal" (Parker et al., 2020). It is thus possible to envisage a promotion of cycling as part of the awaiting new normality, naturally shifting the focus of the debate away from the economic effects—whether in terms of costs for the changes to the road infrastructure or in terms of the economic benefits ensuing—and now rather focusing on impinged health-related needs imposed by physical distancing. While the arguments concerning the detrimental effects of air pollution on health have proved too distant in time to generate a significant request of change from citizens, the arguments of physical distancing are likely to be felt much more. This introduces a frame that envisages health and well-being as (rightly) predominant in the face of time efficiency, and one that—if fostered well—is not likely to go away once the pandemic emergency is overcome and once a significant number of people who were initially forced to choose the bicycle has been able to appreciate its positive effects. Of course, the high increase in remote working and the forced discovery of grocery stores in one's vicinity are also likely to generate changes in people's commuting and shopping habits.

We argued above that it is important not to classify road users in categories and, as also observed in Caimotto (2020), campaigns promoting an increase in cycling by inviting people to choose a bike as their main means of transport work better when they simply focus on cycling and avoid direct reference to the use of cars and the need to drive less. It is even more problematic when campaigns implicitly suggest that cycling is the smart choice and driving the stupid one, for example the 2006 Love Your Bike advertising campaign that depicted a "fast lane" — on the cycle lane — and a "fat lane" — on the traffic lane, accompanied by the slogan "Burn calories, save cash, get there on time" (Manchester FOE, 2006). While this kind of message is likely to make people who already cycle feel proud, people who believe they are forced by circumstances to use a car might feel offended or despised rather than attracted to the idea of shifting their transport mode. Campaigns that are more recent rather depict simple pictures of people cycling and enjoying their ride while wearing ordinary everyday clothes, like examples from Bristol's "Better by Bike" campaign and the one from Transport for London, some of the messages employed were "When I'm on my bike I'm in a better world" and "Catch up with the bicycle". A popular, grassroots visual created by a Twitter user (Engineer like a Girl, 1 May 2020, 12:09 a.m., Twitter post, 2020) during the pandemic addressed the potential change in terms of a question followed by an exhortation to create "a new normal".

When attempting to reframe the promotion of cycling, it is necessary to be aware of the dominant frames of the automentality we are trying to counter and recognize its deep cultural and social ties with the hegemonic, neoliberal, destructive worldview. It is important to adopt an ecolinguistic approach (Stibbe, 2015) and thus create and reinforce themes and narratives that move away from

Promoting Urban Cycling

Figure 5.2: A popular, grassroots visual created by a Twitter user (Engineer Like a Girl, 1 May 2020, 12:09 a.m., Twitter post, 2020).

the prominence of economic growth and celebrate the centrality of life, the reawakening of bodily senses, the heightened well-being derived from better health and rhythms that are more natural.

Criticizing car dependency should never take the form of sweeping accusations against "drivers", but rather be framed as a structural problem that forces people to feel they have no other choice (Furness, 2010). The alternative should be presented as appealing and desirable; people who use cars should not perceive that something is taken away from them, but rather that they are finally given viable alternatives to a mode of transport which is the most expensive they could choose while also being the most damaging to their health and well-being. The persons benefiting from the new policies should be named "citizens, persons" or referred to by their demonym (e.g. "Londoners"). "Cyclists" and "pedestrians" should not be employed and substituted by "active mobility", "people who cycle", "people who walk", "cycling", "walking", depending on the context. The perception that a person belongs to a single category of road user should always be avoided. "Everyday cycling" should be preferred to "utilitarian cycling", as urban cycling is often utilitarian and leisurely at the same time. The use of private cars should be framed as passive, for example through the nominalization "car dependency". Avoiding verbs to talk about automobility reinforces the association of sedentariness and car use.

When choosing words, it is good to avoid "accidents" and substitute it with "collisions", thus removing the unpredictability conveyed by the word "accident". It is, of course, impossible to predict when and where a collision will happen, but how many are likely to happen is sadly well known and preventable, albeit if prevention requires policy choices that many politicians fear will prove detrimental towards their re-election. The naming of "cycle lanes" implies they are an exception to "normal lanes", reinforcing the view that roads belong to cars. Lanes used by cars can be renamed "traffic lanes". When referring to lanes for cycling "dedicated" or "special" have a more positive prosody than "segregated". The feeling that car users are more entitled than others to use the roads is reinforced by the use of "road tax" (which is actually a tax on the vehicle's emissions and the correct name is "vehicle excise duty"); substituting it with "pollution tax" would better describe what car owners are paying for.

Finally, the general hegemony of business-related language should be avoided. The advantages of cycling should not be described mainly from the perspective of economic savings. As cycling advocates, we do not promote cycling because it could save public money, we do it because we think it could improve quality of life, safety, health, well-being and social equity for us, for the people we love and for all our fellow humans. We simply need to remember this and frame our arguments accordingly, resisting our natural instinct to align to the dominant destructive mentality. When it comes to taking decisions, emotions are much more relevant than rationality, and conveying the emotions we associate with cycling and activating the right frames in our recipients is likely to be the most effective strategy.

References
Aldred, R. (2012). Cycling cultures: Summary of key findings and recommendations. https://westminsterresearch.westminster.ac.uk/item/8z5y3/cycling-cultures-summary-of-key-findings-and-recommendations
Aldred, R. (2015). A matter of utility? Rationalizing cycling, cycling rationalities. *Mobilities*, 10(5), 686–705.
Aldred, R. et al. (2020). [open letter] Retrieved from https://docs.google.com/document/d/e/2PACX-1vR5AdOmF2effrg-lpBXtvh0stbxM0W6xTDwV2J-xIgHB8rPfZl5bLVR5eL7VV2m_W9xx5PgH26TB0vq/pub
Brezina, V., Timperley, M., & McEnery, T. (2018). #LancsBox v. 4.x [software]. Available at: http://corpora.lancs.ac.uk/lancsbox
Caimotto, M. C. (2020). *Discourses of cycling, road users and sustainability. An ecolinguistic investigation*. Palgrave Macmillan.
CCNow. (2019). https://www.coveringclimatenow.org/
Charteris-Black, J. (2014). *Analysing political speeches: Rhetoric, discourse and metaphor*. Palgrave Macmillan.
Dalziel, P., Saunders, C., & Saunders, J. (2018). *Wellbeing economics: The capabilities approach to prosperity*. Palgrave Macmillan.
ECF—European Cyclists' Federation. (2017). EU cycling strategy: Recommendations for delivering green growth. https://ecf.com/eu_cycling_strategy
Engineer Like A Girl (@LikeEngineer). (2020, 1 May, 12:09 a.m.). "I drew a thing". Tweet. https://twitter.com/LikeEngineer/status/1255982607919177728
EHN—Environmental Health News. (2020). Coronavirus, climate change, and the environment https://www.ehn.org/coronavirus-environment-2645553060.html

Furness, Z. (2010). *One less car: Bicycling and the politics of automobility*. Temple University Press.

Guardian, The. (2019). *The Guardian*'s environmental pledge. https://www.theguardian.com/environment/ng-interactive/2019/oct/16/the-guardians-climate-pledge-2019

Halliday, M. A. K. (2001). New ways of meaning: The challenge to applied linguistics. In A. Fill & P. Mühlhäusler (Eds.), *The ecolinguistics reader: Language, ecology and environment* (pp. 175–202). Continuum.

Harvey, D.. (1989). *The condition of postmodernity: An enquiry into the origins of cultural change*. Wiley-Blackwell.

Jackson, T. (2017). *Prosperity without growth: Foundations for the economy of tomorrow*. Earthscan.

Jacobsen, P. L. (2003). Safety in numbers: More walkers and bicyclists, safer walking and bicycling. *Injury Prevention*, 9, 205–209.

Laker, L. (2020). World cities turn their streets over to walkers and cyclists. *The Guardian*. https://www.theguardian.com/world/2020/apr/11/world-cities-turn-their-streets-over-to-walkers-and-cyclists

Lakoff, G. (2010). Why it matters how we frame the environment. *Environmental Communication*, 4(1), 70–81.

Lakoff, G., & Johnson, M. (2003). *Metaphors we live by*. University of Chicago Press.

LCC – London Cycling Campaign. (2020a). How we're run. https://www.lcc.org.uk/how-were-run/

LCC – London Cycling Campaign. (2020b). Climate Safe Streets report launch. https://lcc.org.uk/articles/climate-safe-streets-report-launch

Manchester FOE. (2006). Fast lane fat lane (advertising campaign). https://www.manchesterfoe.org.uk/loveyourbike/fast-lane-fat-lane-ad-campaign-2006

Martin, J. R. (2004). Positive discourse analysis: Solidarity and change. *Revista Canaria de Estudios Ingleses*, 49, 179–200.

Mautner, G. (2010a). The spread of corporate discourse to other social domains. In H. Kelly-Holmes & G. Mautner (Eds.), *Language and the market* (pp. 215–225). Palgrave Macmillan.

Mautner, G. (2010b). *Language and the market society: Critical reflections on discourse and dominance*. Routledge.

Mautner, G. 2014. The privatization of the public realm: A critical perspective on practice and discourse. In C. Hart & P. Cap (Eds.), *Contemporary critical discourse studies*, (pp. 461–478). Bloomsbury Academic.

Mayor of London. (2018). Mayor's Transport Strategy. Greater London Authority. https://www.london.gov.uk/what-we-do/transport/our-visiontransport/ mayors-transport-strategy-2018.

Meadows, D. H. (2008). *Thinking in systems: A primer* (edited by Diana Wright). Earthscan.

Oosterhuis, H. 2019. Entrenched habit or fringe mode: Comparing national bicycle policies, cultures and histories. In T. Myllyntaus & T. Männistö-Funk (Eds.), *Invisible bicycle: Parallel histories and different timelines*. Brill.

Parker G., Staton B., & Bounds A. (2020, 17 April). Lockdown legacy likely to "turbo-charge" UK trends. *Financial Times*. https://www.ft.com/content/99ca659a-19ea-49e3-9dbe-a7885759b41f

Poli, C. (2011). *Mobility and environment: Humanists versus engineers in urban policy and professional education*. Springer.

Popan, C. (2019). *Bicycle utopias: Imagining fast and slow cycling futures*. Routledge.

Raworth, K. (2017). *Doughnutnomics: Seven ways to think like a 21st-century economist*. Chelsea Green Publishing.

Spinney, J. (2021). *Understanding urban cycling: Exploring the relationship between mobility, sustainability and capital*. Routledge.

Stibbe, A. (2014a). An ecolinguistic approach to critical discourse studies. *Critical Discourse Studies*, 11(1), 117–128.

Stibbe, A. (2014b). Ecolinguistics and erasure: Restoring the natural world to consciousness. In C. Hart & P. Cap (Eds.), *Contemporary critical discourse studies* (pp. 583–602). Bloomsbury Academic.

Stibbe, A. (2015). *Ecolinguistics: Language, ecology and stories we live by*. Routledge.

Stibbe, A. (2018). Positive discourse analysis: Rethinking human ecological relationships. In A. F. Fill & H. Penz (Eds.), *The Routledge handbook of ecolinguistics* (pp. 165–178). Routledge.

Stibbe, A. (2020). Day 12—Arran Stibbe: Ecolinguistics and erasure (an extract) https://climatecultures.net/quarantine-connection/week-3/

TfL — Transport for London. (2018). *Cycling action plan.* http://content.tfl.gov.uk/cycling-action-plan.pdf.

Urry, J. (2004). The "system" of automobility. *Theory, Culture & Society, 21*(4/5), 25–39.

van Dijk, T. A. (2001). Multidisciplinary CDA: A plea for diversity. In R. Wodak & M. Meyer (Eds.), *Methods of critical discourse analysis* (pp. 95–120). Sage.

Ventura, R. A. (2020). « Face à la catastrophe en Lombardie », une conversation avec la virologue Ilaria Capua. https://legrandcontinent.eu/fr/2020/03/19/coronavirus-ilaria-capua/

Walks, A. (Ed.). (2015). *The urban political economy and ecology of automobility: Driving cities, driving inequality, driving politics.* Routledge.

WWF — World Wildlife Fund. (2020). *The loss of nature and rise of pandemics. Protecting human and planetary health.* https://wwf.panda.org/?361716

CHAPTER 6
ADULT BEGINNER CYCLISTS IN FRENCH CITIES

Thomas Buhler

Adult Beginners as a Blind Spot in the Literature on Utility Cycling
Bicycle use in French cities declined significantly between the 1970s and the 2000s but has been slowly but surely on the rise since, reaching a modal share of 2% in 2013 (CERTU, 2013). This return of the bicycle has multiple causes, two of which are changes in the image projected by riders of higher social status, and the partial redevelopment of public space by local authorities (Buhler, 2011, 2015). However, this (re-)appropriation of cycling skills by certain social groups raises questions about the social conditions surrounding individual incentives for cycling on a daily basis in the city.

The proficiency of urban cyclists is closely correlated with their initial learning of the activity, gender, and membership of certain social groups (Aldred, 2013; Heinen et al., 2010; Sayagh et al., this volume; Stehlin, 2014). Most of the literature on these questions seeks to describe and explain the profile of regular cyclists who are predominantly men from social groups with substantial cultural capital (Quaglione et al., 2019). To our knowledge, there are relatively few papers on the emerging population of "adult beginner cyclists", that is, adults beginning urban utility cycling but with no particular skills, past experience, or relatives with a favourable attitude towards it (Johnson & Margolis, 2013; Telfer et al., 2006; van der Kloof, 2015).

Although only very recently a subject of interest in mobility policies, "adult beginner cyclists" (ABCs) are gradually becoming an issue for urban mobility actors in France for two main reasons. The first is the lack of cycling skills among quite a large part of the population in France. A national survey by the French "cycling cities" association and a polling agency in 2012 shows that 2.1% of adults declare they "cannot cycle at all", 4% declare they "knew but forgot", and 15.6% know how to cycle "a little". Of the 3,945 participants, 78.2% declare they feel confident about cycling, but unfortunately, no further investigation was made to differentiate these levels of confidence between leisure cycling in quiet conditions and utility cycling in urban traffic (CVTC, 2013). This last figure might well have been lower had the question explicitly concerned urban utility cycling. Although incomplete, then, these figures are largely congruent with the profiles generally identified by cycling instructors working with adults. They fall into three categories: (1) "true beginners" who never learned and want to acquire basic skills such as how to stop and start; (2) "false starters" who look to reactivate skills or improve their confidence in basic cycling tasks and knowledge; (3) people at ease cycling for leisure in calm environments, but looking for advanced tips and instructions on how to handle urban traffic better.

This chapter aims at characterizing "adult beginner cyclists" (ABCs) engaged in utility cycling in urban environments. ABCs are people who know how to cycle but do not feel confident in general and even less so in urban traffic. In practice this corresponds mostly to the previously described profiles (2) ("false starters") and (3) ("people intending to be utilitarian cyclists"). It is hard to imagine people corresponding to profile (1) ("true beginners") taking up cycling in a city without knowing how to start and stop in a straight line with no traffic.

This general overview on the lack of cycling skills in the French population leads to a second point. A growing interest in tutorials, instructions, or actual courses whether in online videos or taught at cycling schools, classes or clubs for adults is observed in France as in many European countries. For example, almost one million views were registered for the YouTube video "How to teach an adult to ride a bike quickly and simply" by CTC/Cycling UK. The general interest in cycling ability in France has led to the number of cycling schools for adults almost doubling in four years (from 60 in 2014 to

Adult Beginner Cyclists in French Cities

107 in 2018) according to the national bicycle users' association (*Le Parisien*, 2018). Mundler and Rérat (2018) observe similar growth in Switzerland. The health crisis related to Covid-19 has multiplied this interest in training and tutorials, as cycling has been promoted as an alternative solution to the risks linked to co-presence in public transportation (see Cox, this volume).

These two points mean that, theoretically at least, a number of adults who are insecure with the idea and practice of cycling actually cycle regularly in the city. ABCs will not initially have clearly identified their routes around the city or road hazards such as car doors opening or pedestrians changing direction. In addition to these cognitively charged conditions, like other cyclists, ABCs often face a series of physical obstacles such as hills, and the dangers of urban environments not generally planned for cycling. All these physical, cognitive and emotional elements make continued bike use by ABCs very uncertain in theory.

These various observations help us to formulate the following three hypotheses tested in this chapter.

Hypothesis 1: "ABCs exist". That is, there is such a profile of cyclists in the French urban population combining regular bike use with difficulties, embarrassment and discomfort. In terms of numbers, this profile represents a small but not insignificant group.

Hypothesis 2: This group has specific social features that are closely linked to gender, age and cultural capital.

Hypothesis 3: As they face the difficulties of cycling in the city with minimum proficiency, ABCs are less likely to continue cycling than proficient cyclists. Consequently, the percentage of ABCs still cycling one year on will be lower than for proficient cyclists.

Identifying ABCs and Other Cycling-Related Profiles
In order to identify ABCs and to monitor their bike use over time, we analyse a web-based, self-administered panel survey ("PaNaMo: Panel National Mobilité"). The first two waves analysed in this chapter

are dated March 2018 and 2019 and include more than 2,290 people, statistically representative of the French population. "PaNaMo" is the first representative panel survey in France to focus exclusively on mobility issues for both descriptive and explanatory purposes (description of trips, modes and so on, together with questions about habits, intentions and norms). This survey is conducted on a large panel (ELIPSS Science-Po Paris) whose panellists respond to various questionnaires once a month in exchange for the use of a tablet and a free internet connection. Therefore, several data not directly related to daily mobility issues have been matched to our data set. These data mainly result from an annual survey covering a wide range of topics: political affiliation, consumption, revenues, household composition, occupational or personal changes in the course of the preceding year, and so on.

As our focus is on urban utility cycling, we began by reducing the data set to cover only people living in dense urban settlements. This includes people living in neighbourhoods with high-rise buildings, large housing estates, and townhouses in the core of urban areas of 50,000 to 10,000,000 inhabitants (N = 1,113, representing here 52% of the total French population, i.e. almost 35 million people).

Identifying People Using Bikes for Utilitarian Reasons
Following the logic of household travel surveys, participants were asked to indicate their reasons for making trips in the previous week (from a list of the 14 most common purposes such as going to work, shopping, escorting children to school). Next, participants were asked to state modes, modal share, duration, frequencies and so on associated with each of those purposes. This semi-aggregated approach enabled us to obtain satisfactory results without taking up too much of the participants' time (the average time for the travel description module was five minutes versus one hour for household travel surveys). After combining the semi-aggregated indicators, we calculated "equivalent trips". Modal shares and mobility indicators were calculated on this basis and found to be

Adult Beginner Cyclists in French Cities

very similar to the latest national transport and mobility survey dated 2008 (Buhler, 2019). As the focus was on utility cyclists in general and their diversity, we set the minimum frequency of bike use for utilitarian reasons at once a month. This criterion divides the French urban population into two groups: cyclists ($N = 287$ or 26%) and non-cyclists ($N = 826$ or 74%). By way of comparison, a national survey incorporating data from household travel surveys for 14 French cities indicated that 11% of the population declare they make at least two journeys by bicycle per week (CERTU, 2013). This is consistent with our result of 26% of "cyclists", as our recruitment threshold is much lower (i.e. once a month).

Identifying People Intending to Cycle in the Next Year
"PaNaMo" is designed as a longitudinal survey where intentions are measured in terms of intended use frequencies for the six principal modes (cycling, walking, car-as-driver, car-as-passenger, public transport, motorized two-wheelers) and for mobility generally. Participants declare their modal intentions for the coming year, for weekdays and weekends. These figures can be compared to the (actual) modal behaviour declared in the next wave during the following year. The question we used here was worded "How often do you plan to cycle for everyday travel in the coming year?" Suggested answers were global frequencies "more than once a day"; "once a day"; "three to four times a week", etc. We considered people intending to cycle when the frequency was at least once a month. This criterion divided our population into two sub-groups: people intending to cycle in 2019 ($N = 777$ or 70%) and people not intending to cycle in 2019 ($N = 336$ or 30%).

Identifying People with Rather Low Cycling Skills
Measuring cycling skills is more complex than the previous two items. In order to measure ability, ease-of-use, and confidence when using the six principal modes, we designed a specific habit test. This test was applied for each mode separately in each wave (year).

Why focus on "habit" to measure abilities or feelings of confidence? Briefly, "habit" in social psychology does not refer to frequently repeated behaviour as in the everyday definition. "Habit" (as a social science concept) is defined as a propensity to behave (act or think) in a particular way, based on scripts and in a particular class of situations (Gärling et al., 2001; Hodgson, 2010; Verplanken & Aarts, 1999). Habits are acquired through education and repeated experiences of the behaviour that lead after a certain time to consistent dexterity and confidence in the practice (Bissell, 2012; Brette et al., 2014; Buhler, 2015; Schwanen et al., 2012). In social psychology, "habit" is identified as a strong predictor of future behaviours (Verplanken & Aarts, 1999). Since we want to ascertain people's level of ability and confidence in making utilitarian cycle trips, the level of utility cycling habit is here a good quantified descriptor.

The operationalization of habit measurement was and still is a subject of debate within the social psychology community. A first suitable and reliable measurement was the SRHI (Self-Reported Habit Index) (Verplanken & Orbell, 2003). This protocol proposes 12 statements to participants who have to express their level of agreement on a 7-item Likert scale. These statements cover all the facets of habit-as-a-concept: history of repetition, lack of awareness, lack of control, self-identity, and mental efficiency. SRHI has proved reliable when measuring the strength of a habit. The principal criticism concerns the difficulty in operationalizing it in surveys. According to Gardner et al. (2012), many survey participants perceive some of the 12 statements as being very similar or almost synonymous, and consequently tend to respond in the same way to some assertions. This observation led to a need for a parsimonious protocol for measuring habits. This was materialized with the SRBAI (Self-Reported Behaviour-Automaticity Index) (Gardner et al., 2012), an abridged version of the SRHI limited to five questions focusing on automaticity, history of repetition and lack of control (see Table 6.1). The 5-item SRBAI has been successfully included in

Adult Beginner Cyclists in French Cities

Table 6.1: Six statements composing our "SRBAI+id" test of a habit for six transport modes.

"For everyday travel, cycling is something …"	Components of habit	Type of answer
1. I have been doing for a long time.	History of repetition	7-item Likert-scale between 1: "I totally disagree" to 7: "I totally agree"
2. I do automatically.	Lack of awareness	
3. I do without thinking.		
4. I have no need to think about doing.		
5. I start doing before I realize I'm doing it.	Lack of control	
6. That's typically "me"	Expressing self-identity	

several surveys of hundreds of participants covering very diverse questions such as active travel, snacking or alcohol consumption. It has displayed the same level of reliability and predictive utility as to future behaviour as the full 12-item SRHI.

As the question of "identity" was present in the SRHI, and was of interest as it has been proven the ultimate stage of habituation (Kaufmann, 2001), we also put the assertion ("Behaviour X is something … that's typically 'me'") to participants. The five items of the SRBAI together with this item concerning identity composed what we may call the "SRBAI + id" test.

In this chapter, we use the general mean of these six answers concerning cycling (see Table 6.1). This mean includes responses that differ slightly from each other. It is noteworthy that answers to statements 1 and 4 are generally higher (respectively $M = 3.3$ and $M = 3.1$), reflecting the ideas that cycling is something that was acquired a long time ago (1) and something considered as a basic knowledge for the majority of the population (4). The general mean calculated with the six answers has a particular distribution within

Becoming Urban Cyclists

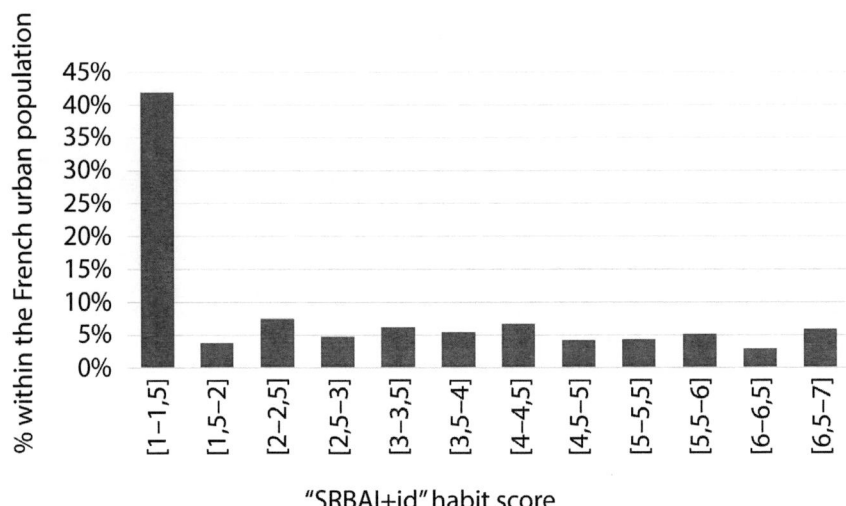

Figure 6.1: Distribution of the level of cycling habits among the French urban population (2018).

the French urban population (see Figure 6.1): for 42% utility cycling scores very low as a habit, between 1 and 1.5 (out of 7). Above 1.5 the numbers are rather low for each class and are relatively stable through to the last group with a cycling habit level of 7 (see Figure 6.1). Considering this distribution of the cycling habit level in 2018 and the general mean (M = 2.76), a threshold of 2.5 was defined to identify people with weak cycling habits (N = 611 or 55%) and people with moderate to strong cycling habits (N = 502 or 45%).

ABCs as a Group With Potential to Enhance Cycling Modal Share
Combining These Criteria to Identify ABCs and the Other Cycling-Related Profiles
In order to make a count of ABCs and other possible types of profiles, the three indicators described above were combined (see Table 6.2). Five different profiles result from this combination between cycling practice, skills and intentions (out of 23 = 8 theoretical possible combinations):

Table 6.2: Five profiles resulting from the combination of the three criteria: current use, cycling skills and intentions (with ABCs highlighted).

Typology regarding urban utility cycling (wave 2018)	Profile 1: Cyclists with skills	Profile 2: ABCs	Profile 3: Non-cyclists with skills and intentions	Profile 4: Non-cyclists intending to be ABCs	Profile 5: Non-cyclists with no skills nor cycling intention
Cycling practice in 2018 "Do they use their bike for utilitarian reasons?" (at least once a month)	x	x			
Cycling skills in 2018 "Do they have low cycling skills?" (mean <2.5/7)		x		x	x
Cycling intentions for 2019 "Do they intend to cycle in the next year?"	x	x	x	x	
N = (and %)	48 (22%)	37 (3%)	216 (19%)	276 (25%)	336 (30%)

- "Cyclists with skills": are people who cycle on a regular basis, have above-average skills, and intend to continue cycling in the future. This corresponds to 248 people in the panel (22%).

- "ABCs" is the smallest group (N = 37; 3%) but it still represents 13% of cyclists.
- "Non-cyclists with skills and intentions": they represent theoretically a group of potential future cyclists as they have above-average cycling skills generally acquired in leisure cycling. This group is quantitatively comparable to the number of actual cyclists (with skills) in 2018 (N = 216; 19%).
- "Non-cyclists intending to be ABCs": this large group (N = 276; 25%) covers profiles of people who want to take up cycling but have no particular skills.
- "Non-cyclists with no skills nor cycling intention": this is the largest group of people not cycling, having poor skills, and no intentions of taking it up (N = 336; 30%).

Interestingly three profiles are not found in the French population: two (theoretical) groups of cyclists (with skills and without) not wanting to continue cycling; and a group of non-cyclists with skills but with no intention. These missing groups, which share an absence of intention, might be a sign of emerging social norms in favour of cycling.

In the light of these numerical results, it appears that the ABCs do indeed constitute a minority group in percentage terms on the scale of the French population. This group is not negligible when we consider that these 3% represent approximately one million urban residents in France. To understand better the potential importance of these ABCs, this figure must be compared with the average 2% (2013 data) modal share of cycling in French cities (CERTU, 2013).

Once the ABC population has been estimated and found to be not insignificant, their social and economic features have to be determined in order to understand their profile better. Thus, we address the predominant characteristics of the different groups identified here with multivariate statistics.

Adult Beginner Cyclists in French Cities

A Multinomial Logistic Regression to Determine Social and Economic Features of the Groups

In order to test the probable socio-economic features of the five groups (see hypothesis 2, p. 131) we conducted a multinomial logistic regression of four profiles compared to "non-cyclists with no skills nor intentions" (number 5). Logistic regression is frequently used in social sciences because it allows "all else equal" reasoning. In other words, the logistic regression seeks to isolate the effects of each explanatory variable (e.g. gender, age, income and so on) on each modality of the variable to be explained (here the cycling-related profiles). Seventeen different explanatory variables were included in the model. Some variables are derived from the literature (e.g. gender, age, income), others from hypotheses formulated beforehand (e.g. environmental perceptions, children living at home). After this first model, we performed another logistic regression to identify the characteristics of profile 5 compared to the rest of the panel using the same 17 explanatory variables.

Each of these five groups have particular socio-economic characteristics (Table 6.3 overleaf). Unlike the other four groups, ABCs have few significant social and economic determinants. This result is highly original in the literature, which tends to associate cycling with particular social groups.

For ABCs reported health status plays a major role. Someone who claims to be in "good" health will be six times more likely to be an ABC than someone reporting they are in "average" or "poor" health. In the world of cycling, where practices (and lack of practices) are often socially determined, this virtual absence of a statistically significant explanation underlines above all the variety of profiles among ABCs. ABCs is the only group that is very balanced in terms of gender, income or activity programmes. Another explanation could be the relatively small size of the group. This makes statistical significance more difficult to achieve. Age, cultural capital, and the presence of a child at home seem to play a role in being an ABC. This result could be tested later on a larger population.

Becoming Urban Cyclists

Cycling-related profile (ref: "Non-cyclists with no intentions nor skills")		Cyclists with skills and intentions		ABCs		Non-cyclists with skills and intentions		Non-cyclists intending to be ABCs		Non-cyclists with no intentions nor skills (ref: other profiles)	
Variable	Modality	Odds ratio	Sig.	Odds ratio	Sig.	Odds ratio	Sig.	Odds ratio	Sig.	Odds ratio	Sig.
Cultural Capital	High	(ref.)		(ref.)		(ref.)		(ref.)		(ref.)	
	Low	0.819		0.565		0.763		0.746		1.276	
Social Capital	High	(ref.)		(ref.)		(ref.)		(ref.)		(ref.)	
	Low	0.673		0.878		0.403	**	1.072		1.330	
Income	High (>1900€/pers.)	(ref.)		(ref.)		(ref.)		(ref.)		(ref.)	
	Low (<)	0.570	**	1.018		0.771		0.682		1.481	*
Perceived financial situation	Difficult	(ref.)		(ref.)		(ref.)		(ref.)		(ref.)	
	OK	0.705		1.157		0.944		0.723		1.276	
Gender	F	(ref.)		(ref.)		(ref.)		(ref.)		(ref.)	
	M	3.402	***	1.015		2.423	***	1.642	**	0.457	***
Reported Health Status	Poor or moderate	(ref.)		(ref.)		(ref.)		(ref.)		(ref.)	
	Good	1.856		6.317	**	1.494		1.213		0.645	**
Diploma	High-school dipl.	(ref.)		(ref.)		(ref.)		(ref.)		(ref.)	
	University dipl.	1.185		0.741		0.880		0.669		1.177	
	Technical dipl.	1.201		0.932		0.860		0.778		1.101	
Age	>65	(ref.)		(ref.)		(ref.)		(ref.)		(ref.)	
	35 to 64	1.346		0.651		1.831	*	1.917	**	0.622	**
	<35	0.735		1.650		1.996		1.686		0.701	
Children living at home?	No	(ref.)		(ref.)		(ref.)		(ref.)		(ref.)	
	Yes	2.931	***	2.231		1.763	*	2.375	**	0.418	***
Type of city	Paris and close suburbs	(ref.)		(ref.)		(ref.)		(ref.)		(ref.)	
	Other cities	1.962	**	1.385		1.377		1.030		0.723	
Is car main travel mode? (>75% trips)	Yes	(ref.)		(ref.)		(ref.)		(ref.)		(ref.)	
	No	2.464		0.530		0.355	**	0.479	*	1.770	*
Is there an almost exclusive mode? (>75% trips on the whole week)	Yes	(ref.)		(ref.)		(ref.)		(ref.)		(ref.)	
	No	4.611	***	2.253		2.022		1.842	*	0.396	**
Political affiliation	Far-right	(ref.)		(ref.)		(ref.)		(ref.)		(ref.)	
	Far-left	1.584		0.428		2.728		1.671		0.634	
	Left	1.343		0.229		4.057	**	1.048		0.758	
	Centre	1.336		0.544		3.622	*	1.218		0.723	
	Right	0.829		0.453		2.685		1.082		0.932	
No of trips per week	Light or medium (<3 trips a day)	(ref.)		(ref.)		(ref.)		(ref.)		(ref.)	
	Intense (>3)	1.882	**	1.103		1.514		1.478		0.638	**
Car-use habit [SRBAI+id]	High (>6)	(ref.)		(ref.)		(ref.)		(ref.)		(ref.)	
	Medium and low (<6)	1.624	*	0.854		1.967		1.184		0.694	*
Environmental perceptions (5 NEP questions)	People involved	(ref.)		(ref.)		(ref.)		(ref.)		(ref.)	
	People awaiting for actions from gov. and economic actors	0.898		1.923		0.873		0.988		1.045	
	Sceptical people	0.754		0.361		0.651		0.847		1.330	
Motility	High (>average)	(ref.)		(ref.)		(ref.)		(ref.)		(ref.)	
	Low	0.889		1.561		1.004		0.997		1.021	

Adult Beginner Cyclists in French Cities

Table 6.3 (opposite): Socio-economic features of the five cycling-related profiles.

Apart from ABCs, results concerning other profiles are also of interest. Major results are in line with the existing literature on cycling. Gender happens to be the first source of explanation for belonging to a certain profile: men will be 3.4 times more likely to be "cyclists with skills and intentions", while women are (1/0.457) 2.18 times more likely to be non-cyclists without intentions or skills.

This result is consistent with recent findings on gender and urban utility bicycle use in France (Heinen et al., 2010; Sayagh, 2018). That said, this result also includes a second effect of gender: it affects not only women's bicycle use and skills, but it also tends to minimize their intentions to take up cycling.

Having one or more children at home also seems to play an important role with odds ratios comparable to the variable "gender". This result is more unusual in the literature. Independently of age, people with a child/children at home are 2.931 times more likely to be a "cyclist with skills and intentions" and (1/0.418 =) 2.39 times less likely to be a "non-cyclist with no skills nor intentions". A possible interpretation of this result would be that adults with children at home, presumably occupied with additional household duties, tend to favour utility cycling as a total or partial substitute for leisure sports.

Other classical variables play a role in the membership of a particular group. Elderly and poor people are more likely to be "non-cyclists with no skills nor intentions". People with an intense activity programme, a diverse modal use, and a lower car-use habit are more likely to be "cyclists with skills and intentions". For all these cases, the reverse result is also true adding importance to the variables age, income, activity programmes, diverse or exclusive modal profile, and car-use habits.

Other variables have a more ad hoc role, such as living in a provincial town for profile 1, high social capital and being politically in the centre or on the left for profile 3. Contrary to some recent findings on the Italian population (Quaglione et al., 2019), we do not find cultural capital significant. It seems to have a positive effect on cycling practice and skills but with no statistical significance. This may be because cultural capital has a weaker effect on the transition to cycling among the French urban population. Alternatively, it may be due to the model's limitations: a rather simple indicator and binary were used. Other variables (perceived financial situation, diploma, environmental perceptions and motility) seem to have no effect or at least no significant effect when distinguishing among profiles.

Monitoring Bike Use Over Time: Continuation and Uptake
After identifying, counting and describing the main cycling-related profiles, we propose here to study the rate of continuation of cycling at one year (threshold: at least once a month).

The results support hypothesis 3 insofar as people with profile 1 show a greater (almost double) persistence in cycling (see Table 6.4). Cyclists with skills have a 67% persistence rate, while that rate is 35% for ABCs. Thus, this group exhibits a higher rate of defection, which is problematic considering the difficulties of policies and incentives for "getting people on their bikes". As two out of three ABCs abandon during the first year, such efforts do not seem to be yielding much in terms of results. The ABCs abandoning cycling during the year are statistically correlated with gender and age (women and younger people stop cycling more frequently). Again, such results require testing on a larger population so as to be less dependent on the behaviour of a few individuals.

One could also compare this figure with that of people with skills and intentions but who were not cyclists in 2018 (profile 3, 16%). The ABC rate is almost double. When people are already on their bikes — whatever their skills — they are significantly more likely to continue cycling the next year than people with cycling skills and intentions but who were not cyclists in 2018. In other words, having

Table 6.4: Persistence in bicycle use for groups of cyclists in 2018 (P1 and P2) and percentage of cycling newcomers for the other three groups.

Typology regarding urban utility cycling (wave 2018)	Profile 1: Cyclists with skills	Profile 2: ABCs	Profile 3: Non-cyclists with skills and intentions	Profile 4: Non-cyclists intending to be ABCs	Profile 5: Non-cyclists with no skills nor intentions
% of the category actually cycling in 2019	67%	35%	16%	9%	2%

previous experience seems to be more important than having strong cycling skills.

The rest of the results can be read as follows: "the fewer cycling skills there are, the fewer new utility cyclists there will be": people with profile 4 have a 9% persistence rate, to be compared with 16% for profile 3. Cycling skills (probably acquired from leisure cycling and prior experience) help people intending to take up utility cycling.

Although they combine many disadvantages in the transition to cycling, and no intention to take it up, 2% of people with profile 5 nevertheless have taken up cycling one year later. This is a good example of the limits of intentions and skills in accurately predicting human behaviour.

The persistence rate is a rather efficient indicator for addressing questions of defection and potential for new cyclists. That said, monitoring flows between profile categories over a one-year period extends these initial findings (see Figure 6.2 overleaf). A far more complicated structure emerges. Although most people tend to remain in their profile category over the year ($N = 594$ or 53%), there are flows that link all profiles.

Two general trends can be first identified: a general decrease in the number of cyclists (-24 people with profile 1 and -17 with profile

Becoming Urban Cyclists

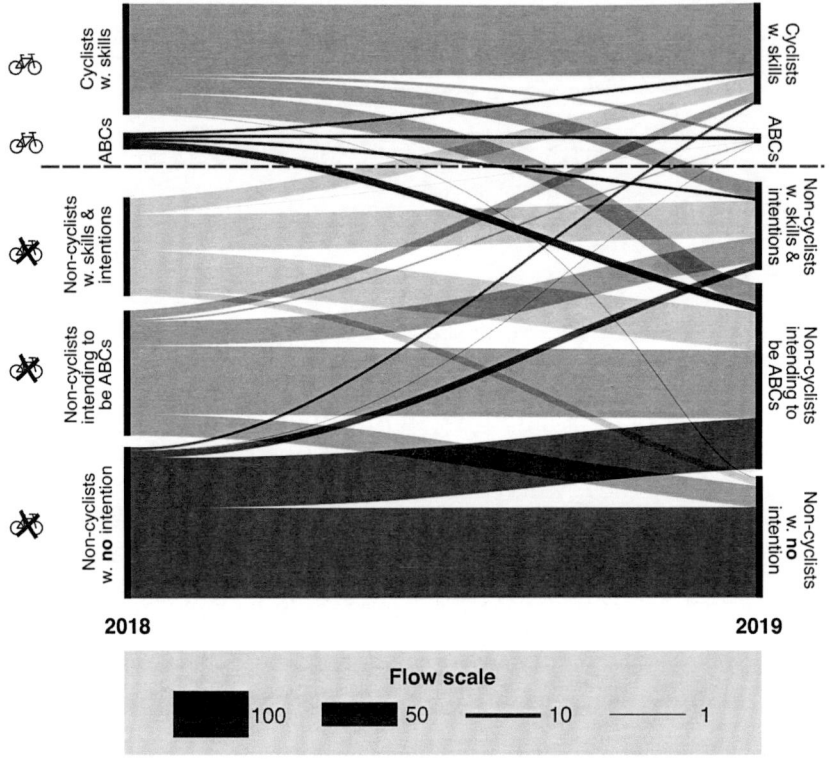

Figure 6.2: Flows of people persisting or changing profile category between March 2018 and March 2019.

2) and an increase in numbers with profile 4 (non-cyclists with no skills but intending to become cyclists) with a 49% increase (+135 people).

Figure 6.2 shows interesting potential of profiles 3 ("non-cyclists with skills and intentions") and 4 ("intending to be ABCs") to "recruit" new cyclists (with skills). Although their percentage of transition to cycling remains low (as seen above) the mass of people concerned offset this and so form comparatively large flows.

Once again, ABCs present an original profile as over the year this category recruited people who formerly belonged to other groups. Some people becoming ABCs are cyclists with average skills who stopped cycling for a while and resumed cycling with lower skills. Other possibilities exist, such as people with intentions and few skills who actually put into effect their former intention. This particular feature is in addition to the strong social diversity of this group seen above. This characterizes a particularly diverse group on which many social expectations are based to materialize a transition to daily cycling.

ABCs as a Group with Underused Potential for Mobility Transition Policies

The proposed method makes it possible to identify, count and track ABCs and their cycling behaviour. To the best of our knowledge, these results are quite unusual in the literature.

The results might also be of interest for practitioners insofar as ABCs are found to be a minority, but a large minority. Small percentages of between 1.8% (in 2019) and 3% (in 2018) nonetheless correspond to between 600,000 and one million ABCs in France. When these relative figures are applied to typical populations of medium-sized French cities (c.100,000 inhabitants), they actually represent around 2,000 to 3,000 cyclists. These figures are far too high not to be taken seriously by mobility actors who are often searching for ways or approaches to enable individual transitions to cycling (or walking). Theoretically, if these ABCs were to take up cycling for all their journeys, the modal share of cycling in French cities would double. Such an increase is equivalent to the objectives expressed in many French local transport plans at the horizon 2025/2030.

That said, ABCs currently have a high rate of defection with two out of three abandoning in the course of the year. It should be pointed out that nothing is being done today for these people in French cities. Helping ABCs to stay with cycling could be a new target for public policies. The help of a dedicated instructor, tutorials or tool-kits designed for beginners could be ideas for new actions for urban utility cycling. The large flows between profile categories reveals great potential for stabilizing ABCs as "cyclists with skills", as new generations of ABCs regularly appear.

In terms of profiles, ABCs are obviously a group with very few social determinants. Their only common characteristic seems to be a "good" reported health status (OR = 6.317**). In other words, generally under-represented people in cycling (women, older people, disadvantaged people) are—for once—represented as much as others. As the profiles identified seem to be quite dissimilar, the trajectories to become ABCs seem to be rather erratic now. We can think of many very different—potential—favourable contexts that should be tested in future work, such as being given a bicycle, experiencing a major change in family structure, knowing someone close who helps to make the leap, or finding oneself in a new occupational group that is normatively favourable to cycling. Even if origins of ABCs remain blurry, helping identified ABCs to continue would certainly be a challenging way to bring about more inclusive urban utility cycling, a task that seems difficult to achieve in other contexts such as the USA (Stehlin, 2014).

By taking a qualitative approach to understanding adult beginner cyclists, examining purposes, personal contexts and motivations, the study has opened new perspectives on transitions to regular cycling. One final observation on these findings is to suggest that they might be fruitfully used in conjunction with existing intervention techniques. "Commented route" methods follow volunteers in real-time conditions. Comments are elicited on two different routes: a "well-known one" (for example home-to-work) in order to identify their anticipations and emerging habits, and a "surprise one" where only a name of a place is given to the cyclist who is expected to improvise in an unfamiliar environment (Caillot et al., 2018). The profiling work of this study would augment situational discourses of route commentaries and reveal the allied social or physical obstacles. Identifying and helping out ABCs thus seems to be a promising path for better understanding transitions to utility cycling and for helping it to attain a higher modal share.

References
Aldred, R. (2013). Incompetent or too competent? Negotiating everyday cycling identities in a motor dominated society. *Mobilities, 8*(2), 252–271. https://doi.org/10.1080/17450101.2012.696342
Bissell, D. (2012). Agitating the powers of habit: Towards a volatile politics of thought. *Theory & Event, 15*(1). https://doi.org/10.1353/tae.2012.0000
Brette, O., Buhler, T., Lazaric, N., & Marechal, K. (2014). Reconsidering the nature and effects of habits in urban transportation behavior. *Journal of Institutional Economics, 10*(3), 399–426. https://doi.org/10.1017/S1744137414000149
Buhler, T. (2011). Sustainable mobility in Lyon: Should we hang private car drivers? TeMA. *Journal of Land Use, Mobility and Environment, 3.* https://doi.org/10.6092/1970-9870/497
Buhler, T. (2015). *Déplacements urbains : Sortir de l'orthodoxie : plaidoyer pour une prise en compte des habitudes.* Presses Polytechniques et Universitaires Romandes.
Buhler, T. (2019). *Panel National Mobilité. Une enquête interdisciplinaire et longitudinale pour décrire et comprendre les pratiques de mobilité quotidienne.* Laboratory ThéMA internal seminar, 15 March 2019, Besançon.
Caillot, A., Buhler, T., & de Sède-Marceau, M.-H. (2018). *Les cyclistes et leurs environnements. Observations et discours in situ.* Les 1ères Rencontres Francophones Transport-Mobilité (RFTM), 6-8 juin 2018, Lyon/Vaulx-en-Velin.
CERTU—Centre d'Études sur les Réseaux, les Transports, l'Urbanisme et les Constructions Publiques.(2013). *L'usage du vélo en milieu urbain : Une pratique qui se développe, des freins à desserrer.* http://www.corse.developpement-durable.gouv.fr/IMG/pdf/l_usage_du_velo_en_milieu_urbain.pdf

Compagnon, S. (2018, 15 Septembre). Plan vélo : Ces adultes qui n'ont pas appris à pédaler, *Le Parisien*. https://www.leparisien.fr/societe/plan-velo-ces-adultes-qui-n-ont-pas-appris-a-pedaler-14-09-2018-7888209.php

CTC—Cycling Touring Club/Cycling UK. *How to teach an adult to ride a bike quickly and simply*. https://www.youtube.com/watch?time_continue=1&v=wqmzwVrkTU4&feature=emb_logo

CVTC—Club des Villes et Terroires Cyclables. (2013). *Les Français et le vélo en 2012*. http://www.villes-cyclables.org/modules/kameleon/upload/1LesFrancaisetLeVelo_v3.pdf

Gardner, B., Abraham, C., Lally, P., & de Bruijn, G.-J. (2012). Towards parsimony in habit measurement: Testing the convergent and predictive validity of an automaticity subscale of the Self-Report Habit Index. *International Journal of Behavioral Nutrition and Physical Activity*, 9(1), 102. https://doi.org/10.1186/1479-5868-9-102

Gärling, T., Fujii, S., & Boe, O. (2001). Empirical tests of a model of determinants of script-based driving choice. *Transportation Research Part F: Traffic Psychology and Behaviour*, 4(2), 89–102. https://doi.org/10.1016/S1369-8478(01)00016-X

Heinen, E., van Wee, B., & Maat, K. (2010). Commuting by bicycle: An overview of the literature. *Transport Reviews*, 30(1), 59–96. https://doi.org/10.1080/01441640903187001

Hodgson, G. M. (2010). Choice, habit and evolution. *Journal of Evolutionary Economics*, 20(1), 1–18. https://doi.org/10.1007/s00191-009-0134-z

Johnson, R., & Margolis, S. (2013). A review of the effectiveness of adult cycle training in Tower Hamlets, London. *Transport Policy*, 30, 254–261. https://doi.org/10.1016/j.tranpol.2013.09.005

Kaufmann, J. C. (2001). *Ego : Pour une sociologie de l'individu*. Nathan.

Mundler, M., & Rérat, P. (2018). Le vélo comme outil d'empowerment. Les impacts des cours de vélo pour adultes sur les pratiques socio-spatiales. *Cahiers Scientifiques du Transport*, 73, 139–160.

Quaglione, D., Cassetta, E., Crociata, A., Marra, A., & Sarra, A. (2019). An assessment of the role of cultural capital on sustainable mobility behaviours: Conceptual framework and empirical evidence. *Socio-Economic Planning Sciences*, 66, 24–34. https://doi.org/10.1016/j.seps.2018.07.005

Sayagh, D. (2018). *Pourquoi les filles ont moins de possibilités réelles de faire du vélo que les adolescents. Approche sociologique.* [Thèse]. Université Paris-Est Marne-la-Vallée.

Schwanen, T., Banister, D., & Anable, J. (2012). Rethinking habits and their role in behaviour change: The case of low-carbon mobility. *Journal of Transport Geography, 24,* 522–532. https://doi.org/10.1016/j.jtrangeo.2012.06.003

Stehlin, J. (2014). Regulating inclusion: Spatial form, social process, and the normalization of cycling practice in the USA. *Mobilities, 9*(1), 21–41. https://doi.org/10.1080/17450101.2013.784527

Telfer, B., Rissel, C., Bindon, J., & Bosch, T. (2006). Encouraging cycling through a pilot cycling proficiency training program among adults in central Sydney. *Journal of Science and Medicine in Sport, 9*(1–2), 151–156. https://doi.org/10.1016/j.jsams.2005.06.001

van der Kloof, A. (2015). Lessons learned through training immigrant women in the Netherlands to cycle. In P. Cox (Ed.), *Cycling cultures* (pp. 78–105). University of Chester Press.

Verplanken, B., & Aarts, H. (1999). Habit, attitude, and planned behaviour: Is habit an empty construct or an interesting case of goal-directed automaticity? *European Review of Social Psychology, 10*(1), 101–134. https://doi.org/10.1080/14792779943000035

Verplanken, B., & Orbell, S. (2003). Reflections on past behavior: A self-report index of habit strength. *Journal of Applied Social Psychology, 33*(6), 1313–1330. https://doi.org/10.1111/j.1559-1816.2003.tb01951.x

CHAPTER 7
IMMIGRATION BACKGROUND AND CYCLING – FINDINGS FROM GERMANY

Janina Welsch

Introduction

In today's highly mobile society, transport and mobility are ubiquitous, but at the same time represent major threats to the urban quality of life, to health and to the environment. Knowledge about individual behaviour, its influencing factors, underlying motives and mobility needs is an important basis for supporting the use of sustainable means of transport, such as cycling. In general, cycling is seen as an individual, flexible and low-cost transport mode that theoretically could be used by almost everybody. It allows for longer distances than walking and unlike the car it is inexpensive and no legal allowance is required for its use. Generally, the share of urban cycling differs between countries or cities where relevant factors vary as well such as spatial, infrastructural or weather conditions (European Commission, 2013; Pucher & Buehler, 2012).

According to the latest German national travel survey, most trips tend to be rather short and are therefore generally suitable for bicycle trips (81% of those < 5km). Thirty-five per cent of all trips are shorter than 2km; another 23% are between 2km and 5km long. A total of 46% of all trips undertaken by car are in these categories and thus have the potential to be replaced by bicycle (BMVI/ MiT, 2017). Overall, the car remains by far the most important transport mode, even though the number of people who cycle, the cycling trip length and the modal split for cycling grew slightly in comparison to almost a decade ago. Regions with higher shares of bicycle use (traffic volume) are located in the rather flat northern part. Nevertheless, cycling cities where a high share of participants cycled on the reporting day, such as Münster (29%), Karlsruhe or Freiburg (both 26%), are found all over the country. More people rate local cycling conditions as (very) good in such cities and a strong local cycling culture is likely to be relevant. Dortmund, where one of the studies examined was conducted, has rather low shares (9%) (Nobis, 2019). According to the German Mobility Panel, about 70% of adults own a bicycle and about one-third use it at least once per week (Eisenmann et al., 2018).

As in other countries, transport behaviour in Germany changed drastically due to the Covid-19 pandemic, especially in times of a restrictive period like lockdown with reduced traffic volumes overall. Many people, who normally would use public transport, tried to avoid it out of fear of infections and car use increased instead (Kolarova et al., 2021; Zehl et al., 2020). These changes are unequally distributed, i.e. particularly people with high and middle income tend to use the car more often. People with low income and especially those without a car available rely to a much greater extent on public transport and often they do not work in sectors where a shift towards home working is possible. According to Zehl et al. (2020), the modal split for bicycle stayed more or less the same, while BMVI (2020) and, to a smaller extent, Kolarova et al. (2021), show an increase in walking and cycling. So far, it is open to debate whether there is a lasting cycling boom or if the car will gain even more dominance, which would increase existing spatial and environmental injustice and inequalities even further (UBA, 2020). Nevertheless, the crisis also offers a new window of opportunity for politicians, planners, administrations and organizations to act (if they move quickly enough) in favour of supporting more sustainable transport modes (Bauer et al., 2020; Cox, this volume; Gehrs & Tiemann, 2020). In some places, bicycle traffic increased rapidly in 2020. In order to cope better with the coronavirus crisis, many cities responded and dedicated road space, which was formerly used for car traffic or parking, for walking and cycling, or other public uses in order to facilitate physical distancing and to increase resilience (ITF, 2020). Rapidly installed new bicycle infrastructure, such as the so-called pop-up bike lanes, were a highly visible and often contended measure. Berlin was the first city in Germany to build several new protected bike lanes with barriers against the car traffic in order to facilitate safe cycling. Even though they were announced as temporary infrastructure, it is planned to convert them into long-term solutions.

Such (newly) dedicated, spacious walking and cycling infrastructure can support the adoption of these transport modes, especially if accompanied by speed limits and integrated in neighbourhood- or city-wide approaches. As Cox (this volume) points out, they can provide space for people, not just utilitarian traffic. If they are easy and safe to use by all people, not only skilled cyclists or particular user groups such as commuters, they have the potential to transform urban space. A sustainable city and a sustainable transport system need to be equally accessible and usable for all population groups, independent of economic status, gender, age or ethnic background.

In Germany, demographic change can be characterized by an overall shift towards older age groups, a general population decline and a diversification of lifestyles. At the same time, ethnic diversity and diversity in terms of nationalities and origins is increasing, especially in urban areas and large cities (Körner-Blätgen & Sturm, 2015). The further increase of ethnic diversity in Germany is reflected in the growing number and proportion of people with a family immigration background (Figure 7.1). Germany's micro-census introduced the categorization of people with an "immigration background" in 2005 to refer to those people who do not hold German citizenship from birth, or who have at least one parent without German citizenship from birth. "Immigration background" therefore has a particular definition and meaning within the context of German population studies and this chapter uses the specific terminology to explore the potential data correlations that it makes possible.

In 2018, about two-thirds of the people with an immigration background were born outside Germany, predominantly in Europe.

Immigration Background and Cycling

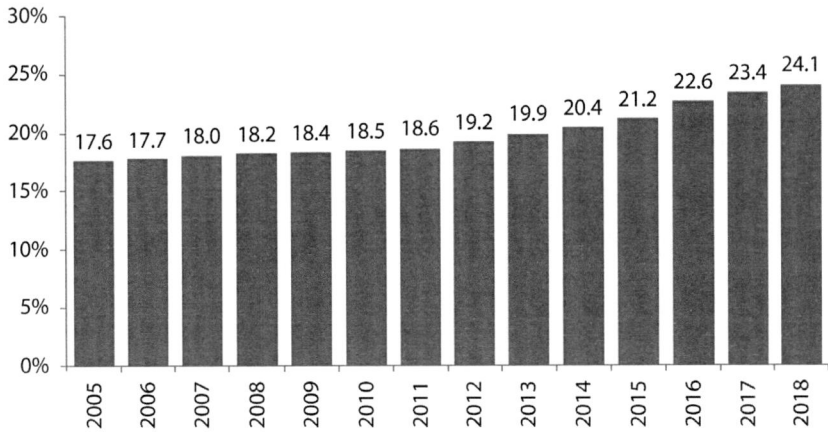

Figure 7.1: Percentage of the population with an immigration background between 2005 and 2018 (source: Statistisches Bundesamt, 2019).

Table 7.1 (overleaf) shows the main countries of origin, the average length of stay and age at arrival, all factors which relate to immigration history. Southern Europe and Turkish origins represent the early workforce immigration (with long duration of stay and smaller shares of first-generation immigrants) while later, a number of immigrants arrived from Eastern Europe, due to their German ancestry or recent membership of the European Union. The presence of Syria as a specific origin highlights recent events resulting in protection seekers coming into Germany. Tables 7.2 and 7.3 (on pp. 155–156) show that people with an immigration background are more likely to be still in education, live in bigger households, are more frequently looking for employment and have a lower household income per person.

In Germany, very few studies refer explicitly to transport or mobility behaviour of people with an immigration background, despite its history as an immigration country. Therefore, the following text combines available empirical findings on cycling behaviour of people with an immigration background in Germany.

Table 7.1: Population with an immigration background in Germany (*N* = 20.8 million) by main countries of origin, i.e. their own or their parents' country of birth (source: Statistisches Bundesamt, 2019).

Country of origin	Share of the total with an immigration background	First-generation immigrants		
		Share of the total with the same origin	Average duration of stay [years]	Average age at arrival [years]
Turkey	13%	48%	31	19
Poland	11%	74%	25	24
Successor states of Yugoslavia	9%	66%	24	22
Russian Federation	7%	79%	21	28
Kazakhstan	6%	76%	23	24
Romania	5%	81%	17	27
Italy	4%	59%	29	21
Syria	4%	87%	5	23

The first quantitative survey is the national travel survey (BMVI/MiD, 2017), the second, an ILS-funded telephone survey, conducted in Offenbach am Main in 2010 (Welsch, 2019). Additionally, a 2014 qualitative survey with Turkish origin interviewees, conducted in Dortmund and the surrounding Ruhr area, is analysed (Klausing, 2015). A literature review and a short description of the different survey data and methodology follow the introduction. First, quantitative descriptive results on bicycle availability, cycling behaviour, attitudes and socialization are presented. They are backed up by a logistical model in order to take a closer look at influencing factors. Second, qualitative results are presented, which focus on statements about the importance of bicycles for everyday use and on the status of bicycles. The last section provides a combined discussion and conclusion.

Immigration Background and Cycling

Table 7.2: Characteristics of population by immigration background and immigrant generation (source: Statistisches Bundesamt, 2019).

Population characteristics	With an immigration background		Without an immigration background (N = 60.8 million)
	First-generation immigrants (N = 13.5 million)	Immigrant descendants (N = 7.3 million)	
Female	49%	48%	51%
Average age in years	44.2	19.5	47.4
School-leaving certificates			
Not yet/still in school	8%	55%	13%
No certificate	14%	2%	1%
With certificate (university entrance qualification)	42% (43%)	77% (42%)	85% (33%)
Employment status			
Non-active (e.g. retired, children <15 years)	40%	65%	46%
Workforce population (15+ years)(unemployed/ looking for a job)	60% (5.9%)	35% (5.5%)	54% (2.6%)

Literature Review

As stated above, different determinants can influence bicycle use such as socio-demographic and economic factors, trip purposes or distances, and characteristics of the environment, such as cycling infrastructure or weather. Additional factors are individual attitudes, habits, and norms or other aspects of the social environment (Heinen et al., 2010; Ton et al., 2019; Willis et al., 2014). Cycling is also influenced by perception, which varies according to experience, age or gender. Women are often less likely to cycle, especially in

Table 7.3: Household size and income by immigration background (source: Statistisches Bundesamt, 2019).

Household characteristics	At least one member with an immigration background (N = 2.6 million)	All members with an immigration background (N = 7.6 million)	All members without an immigration background (N = 31.2 million)
Average number of persons	2.8*	2.2	1.9
Average number of children (up to the age of 17 years)	0.7	0.5	0.2
Average equivalent scale income (€)	2,293	1,550	2,002
Average net income per person in household (€)	1,567	1,257	1,653

* By definition without 1-person households

countries with a less bicycle-friendly infrastructure and low levels of everyday cycling. They are more sensitive to perceived risks related to accidents or safety and to the absence of (safe) cycling infrastructure (Akar et al., 2013; Forsyth & Krizek, 2011; Garrard et al., 2012). Sayagh et al. (this volume) point towards additional and multifaceted reasons that hinder or support cycling for (young) women, including biographical events and gender related identity, cycling socialization or cultural norms. Consequently, individuals but also population groups vary in their cycling behaviour.

Baslington (2008) points out that children do not learn aspects of mode-choice and mobility behaviour differently from other cultural aspects. Socialization, especially in childhood and youth, influences the learning of appreciated skills, values and roles in a group or society. Important socialization agents in the process of growing up are families or peer groups. Their values and norms are strongly influenced by the formative culture(s) (Veith, 2008). Similarly, mobility culture determines the framework in which mobility socialization and the development of habits take place (Aldred & Jungnickel, 2014; Klinger & Lanzendorf, 2016). Habits that influence everyday transport decisions are formed by previous behaviour and experiences. Strong habits make it unlikely that alternative modes are taken into account (Friedrichsmeier et al., 2013). According to Tully and Baier (2006), individual mobility habits begin to form in childhood and especially in adolescence. In Germany and other industrialized countries, the acquisition of a driving licence can function as an initiation into the adults' world of mobility and as a sign of coming of age. Klöckner (2004) notices that its acquisition and the first car purchase are two of the most important events that influence habitual car use. However, habits can also be altered during the life course by different events that require a reorientation. In the case of upheavals, such as the loss of a driving licence, it is possible to reactivate earlier (car-free) routines (Schwanen et al., 2012). Likewise, strong emotional references to cycling in childhood were found in women who rediscovered cycling for themselves later in life (Bonham & Wilson, 2012).

Socialization goals, values and norms (can) differ between countries, but also between individuals. The particular cultural context defines what is considered to be a desired or undesired socialization result and discrepancies can occur when people act on the basis of different values (Citlak et al., 2008; Robinson & Harris, 2013). In summary, mobility socialization is assumed to have a long-lasting effect, but norms and habits are not unchangeable. It is seen as an additional determining factor accounting for differences in (mobility) behaviour of groups such as people with and without an immigration background.

In comparison to the USA, little is known about differences in mobility behaviour according to immigration background in Germany and other European countries. In the United States, immigrants, ethnic minorities and the issue of transport assimilation are investigated empirically. In general, immigrant populations use public transport and the car as passengers more often, but they use the car less (alone) as drivers. However, car use still dominates, albeit to a lesser extent (Asgari et al., 2017; Chatman, 2014; Handy et al., 2008). European studies show similar trends: immigrants (and their descendants) tend to use public transport more, cars less frequently, and they walk more often. However, European transport surveys seldom include relevant information on population origin, nationality or ethnicity (Fassmann & Reeger, 2014; Harms, 2007; Kasper et al., 2007; Tsang & Rohr, 2011; Welsch et al., 2014). For a notable exception to this trend, see the analysis of cycle trips in The Netherlands by van der Kloof (2015). With regard to cycling, results are somewhat inconsistent. Cycling accounts only for a very small portion of trips in the US; overall, immigrant populations tend to cycle more often, especially when newly arrived, but cycling also varies by region of origin (Smart, 2010). A study among low-income Latino immigrants showed that they have limited access to bicycles and do not often consider cycling, being more likely to walk, especially for shorter trips. In addition, immigration experiences and cultural narratives influence their perceptions of (not) belonging as a cyclist in their neighbourhood (Barajas, 2018).

Cycling shares vary widely across European countries, as does the proportion of immigrants (European Commission, 2013; Migration Data Portal, 2019). The Netherlands and Denmark have the highest shares of cycling. There, people with an immigration background do cycle slightly less than native-born peoples overall, but the data is heavily shaped by gender, location and region of origin (de Munter et al., 2013; van der Kloof et al., 2014). For example, van der Kloof (2015) shows that in The Netherlands, men with non-Western origins in urban areas have the highest cycling travel time of any population group and women of non-Western origin in little urbanized areas have the second highest cycle travel times. Both are offset in the overall data by very low levels in other locations. Part of the explanation is that cycling probability decreases for individuals who live in neighbourhoods with a higher share of people of non-Western origin. Haustein et al. (2019) assume that the (national) norm to cycle is less salient there and cultural norms mediated by parents play a relevant role. In Germany and Austria, cycling is also an integral part of the mobility culture but to a lesser extent. Similar to The Netherlands, people with an immigration background, especially women, tend to use bicycles less often (Fassmann & Reeger, 2014; Welsch et al., 2018). Cycling socialization in childhood measured by parents' cycling behaviour was found to vary by region of origin. In addition to other factors, it had a small but significant effect on cycling probability (Welsch, 2015). In summary, immigrants and their descendants show signs of transport assimilation in their new home countries notably regarding car use, but to a lesser or no extent with regards to cycling. Here, differences in socialization/mobility culture in which people grew up could be an additional but often unobserved explanation.

Survey Data and Methods
The first data source is the German national travel survey (BMVI/MiD, 2017) conducted at irregular intervals. Household members are asked to volunteer transport-related information. However, only in 2017 was a self-reported immigration background included, and then only in the online/telephone module. The proportion of participants with an immigration background is rather small (8%). No further information such as country of birth, duration of stay or nationality is included in the data set. Free accessible online data and tables (BMVI/MiT, 2017) were used to analyse cycling-related information and differences between people with/without an immigration background, based on valid indications of participants who are 14 years and older. Selectable and analytical options are limited, results are weighted automatically and exported, e.g. as cross-tabulations as percentages without decimals.

The second data source is a quantitative transport survey conducted via telephone in 2010 among citizens of Offenbach am Main aged 18 years and older (for details of this "ILS-study 2010" see Welsch, 2019). The city is located in the western part of Germany on the banks of the river Main. In 2010, more than half of the 120,000 inhabitants have an immigration background. The survey included additional information related to immigration and mobility socialization. The latter relies on participants' childhood memories about their parents' mobility behaviour and their own attitudes towards the car in their youth. The analyses for the two main groups with and without an immigration background use a weighting of the sample by sex, age groups and region of origin to match population statistics. An age limit of 66 years was introduced in order to re-analyse information on cycling in combination with childhood-related mobility socialization and immigrant generations ($N = 1{,}557$).

The qualitative ILS-study/Klausing, 2015 is the third data source. Interviews were conducted in 2014 in Dortmund and the surrounding Ruhr in the course of a Master's thesis, supported by the ILS (Klausing, 2015). Transcripts of 32 interviews with people of Turkish origin are the base for the present re-analysis, which focuses on importance and status of the bicycle as a transport means.

Little and Unloved? Cycle Use by People with an Immigration Background

Overview Based on The German National Travel Survey (BMVI/ MiD, 2017)

In the available online data of the German travel survey participants aged 14 years and older are included. Those with an immigration background represent about 8% of the sample, in comparison to 23% of the overall population (aged 15 and older, Statistisches Bundesamt, 2019). They are on average younger, and they live in bigger households. The share of the educational degrees is fairly

Immigration Background and Cycling

Table 7.4: Sample characteristics by immigration background (source: BMVI/MiT, 2017).

Sample characteristics	With an immigration background (N = 12,227)	Without an immigration background (N = 142,724)
Female	48%	50%
Average age in years	39.5	49.3
Educational degrees[a]		
No/not yet school degree	8%	4%
School-leaving certificate (college/university entrance qualification)	18%	14%
School-leaving certificate (all other)	44%	58%
University/college degree	29%	23%
Average number of persons per household	3.0	2.5
Economic status (households)[b]		
very low/low	33%	21%
middle	37%	42%
high/very high	30%	37%

[a] $\chi^2(3, N = 154829) = 1061.2$, $p<.001$, Cramer's V = .08
[b] $\chi^2(2, N = 154951) = 958.0$, $p<.001$, Cramer's V = .08

similar, possibly due to sampling methods (e.g. landline telephone, mainly German language). The economic situation of the households differs; more people without an immigration background tend to have middle or high economic status, based on predefined net-income categories in combination with household size (Table 7.4).

Cycling requires certain preconditions; individuals need to have the required skills and a functional bicycle, and the city should not have too hilly a topography and should provide basic infrastructure. The travel survey does not include information on the ability to cycle. The average number of bicycles per household in Germany is 1.8. It differs by income and varies between 0.8 for

Table 7.5: Bicycle availability by immigration background and gender (source: BMVI/MiT, 2017).

Bicycle availability (yes)	With an immigration background (N = 12,227)	Without an immigration background (N = 142,724)
General share[a]	68%	76%
Male	71%	79%
Female	65%	74%

[a] $\chi^2(1, N = 154951) = 444.0$, $p<.001$, Cramer's V = .05
[a/sex] $\chi^2(3, N = 154931) = 982.5$, $p<.001$, Cramer's V = .08

the two lowest net-household income groups (below 900€ per month) and 3.6 for the second highest (6,000–7,000€). Seventy-five per cent of all households own at least one bicycle. No information is available for households with/without an immigration background. The bicycle availability differs between the two groups but also between men and women. Overall, women with an immigration background have the lowest bicycle availability (Table 7.5).

Some participants were asked whether they like to cycle: "In general, I like to cycle" (agreement on a 5-point Likert scale). A high proportion (fully) agrees. The highest level of agreement is found among the male participants without an immigration background. Interestingly, this pattern does change partially when people are asked to assess the overall (traffic) situation at their location for bicycles: "How do you rate the general traffic situation at your location?" (German school grading system, from 1 = very good to 6 = insufficient/failure). A higher percentage of people with an immigration background assessed the situation positively, but women to a lesser extent than men (Table 7.6).

The available online data does not allow for a deeper insight (for example, by trip diaries) into the use of the bicycle by people with an immigration background. However, general frequency of use can be accessed. All participants were asked about their bicycle

Immigration Background and Cycling

Table 7.6: Cycling attitude and traffic situation assessment by immigration background (source: BMVI/MiT, 2017).

	With an immigration background (N = 7,256[a], 3754[b])	Without an immigration background (N = 84,003[a], 42,071[b])
Bicycle attitude (fully agree/agree)[a]	55%	60%
Male	59%	64%
Female	50%	58%
Traffic situation (very good/good)[b]	61%	54%
Male	63%	55%
Female	57%	53%

All p<.001; [a]χ^2(1, N = 91259) = 96.9, Cramer's V = .03; [a/sex]χ^2(3, N = 91255) = 522.4, Cramer's V = .08
[b]χ^2(1, N = 91259) = 100.4, Cramer's V = .03; [b/sex]χ^2(1, N = 45825) = 98.5, Cramer's V = .05

use regardless of ability or availability. Thirty-one per cent of people with an immigration background, in comparison to 36%, stated that they frequently cycle, i.e. at least on a weekly basis. Table 7.7 (overleaf) shows the percentages for male and female participants separately. Overall, women tend to cycle less often than men, especially those with an immigration background. The share of people who (almost) never cycle is much higher for people with an immigration background, possibly also due to low bicycle availability.

It is worth mentioning that the young age group (14–17 years) is generally the one with the highest share of frequent users but also the one with the most distinct difference between the two main groups. Forty-four per cent of the young people with an immigration background cycles at least once a week in comparison to 57% without, but only 30% and 36% respectively for those aged 18–29. It increases slightly in the older age groups until it drops again to 28% and 31% for those aged 75–79. The lowest shares are

Table 7.7: Bicycle use by immigration background and gender (source: BMVI/MiT, 2017).

Bicycle use	With an immigration background (N = 12,227)		Without an immigration background (N = 142,724)	
	Male	Female	Male	Female
(almost) every day	18%	15%	19%	17%
1 to several times a week	17%	13%	20%	17%
1 to 3 days a month	14%	12%	18%	14%
less than monthly	14%	14%	15%	16%
(almost) never	37%	46%	28%	36%

$\chi^2(12, N = 154931) = 1115.8$, $p<.001$, Cramer's V = .05

for the age group of 80 and older with 15% and 19% respectively. To summarize, it can be stated that the majority of the German population uses the bicycle at least occasionally. A drop in frequent bicycle use occurs at both ends of the age-group spectrum. Young people can get a driving licence for a car at the age of 17 and people can possibly experience physical difficulties in old age. Overall, more than half of the population enjoys cycling and assesses the situation for cycling positively, irrespective of immigration background. In line with the literature, differences occur when factors like gender are taken into account. Women, especially those with an immigration background, tend to have lower shares regarding the above-mentioned aspects. Unfortunately, no further differentiation of the group with an immigration background is possible.

City Cycling and Immigrant Generations – Findings from Offenbach am Main (ILS-study, 2010)
As stated above, the scarce data is the main reason why the ILS-study is revisited and analysed to identify differences in immigrant generation and bicycle use. Various studies speculate about transport

Immigration Background and Cycling

Table 7.8: Country/region of reference by immigration background/ generation and average duration of stay (source: ILS-study, 2010; see Welsch, 2019).

	With an immigration background			Without an immigration background ($N = 719$)
	First generation ($N = 576$)	Second generation ($N = 263$)		
Country/region of reference	avg. duration of stay (years)[a]	share of generations[b]		
Germany ($N = 719$)				100%
Turkey ($N = 134$)	24.8	63%	37%	
Eastern Europe ($N = 210$)	20.2	74%	26%	
Southern Europe ($N = 261$)	29.4	62%	38%	
Asia ($N = 123$)	20.1	83%	17%	
Other ($N = 111$)	22.9	65%	35%	

[a] $F(4,570) = 19.138$, $p<.001$
[b] $\chi^2(4, N = 838$, without Germany$) = 22.620$, $p<.001$, Cramer's V $= .16$

assimilation and differences in cycling socialization and cycling cultures. The ILS-study does offer the opportunity to distinguish between the immigrant generations when analysing cycling-related data. This aspect is of interest especially in the context of cycling socialization but was not analysed in the above-mentioned publications.

The first generation comprises people who are born outside of Germany and migrated between 1959 and 2010. They represent 69% of the sample with an immigration background. About half of them arrived before 1987. The average duration of stay is 24 years, and the average age at arrival is 19 years. Twenty-two per cent came to Germany as children (aged 10 or younger) and 34% as teenagers and young adults (aged 10–20). Table 7.8 shows the main countries/ regions of reference, where either the participant or (one of) their parents has citizenship by birth or acquired it later.

Table 7.9: Sample characteristics by immigration background/generation (source: ILS-study, 2010; see Welsch, 2019).

Sample characteristics	With an immigration background		Without an immigration background (N = 719)
	First generation (N = 576)	Second generation (N = 263)	
Female	48%	48%	51%
Average age (years)[a]	42.7	33.7	44.2
Shares of educational degrees[b]			
No/not yet school degree	3%	5%	0.3%
With school-leaving certificate (other)	52%	43%	48%
With school-leaving certificate (college or university entrance qualification)	45%	52%	52%
Average household size (person)[c]	3.14	3.07	2.47
Average household income (equivalent scale, €)[d]*	1,242€	1,499€	1,811€

All $p<.001$; [a] $F(2,1554)=66.898$
[b] $\chi^2(4, N = 1557) = 29.828$, Cramer's V = .10
[c] $F(2,1554) = 41.157$
[d] $F(2,1554) = 81.057$ *accounts for household members' non-proportional financial needs

As noted previously, people in the immigration background category are younger, live in bigger households and have a lower average household income. The group of the first-generation immigrants tends to live in bigger households with less income and have a lower educational degree (Table 7.9).

The preconditions for cycling are bicycle availability, knowledge of basic transport rules and cycling ability, often already acquired in childhood. Table 7.10 presents the differences for bicycle ownership, availability and cycling ability. Overall, people without an immigration background come first, except regarding the availability

Immigration Background and Cycling

Table 7.10: Preconditions for cycling by immigration background/ generation (source: ILS-study, 2010, see Welsch, 2019).

	With an immigration background		Without an immigration background (N = 719)
	First generation (N = 576)	Second generation (N = 263)	
Percentage of households with at least one bicycle[a]	73%	81%	87%
Average number of bicycles per household[b]	1.7	2.1	2.5
Average number of bicycles per household member[c]	0.6	0.8	1.0
Percentage of persons with cycling ability[d]	90%	97%	97%
Male	95%	97%	99%
Female	84%	97%	95%
Percentage of potential cyclists with bicycle availability[e1/e2]	79%	84%	90%
Male	80%	85%	89%
Female	78%	83%	90%

All p<.001; [a]χ^2(2, N = 1557) = 36.115, Cramer's V = .15
[b]F(2,1551) = 28.662
[c]F(2,1550) = 72.443
[d]χ^2(2, N = 1556) = 32.281, Cramer's V = .14; [d/sex]χ^2(5, N = 1558) = 69.947, Cramer's V = .21
[e]χ^2(2, N = 1462) = 26.152, Cramer's V = .13; [e/sex]χ^2(5, N = 1461) = 26.303, Cramer's V = .13

of bicycles for females, and the second generation are often in the middle. As expected, immigrant women of the first generation are the group with the lowest cycling ability rates, and most of them are in the older age group (40–66 years). For a better comparability with MiD, bicycle availability and bicycle use were re-analysed. People without cycling ability count for the group with no bicycle availability, "not applicable" is used for those with no ability and

Table 7.11: Bicycle use by immigration background/generation and gender (source: ILS-study, 2010; see Welsch, 2019).

Bicycle use	With an immigration background				Without an immigration background (N = 719)	
	First generation (N = 576)		Second generation (N = 263)			
	Male	Female	Male	Female	Male	Female
(almost) every day	12%	12%	10%	14%	22%	18%
1 to several times a week	29%	18%	27%	18%	32%	30%
1 to 3 days a month	12%	7%	16%	17%	15%	10%
less than monthly	10%	11%	15%	14%	8%	13%
(almost) never	12%	17%	13%	17%	11%	15%
no ability/availability	25%	35%	20%	20%	13%	14%

$\chi^2(25, N = 1556) = 107.590$, $p<.001$, Cramer's V = .12

no availability. The resulting bicycle use is the highest for people without an immigration background of both sexes. The first and second generation cycle to a similar degree, but the first generation has a higher share of participants without cycling ability/bicycle availability (Table 7.11).

Participants who do not cycle frequently were asked to state their (multiple) reasons. The most frequent ones (Table 7.12) include that cycling is too slow or destinations are too far away. Other reasons refer to a lack of safe bicycle paths/parking facilities, health reasons or that people do not enjoy cycling. Cycling is perceived as inconvenient to transport shopping or (small) children. Furthermore, people with an immigration background were more likely to state that they do not have access to a (functional) bicycle, partially due to theft.

All participants were asked to remember (at the age of 10) to what extent their parents used different transport modes and socialization factors were derived. Table 7.13 (overleaf) shows the averages

Immigration Background and Cycling

Table 7.12: Share of responses by reason by immigration background/ generation (multiple entries) (source: ILS-study, 2010; see Welsch, 2019).

Reason for not cycling	With an immigration background		Without an immigration background ($N = 79$)
	First generation ($N = 172$)	Second generation ($N = 99$)	
	242 entries	146 entries	127 entries
Too slow, destinations far away	19%	27%	17%
(no) Cycling infrastructure	21%	26%	26%
Do not like cycling, too lazy	11%	12%	16%
No personal functional bicycle, bicycle theft	11%	9%	5%
Impractical, difficult (children, shopping)	10%	5%	6%
Own physical condition/ill health	7%	5%	10%
Fear of accidents, safety concerns	6%	4%	7%
Other transport modes available/preferred	2%	4%	4%
Weather	4%	3%	1%
Other reasons	2%	3%	2%
Destinations reachable by walking	6%	2%	7%

for each group. Differences between car and bicycle use become clear, especially in socialization experiences of the first generation. In addition to the combined cycling socialization factor, the underlying single items are also presented. The results show a rather mixed picture. Besides the first generation's low average for car and cycling socialization factor, the underlying single items are also presented.

A logistic regression model for cycling use (at least weekly yes/no) offers further insight into underlying factors that influence

Table 7.13: Mobility socialization (factor/item average) by immigration background and generation (source: ILS-study, 2010; see Welsch, 2019).

Mobility socialization	With an immigration background		Without an immigration background (N = 689–714)
	First generation (N = 503–560)	Second generation (N = 252–260)	
Car initiation (age 19)[a]	3.6	3.6	3.8
Car socialization (age 10)[b]	2.2	3.3	3.1
Public transport socialization (age 10)[c]	2.4	3.0	2.4
Cycling socialization (age 10)[d]	2.1	2.4	2.5
Mother often used to cycle[d1]	2.0	2.4	2.8
Father often used to cycle[d2]	2.4	2.4	2.5
Often accompanied by parents when cycling[d3]	2.0	2.5	2.2

[a]$F_{(2,1554)}$ = 4.006, $p<0.018$; all other $p<.001$, [b]$F_{(2,1554)}$ = 78.844, [c]$F_{(2,1554)}$ = 40.421, [d]$F_{(2,1554)}$ = 16.084, [d1]$F_{(2,1530)}$ = 38.460, [d2]not significant, [d3]$F_{(2,1440)}$ = 11.110

cycling behaviour (Table 7.14). It is based on previous work by Welsch et al. (2018), but varies with regards to immigrant generation. Most independent variables were used as dummy variables; the reference group is indicated in italic letters. Numeric variables are bicycles per household, a distance factor, the socialization factors and a statement addressing participants' feeling of security in their own neighbourhood. The estimates for regression coefficient B (reg. coeff. β), odds ratio (OR) and average marginal effects (AME) for each estimated parameter are presented.

By far the largest positive influence on the probability of riding a bicycle at least weekly is the existence of an additional bicycle in the household. Positive effects can be observed for belonging

Immigration Background and Cycling

Table 7.14: Parameter estimation for bicycle use (at least weekly: yes/no) (source: ILS-study, 2010; see Welsch, 2019).

Independent variable	reg. coeff. β	OR	AME
Sex female (*male*)	-.248*	.781	-.048
Age groups (*18–33 years*)			
34–49 years	.313*	1,367	.060
50–66 years	.392*	1,480	.075
Household with children (*without children*)	-.553***	.575	-.103
Number of bicycles in household	.604***	1,830	.116
Ln mean distance (workplace, education, grocery)	-.141*	.869	-.027
Feeling secure in the neighbourhood even when it gets dark	.161***	1,175	.031
Bicycle socialization	.247***	1,281	.047
Immigration background (*no immigration background*)			
First generation	-.134	.875	-.026
Second generation	-.437*	.646	-.083
Constant	-2,388***	.092	

N = 1,557; Nagelkerkes pseudo-r-squared: .279; Level of significance: *p<.05; **p<.01; ***p<.001

to one of the two older age groups and for an increase in the bicycle-socialization factor. Similar but to a lesser extent is the neighbourhood statement about feeling secure even when it gets dark. A decrease in probability can be observed for women and for living together with children. Average further distances to locations for work, education or grocery shopping also affects regular bicycle use in a negative way. A small negative effect is associated with belonging to the group of people with an immigration background, but it is only significant for the second generation.

To sum up, participants of the study in Offenbach am Main tend to differ by immigration background with regards to cycling. Having an immigration background is generally associated with fewer bicycles per household and lower personal bicycle availability. Bicycles are used less frequently, if at all. The second generation seems to hold a middle position between the other two groups in many aspects. However, belonging to this group makes people less likely to cycle frequently according to the multivariate analysis.

Importance and Status of the Bicycle for People with a Turkish Background — Findings from the Dortmund and Ruhr Area (ILS-study/Klausing, 2015)
Mobility culture is often discussed as an additional explanatory factor for differences in cycling behaviour between immigrants and native born, and those norms and values are considered to be reflected in the perceived status (Harms, 2007; Kaplan et al., 2018). The following insights into the status of transport modes are gained by re-analysing qualitative interviews with 32 participants of a Turkish immigration background. They were recruited via a snowball sampling in Dortmund and the surrounding Ruhr area, a (formerly) highly industrialized region with rather low shares of cycling in West Germany. It includes a mix of age, gender and immigration generation, but participants with a lower economic or educational status were hard to find. Participants are aged 19–55, many are highly educated (19 women, average age: 32 years, 14 students, all of whom also work part-time).

The analysis includes 31 participants, who were asked explicitly to rank pictograms of different transport means by importance for everyday transport and status and to talk freely about the selection, ranking orders and related aspects. The status represents the personal views of participants and in addition a ranking according to the perceived status for the overall society. Numbers between one and seven represent the rank. The frequency of the ranking number is presented in Table 7.15, Table 7.16 (both opposite) and Table 7.17 (overleaf). In order to come to relative ranks for each transport mean, each rank was weighted according to its position, e.g. all entries for rank 1

Immigration Background and Cycling

Table 7.15: Rank for importance of transport means (source: ILS-study/Klausing, 2015).

Importance	Walking	Bicycle	Car	Metro/Tram	Bus	Train	Motorbike
Rank 1	8	2	12	5	0	4	0
Rank 2	8	2	3	9	3	5	1
Rank 3	7	8	0	7	4	4	1
Rank 4	4	3	4	5	6	9	0
Rank 5	3	6	5	3	9	4	1
Rank 6	1	10	7	1	7	5	0
Rank 7	0	0	0	1	2	0	28
Weighted rank	*1*	*5*	*3*	*2*	*6*	*4*	*7*

Table 7.16: Rank for status of transport means — self (source: ILS-study/Klausing, 2015).

Status — self	Walking	Bicycle	Car	Metro/Tram	Bus	Train	Motorbike
Rank 1	8	4	16	0	0	2	1
Rank 2	4	4	7	4	2	2	8
Rank 3	6	7	2	4	5	5	2
Rank 4	6	7	2	5	2	9	0
Rank 5	2	4	0	13	4	7	1
Rank 6	3	3	4	4	12	4	1
Rank 7	2	2	0	1	6	2	18
Weighted rank	*2*	*3*	*1*	*5*	*7*	*4*	*6*

are weighted by multiplication with 7, all for rank 2 with 6 and so forth. The weighted ranks for each of the three rankings are shown in Figure 7.2 (overleaf).

Table 7.17: Rank for status of transport means — society (source: ILS-study/Klausing, 2015).

Status — society	Walking	Bicycle	Car	Metro/Tram	Bus	Train	Motorbike
Rank 1	0	0	26	1	0	4	0
Rank 2	5	1	2	1	0	6	16
Rank 3	1	9	3	8	1	8	1
Rank 4	6	1	0	9	7	7	1
Rank 5	2	9	0	7	8	4	1
Rank 6	8	6	0	4	7	2	4
Rank 7	9	5	0	1	8	0	8
Weighted rank	*6*	*5*	*1*	*4*	*7*	*2*	*3*

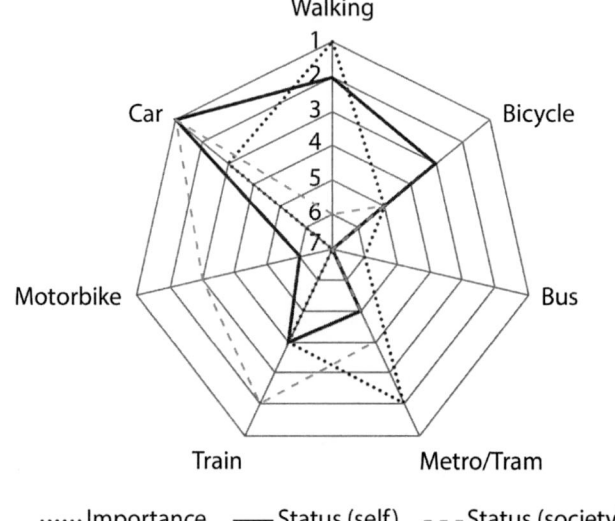

Figure 7.2: Rank of transport means by importance for everyday transport, status for oneself and status for the general society (source: own illustration based on data from ILS-study/Klausing, 2015).

Immigration Background and Cycling

Many of the second- or third-generation interviewees explain that their grandparents or parents do not have cycling abilities. They refer to the situation (then) in Turkey where there was no cycling and bicycles were too expensive. Nowadays, cycling is often seen as too risky in the traffic situation, with the exception of the holiday regions or islands.

In general, there is no doubt that the car is most highly ranked by the participants themselves and even more so for society. "To own a car is very important in any case, yes, you just have to show what you own" (female, third gen., Interview16). Cars are seen as an expression of wealth, achievements and affection. "In my family we always had really beautiful cars" (male, third gen., Int13). Walking represents for many the most important, flexible and enjoyable way to move around in the city. "You are free, choose where you go, which route you take" (female, third gen., Int5). The societal status almost drops almost to the bottom. "… because [people think] you don't even have a bike" (female, third gen., Int18). "He is a bad catch, he walks everywhere" (male, third gen., Int3). The high esteem for the car is stated as culturally grounded and is sometimes connected with the high cost of German manufactured cars, especially in Turkey. Owning an expensive car can be seen as proof of a successful migration. Those stories were communicated from parents to children and might additionally work in favour of the car as a high-status symbol.

The family's attitude towards cycling is most often not stated in detail, but rather indirectly. However, some of the younger mostly well-educated generation describe bicycle use as a means to break away from these status symbols and some think that the status might shift in the future. Generally, the bicycle seems to divide the participants, even though all have the ability and could therefore cycle, in theory. It holds a middle rank regarding importance, but some use the bicycle and give it a high priority, while some appreciate it but only use it sometimes. Some do not cycle at all and usually do not like it. Bicycle users regularly appreciate the flexibility, the low cost and the health benefits. "I definitely think riding a bike is cool. [... Everyone] should definitely learn it" (female, third gen., Int19). "You are as independent as you are with the car [...] a bike is just great [...] you don't have to pay any money if you want to go into town" (female, second gen., Int20). Interviewees mention cycling for leisure, appreciate it as active transport and associate it with sport. "Just for fun and for a little exercise" (female, third gen., Int18). "There's fresh air around you […] I think it is always important to have your own freedom, so I can get on and off the bike whenever I want to and I can also go as fast as I want" (female, third gen., Int10).

The interviews took place in autumn and many participants did not cycle as much as they would in warmer and drier weather. More women than men mention the weather as a barrier and/or do not have or like the protective clothes they have to wear.

> In the summer, if possible, I always prefer cycling […] it saves time and I also find it pleasant to simply cycle, it is also healthier. (female, second gen., Int21)

> In summer and spring, I'm out and about on my bike more often […] but at the moment I really don't like being on my bike because the weather is not so good. (female, second gen., Int25)

> Bicycle, it is so seasonal for me, I don't ride a bike in winter, that's just too cold for me, but then even more so in summer. (female, 1st gen., Int5)

Only one woman mentioned that it is not practical to cycle with a headscarf and that her children felt embarrassed when she put on her husband's rain jacket. But she also referred to cycling as one of the rare sports she can do wearing a headscarf.

> I think out of consideration for my children I let it go, if it rains, I leave my bike at home. […] I just want to move, because especially we women are limited by our outfit [headscarf] in the normal sporting activities here in Germany. (female, second gen., Int12)

Immigration Background and Cycling

The status of bicycles for the participants themselves is relatively high, but very low in regard to the perceived status in society. Reasons for a middle or high rank were that a bicycle has value and status as a property, especially expensive ones, but also because it provides the opportunity to present oneself as active and sporty. In addition, it is described as environmentally friendly, but this aspect is more frequently stated as a well-known fact, but not as a particular reason to use it. The intention to use a bike and to enhance the person's own status was also mentioned in connection with using a more expensive bicycle in the future. "Maybe if I ride a good bike, then maybe it's something else. So, then I might like it a bit more" (male, second gen., Int4).

One of the main barriers and a reason for the low status in society is the perception that the bicycle is not commonly used in the city region and not by people in general. This is especially true for people in their surrounding neighbourhood or those similar to themselves.

> No, Turkish people don't like cycling, they do not know it. (male, second gen., Int15)

> If more people would cycle here, it wouldn't be so bad if I did. (male, first gen., Int27)

Many participants used to cycle when they were (young) children and liked it. But it is not perceived as a serious mode of transport except for children and people use it — if at all — only sometimes in leisure time. "I think that it is also seen [...] childish, when you are on the road with your bike" (female, third gen., Int28). Some state that coming of age is connected to getting their own car, sometimes as a gift from the parents. Having a car and a driving licence is also indirectly connected to the feeling that cycling is something you do not continue with when you are grown up. Also, some participants fear the judgement of other people. In this respect, the bicycle is ranked far below the car and the motorbike and is almost on the same low level as the bus. "Whom can you possibly impress by walking, cycling or taking the bus?" (male, third gen., Int1). In an environment where not many people cycle, also little things like not knowing where to park the bike or a flat tyre can become a barrier to cycling. One participant was asked why he stopped cycling. "No one else around me rides a bike, I don't know how to repair it and then there is nobody else who knows how to do it" (male, third gen., Int13).

Discussion and Conclusion
As stated above, in Germany few mobility and transport-related studies include information on immigration background, country of origin or duration of stay. The current surveys (see introduction), that aim for tracking corona-related changes in travel behaviour, are no exception. Therefore, a (re-)analysis of existing studies on cycling behaviour of immigrants and their descendants was conducted in order to investigate and consider this under-represented group in greater detail.

To summarize, the quantitative analyses showed that people with an immigration background tend to cycle less often. In all groups, women do so less frequently, especially those of non-German origin. Here, those belonging to the first generation are less likely to cycle and tend to have the lowest bicycle availability and the highest share of people without the relevant cycling skills. In contrast, almost every one of the second immigrant generation and those without an immigration background knows how to cycle. Both groups also had parents who cycled more often and accompanied their children on the bicycle. For the first generation the bicycle socialization factor is lower. Interestingly, the second generation takes a middle position, e.g. for bicycle availability and number of bicycles in the household. These findings suggest that there was some sort of transport assimilation with learning how to cycle in childhood, owning bicycles in the household and bicycle availability. Rather unexpectedly, this does not translate into a bigger share of cyclists. Instead, the descriptive results and the logistic model reveal that the second generation tends to cycle less often in comparison to the other two groups. Reasons for not cycling suggest that cycling is not seen as a suitable and practical mode of transport.

Analyses of the qualitative interviews with people with Turkish origins present the importance and the status of the bicycle for participants themselves as well as the perceived status for society. Stated reasons in favour of cycling include that the bicycle is a cheap, flexible and active transport mode. Barriers refer to infrastructural or weather conditions and to the fact that it is (too) slow in comparison to motorized modes and therefore not suitable for longer distances. Interestingly, it is often seen as a mode (only) for children. For adults, the car is the appropriate transport means. Some participants state that Turkish people do not cycle and reject it, as few people like themselves appear to use the bicycle. Cycling has low social status, placed at the bottom of the ranking scale with bus and walking. Such perceived social norms could prevent some people from cycling altogether and some participants point to the differences in Turkish culture, where the possession and usage of a car is valued over all other transport means.

In line with cultural transmission theory (Mchitarjan, 2015), one might conclude that cycling is not considered a practice that "someone is supposed to do", when it is not part of someone's own cultural identity. So, the transmission of cycling as a learned practice in everyday life is not happening and cycling could be perceived as childish or something others do, but not their own family. Immigrant children might thus face the difficulty of (having to) learn how to cycle, despite their own families' non-cycling mobility culture. The same would be true for many children whose families have a car-oriented mobility culture. Cycling is nevertheless very prevalent in children's lives in Germany as cycling skills are often examined at the end of primary school. Whether trends like the fact that more and more children are driven to school by car instead of walking or cycling (Nobis, 2019) will generally lead to less cycling in later life is open to debate.

Cycling courses for immigrant women can reduce the numbers of people who lack skills and widen their local transport options. For some women, who come from (restrictive) non-cycling cultures, undertaking these courses is a deliberate decision towards independent mobility. They enhance social capital and chances for social inclusion, especially for those (now) living in cycling-friendly contexts like The Netherlands (van der Kloof et al., 2014) or Freiburg, Germany (Mohammadi, 2018). However, existing studies show that skills acquisition does not automatically translate to greater independence and social inclusion: continuing further support is also required. Likewise, emphasis on allied health benefits with support from family and friends can help motivate people to continue to cycle after interventions, as shown by Schneider et al. (2018). Indeed, as Sayagh et al. (this volume) point out, cycling alone without company is not only difficult but can be a reason for women to stop altogether. Training courses offer opportunities for individuals, but schools, sports clubs, workplaces and other organizations can offer further support and be sites for intervention planning. In designing programmes, attention also needs to be paid to population diversity (Aldred & Jungnickel, 2014) recognizing different needs and thresholds related to cycling.

Sustainable, liveable cities with a general mobility culture in favour of walking and cycling ease the need for special "cycling skills", as Aldred notes in her afterword (this volume). Urban cycling and walking as enjoyable, zero-emission and active modes of mobility require inclusive and sustainable transport policies and appropriate infrastructure, but still require interventions to support their uptake. A sustainable transport system that allows for pleasant and safe walking and cycling offers the opportunity to do so more often for everyone.

Immigration Background and Cycling

Acknowledgements

The ILS-study (2010) was funded mainly by the ILS—Research Institute for Regional and Urban Development gGmbH and supported by ivm GmbH and the city of Offenbach; I am grateful to Kerstin Conrad, Dirk Wittowksy, Ulrike Reutter and Sonja Haustein with whom I collaborated on this study. Special thanks go to Eva Rademacher for her support and to Rebecca Klausing, who conducted all the qualitative interviews in the course of her Master's thesis (ILS-study/Klausing, 2015). ILS funded a transcript of the interviews, which was re-analysed and partly translated by the author for this publication.

References

Akar, G., Fischer, N., & Namgung, M. (2013). Bicycling choice and gender case study: The Ohio State University. *International Journal of Sustainable Transportation*, 7(5), 347–365. https://doi.org/10.1080/15568318.2012.673694

Aldred, R., & Jungnickel, K. (2014). Why culture matters for transport policy—The case of cycling in the UK. *Journal of Transport Geography*, 34, 78–87. https://doi.org/10.1016/j.jtrangeo.2013.11.004

Asgari, H., Zaman, N., & Jin, X. (2017). Understanding immigrants' mode choice behavior in Florida—Analysis of neighborhood effects and cultural assimilation. *Transportation Research Procedia*, 25, 3083–3099. https://doi.org/10.1016/j.trpro.2017.05.319

Barajas, J. M. (2018). Supplemental infrastructure—How community networks and immigrant identity influence cycling. *Transportation*, 1–24. https://doi.org/10.1007/s11116-018-9955-7

Baslington, H. (2008). Travel socialization: A social theory of travel mode behavior. *International Journal of Sustainable Transportation*, 2(2), 91–114. https://doi.org/10.1080/15568310601187193

Bauer, U., Bracher, T., & Gies, J. (2020). *Ein anderer Stadtverkehr ist möglich—Neue Chancen für eine krisenfeste und klimagerechte Mobilität*. Agora Verkehrswende. https://www.agora-verkehrswende.de/fileadmin/Projekte/2020/Covid19_Stadtverkehr/Agora-Verkehrswende_Ein-anderer-Stadtverkehr-ist-moeglich_1-1.pdf

BMVI/MiD — Bundesministerium für Verkehr und digitale Infrastruktur. (2017). *Mobilität in Deutschland.* http://www.mobilitaet-in-deutschland.de/publikationen2017.html

BMVI/MiT — Bundesministerium für Verkehr und digitale Infrastruktur. (2017). *Mobilität in Tabellen (MiT 2017). Mobilität in Deutschland.* https://www.mobilitaet-in-tabellen.de/mit/

BMVI — Bundesministerium für Verkehr und digitale Infrastruktur. (2020). *Corona-Befragng des Fahrrad-Monitors 2020.* BMVI. https://www.bmvi.de/SharedDocs/DE/Artikel/StV/Radverkehr/fahrradmonitor-2020.html

Bonham, J., & Wilson, A. (2012). Bicycling and the life course: The start-stop-start experiences of women cycling. *International Journal of Sustainable Transportation, 6*(4), 195–213. https://doi.org/10.1080/15568318.2011.585219

Chatman, D. G. (2014). Explaining the "immigrant effect" on auto use: The influences of neighborhoods and preferences. *Transportation, 41*(3), 441–461. https://doi.org/10.1007/s11116-013-9475-4

Citlak, B., Leyendecker, B., Schölmerisch, A., Drießen, R., & Harwood, R. L. (2008). Socialization goals among first- and second-generation migrant Turkish and German mothers. *International Journal of Behavioral Development, 32*(1), 56–65. https://doi.org/10.1177/0165025407084052

de Munter, J. S. L., Agyemang, C., van Valkengoed, I. G. M., Bhopal, R., Zaninotto, P., Nazroo, J., Kunst, A. E., & Stronks, K. (2013). Cross national study of leisure-time physical activity in Dutch and English populations with ethnic group comparisons. *The European Journal of Public Health, 23*(3), 440–446. https://doi.org/10.1093/eurpub/cks088

Eisenmann, C., Chlond, B., Hilgert, T., Behren, S. v., & Vortisch, P. (2018). MOP Bericht 2016/2017: Alltagsmobilität und Fahrleistung. Karlsruher Institut für Technologie (KIT), Institut für Verkehrswesen. https://www.ifv.kit.edu/downloads/Bericht_MOP_16_17.pdf

European Commission. (2013). Attitudes of Europeans towards urban mobility. Wave EB79.4 — TNS Opinion & Social. *Special Eurobarometer, 406.* https://ec.europa.eu/commfrontoffice/publicopinion/archives/ebs/ebs_406_en.pdf

Fassmann, H., & Reeger, U. (2014). Migrationshintergrund und Alltagsmobilität—Mobilitätsverhalten und Verkehrsmittelwahl der österreichischen Bevölkerung. Wien. Österreichischer Automobil und Touring Club (ÖAMTC). https://www.oeamtc.at/thema/verkehr/migrationshintergrund-alltagsmobilitaet-17964357

Forsyth, A., & Krizek, K. J. (2011). Urban design: Is there a distinctive view from the bicycle? *Journal of Urban Design*, *16*(4), 531–549. https://doi.org/10.1080/135809.2011.586239

Friedrichsmeier, T., Matthies, E., & Klöckner, C. A. (2013). Explaining stability in travel mode choice: An empirical comparison of two concepts of habit. *Transportation Research Part F: Traffic psychology and behaviour*, *16*, 1–13. https://doi.org/10.1016/j.trf.2012.08.008

Garrard, J., Handy, S. L., & Dill, J. (2012). Women and cycling. In J. R. Pucher & R. Buehler (Eds.*), City cycling* (pp. 211–234). MIT Press.

Gehrs, B., & Tiemann, M. (05/2020). *Städtische Mobilität nach Corona: Auto-Kollaps oder Fahrrad-Boom?* Greenpeace. https://www.greenpeace.de/sites/www.greenpeace.de/files/publications/s02871_es_gp_mobilitaet_radverkehr_studie_5_20_fin.pdf

Handy, S. L., Blumenberg, E., Donahue, M., Lovejoy, K., Rodier, C., Shaheen, S. A., Shiki, K., & Song, L. (2008). Travel behavior of Mexican and other immigrant groups in California. *Berkeley Planning Journal*, *21*(1), 1–24.

Harms, L. (2007). Mobilität ethnischer Minderheiten in den Stadtgebieten der Niederlande. *Deutsche Zeitschrift Für Kommunalwissenschaften (DfK)*, *46*(2), 78–94.

Haustein, S., Kroesen, M., & Mulalic, I. (2020). Cycling culture and socialisation—Modelling the effect of immigrant origin on cycling in Denmark and the Netherlands. *Transportation*, *47*, 1689–1709. https://doi.org/10.1007/s11116-019-09978-6

Heinen, E., van Wee, B., & Maat, K. (2010). Commuting by bicycle: An overview of the literature. *Transport Reviews*, *30*(1), 59–96. https://doi.org/10.1080/01441640903187001

ITF—International Transport Forum at the OECD. (2020). *Re-spacing our cities for resilience—analysis, facts and figures for transport's response to the coronavirus. Covid 19 Transport Brief.* https://www.itf-oecd.org/sites/default/files/respacing-cities-resilience-covid-19.pdf

Kaplan, S., Wrzesinska, D. K., & Prato, C. G. (2018). The role of culture and needs in the cycling habits of female immigrants from a driving-oriented to a cycling-oriented country. *Transportation Research Record: Journal of the Transportation Research Board, 2672*(3), 155–165. https://doi.org/10.1177/0361198118793242

Kasper, B., Reutter, U., & Schubert, S. (2007). *Verkehrsverhalten von Migrantinnen und Migranten – eine Gleichung mit vielen Unbekannten.* Deutsche Zeitschrift Für Kommunalwissenschaften (DfK), 46(2), 62–77.

Klausing, R. (2015). *Motivationsorientierte Analyse der räumlichen Alltagsmobilität von Personen mit türkischem Migrationshintergrund am Beispiel der Stadt Dortmund* [Unpublished Master's thesis]. Universität Hamburg.

Klinger, T., & Lanzendorf, M. (2016). Moving between mobility cultures — What affects the travel behavior of new residents? *Transportation, 43*(2), 243–271. https://doi.org/10.1007/s11116-014-9574-x

Klöckner, C. A. (2004). How single events change travel mode choice — A life span perspective. 3rd International Conference on Traffic and Transport Psychology. IAAP — Traffic and Transportation Psychology. http://www.psychology.nottingham.ac.uk/IAAPdiv13/

Kolarova, V., Eisenmann, C., Nobis, C., Winkler, C., & Lenz, B. (2021). Analysing the impact of the COVID-19 outbreak on everyday travel behaviour in Germany and potential implications for future travel patterns. *European Transport Research Review, 13*(1). https://doi.org/10.1186/s12544-021-00486-2

Körner-Blätgen, N., & Sturm, G. (2015). Internationale Migration in deutsche Großstädte. *BBSR-Analysen kompakt — Informationen aus der vergleichenden Stadtbeobachtung, 11/2015*, 3–23. Bonn. BBSR-Bundesinstitut für Bau-, Stadt- und Raumforschung. http://www.bbsr.bund.de/BBSR/DE/Veroeffentlichungen/AnalysenKompakt/2015/DL_11_2015.pdf

Mchitarjan, I. (2015). Zur Rolle der Herkunftskultur in Migrantenfamilien. *Migration und Soziale Arbeit, 37*(4), 369–379.

Migration Data Portal. (Ed.). (2019, 18 September). International migrant stock (%). https://migrationdataportal.org

Mohammadi, S. (2018). Social inclusion of newly arrived female asylum seekers and refugees through a community sport initiative — The case of Bike Bridge. *Sport in Society, 22*(6), 1082–1099. https://doi.org/10.1080/17430437.2019.1565391

Immigration Background and Cycling

Nobis, C. (2019). Mobilität in Deutschland – MiD Analysen zum Radverkehr und Fußverkehr. (FE-Nr. 70.904/15). http://www.mobilitaet-in-deutschland.de/publikationen2017.html

Pucher, J. R., & Buehler, R. (Eds.). (2012). *City cycling*. MIT Press.

Robinson, K., & Harris, A. L. (2013). Racial and social class differences in how parents respond to inadequate achievement: Consequences for children's future achievement. *Social Science Quarterly, 94*(5), 1346–1371. https://doi.org/10.1111/ssqu.12007

Schneider, R. J., Kusch, J., Dressel, A., & Bernstein, R. (2018). Can a twelve-week intervention reduce barriers to bicycling among overweight adults in low-income Latino and Black communities? *Transportation Research Part F: Traffic Psychology and Behaviour, 56*, 99–112. https://doi.org/10.1016/j.trf.2018.03.023

Schwanen, T., Banister, D., & Anable, J. (2012). Rethinking habits and their role in behaviour change: The case of low-carbon mobility. *Journal of Transport Geography, 24*, 522–532. https://doi.org/10.1016/j.jtrangeo.2012.06.003

Smart, M. (2010). US immigrants and bicycling: Two-wheeled in Autopia. *Transport Policy, 17*(3), 153–159. https://doi.org/10.1016/j.tranpol.2010.01.002

Statistisches Bundesamt (2019). Bevölkerung und Erwerbstätigkeit. Bevölkerung mit Migrationshintergrund – Ergebnisse des Mikrozensus 2018. https://www.destatis.de/DE/Themen/Gesellschaft-Umwelt/Bevoelkerung/Migration-Integration/Publikationen/Downloads-Migration/migrationshintergrund-2010220187004.pdf

Ton, D., Duives, D. C., Cats, O., Hoogendoorn-Lanser, S., & Hoogendoorn, S. P. (2019). Cycling or walking? Determinants of mode choice in the Netherlands. *Transportation Research Part A: Policy and Practice, 123*, 7–23. https://doi.org/10.1016/j.tra.2018.08.023

Tsang, F., & Rohr, C. (2011). The impact of migration on transport and congestion. http://www.rand.org/content/dam/rand/pubs/technical_reports/2011/RAND_TR1187.pdf.

Tully, C. J., & Baier, D. (2006). Mobiler Alltag – Mobilität zwischen Option und Zwang. Vom Zusammenspiel biographischer Motive und sozialer Vorgaben. VS Verlag für Sozialwissenschaften.

UBA—Umweltbundesamt. (2020). CO2-Fußabdrücke im Alltagsverkehr—Datenauswertung auf Basis der Studie Mobilität in Deutschland. UBA-Texte, 224/2020. www.umweltbundesamt.de/sites/default/files/medien/5750/publikationen/2020_12_03_texte_224-2020_co2-fussabdruecke_alltagsverkehr_0.pdf

van der Kloof, A. (2015). Lessons learned through training immigrant women in The Netherlands to cycle. In P. Cox (Ed.) *Cycling cultures*, (pp. 78–105). University of Chester Press.

van der Kloof, A., Bastiaanssen, J., & Martens, K. (2014). Bicycle lessons, activity participation and empowerment. *Case Studies on Transport Policy*, 2(2), 89–95. https://doi.org/10.1016/j.cstp.2014.06.006

Veith, H. (2008). *Sozialisation*. Ernst Reinhardt Verlag.

Welsch, J. (2015). Alltagsmobilität und Mobilitätssozialisation von Menschen aus verschiedenen Herkunftsländern—Ergebnisse einer Pilotstudie in Offenbach am Main. In J. Scheiner & C. Holz-Rau (Eds.), *Räumliche Mobilität und Lebenslauf—Studien zu Mobilitätsbiografien und Mobilitätssozialisation* (pp. 199–220). VS Verlag für Sozialwissenschaften.

Welsch, J. (2019). *Mobilitätsverhalten von Menschen mit Migrationshintergrund in Deutschland—Annäherungen an eine unbekannte Größe am Beispiel von Offenbach am Main* [Unpublished doctoral dissertation]. Leuphana Universität Lüneburg. http://opus.uni-lueneburg.de/opus/volltexte/2019/14552/

Welsch, J., Conrad, K., & Wittowsky, D. (2018). Exploring immigrants travel behaviour—Empirical findings from Offenbach am Main, Germany. *Transportation*, 45, 733–750. https://doi.org/10.1007/s11116-016-9748-9

Welsch, J., Conrad, K., Wittowsky, D., & Reutter, U. (2014). Einfluss des Migrationshintergrundes auf die Alltagsmobilität im urbanen Raum. Raumforschung und Raumordnung/*Spatial Research and Planning*, 72(6), 503–516. https://doi.org/10.1007/s13147-014-0323-6

Willis, D. P., Manaugh, K., & El-Geneidy, A. (2014). Cycling under influence—Summarizing the influence of perceptions, attitudes, habits, and social environments on cycling for transportation. *International Journal of Sustainable Transportation*, 9(8), 565–579. https://doi.org/10.1080/15568318.2013.827285

Immigration Background and Cycling

Zehl, F., Weber, P., Knie, A., Follmer, R., & Schelewsky, M. (2020). Mobilitätsreport 03 – Ergebnisse aus Beobachtungen per repräsentativer Befragung und ergänzendem Mobilitätstracking bis Ende Oktober. Projekt: 7331 – MOBICOR. WZB – Wissenschaftszentrum Berlin für Sozialforschung gGmbH; infas – Institut für angewandte Sozialwissenschaft. https://www.infas.de/fileadmin/pdf-geschuetzt/infas_Mobilit%C3%A4tsreport_WZB_7331_20201217.pdf

CHAPTER 8
WHAT MAKES WOMEN STOP OR START CYCLING IN FRANCE?

David Sayagh, Clément Dusong and Francis Papon

Introduction

In most countries around the world, women cycle less than men. Most studies that have examined this issue have relied on quantitative methods and have identified the following main factors that explain this phenomenon: (i) labour market positions, (ii) household roles and responsibilities, (iii) life stages, (iv) gender-based perceptions and valorization of safety and risk, (v) cultural norms, (vi) physical barriers such as urban spatial structures that segregate housing from other land uses, (vii) weather and topographical conditions, and (viii) the lack of public transportation systems (Garrard et al., 2008; Krizek et al., 2009; Kunieda & Gauthier, 2007; Lusk et al., 2014; McGuckin et al., 2005; Song et al., 2019, p. 141).

Although there are variations across different territories, it appears that regardless of the scale considered, the lower the bicycle modal share, the lower the proportion of women among the cyclists (Garrard et al., 2012). The proportion of women is particularly low in regions that are less developed for cycling and is higher in regions that are more developed for cycling (Heinen et al., 2010). Countries with the highest modal share of cycling, namely The Netherlands, Germany and Denmark, are the only ones in which women — overall — cycle as much or more than men (Pucher & Buehler, 2008). Some authors have identified that the major reason for the low share of women among cyclists is the fear of motorized traffic, which is associated with dependence on the presence of separate cycling facilities (Garrard et al., 2008; Griffin, 2015; Heinen et al., 2010; Winters & Teschke, 2010). However, important variations in women's cycling practices are also observed according to age, and social and cultural backgrounds. Women

What Makes Women Stop or Start Cycling?

from disadvantaged backgrounds, especially immigrant women from developing countries, are less likely to learn how to bicycle, or to stop doing so after reaching puberty (Assum et al., 2011; Segert & Brunmayr, 2018). Even in The Netherlands, the cycling kingdom, adolescent girls (12–17 years) are almost 28% less likely to cycle to school when compared to adolescent boys (Soemers, 2016), and those born in The Netherlands use bicycles more often than those with origins in non-Western countries (Harms, 2007). Steinbach et al. (2011) suggest that meanings of cycling differ across urban, gendered, ethnic and class identities. We found that in France, residents of underprivileged neighbourhoods tend to equate bicycling with childhood and poverty, whereas certain women with high cultural capital distinguish themselves socially by highlighting the libertarian, health and ecological virtues of their cycling practice (Sayagh, 2018). By considering variations according to territory, age, and social and cultural backgrounds, this chapter aims to understand what makes women stop or start cycling in France.

In most studies, the lack of long-term temporal perspective precludes the understanding of cyclists' behaviours as an outcome of past behaviours and experiences (Jones et al., 2014). A study based on qualitative research stands out for investigating the experiences of cycling among Australian women through the course of their lives (Bonham & Wilson, 2012). It focused on the circumstances under which women started and stopped cycling and the spatial contexts in which this occurred. It began from the premise that an important aspect of a life course approach to cycling is to identify how women's changing travel behaviours challenge and disrupt both transport and existing physical activity norms. The research shows that particular "events" as part of a mix of circumstances, precipitate changes in bicycle biographies including: a shift in residence, change in employment, schooling, social relations and altered physical conditions. Drawing on this approach, the objective of this chapter is to compare the findings of Bonham and Wilson

(2012) with those of studies conducted in France, where the cycling modal share is almost double (around 3% FR versus 1.5% AU) as is the proportion of women cycling (almost 40% FR versus just over 20% AU) (Garrard et al., 2012).

Method
Our analysis is based on three corpuses of formal semi-structured interviews conducted with 84 women aged between 17 and 80 years in various geographical and social settings of the metropolises of Montpellier and Strasbourg (in 2015–2016), and in the inner suburbs of Paris (in 2019). Strasbourg has the most developed cycling network in France. Montpellier is a metropolis of a comparable size (around 500,000 inhabitants), but with a larger car dependency and a lower rate of cycle use (2% modal share, as against Strasbourg's 8%), closer to the national average. The inner suburbs of Paris are interesting because the development of cycling on the outskirts of major cities is a major challenge, particularly with respect to female mobility. Between 2001 and 2010, the number of women cyclists increased by 289% while the number of male cyclists increased by 96% in this area. As Le Vine et al. (2014) noted in the case of London, women are disproportionately responsible for the boom in cycling in the inner suburbs, although men continue to outnumber women among cyclists (Le Vine et al., 2014).

Concerned about obtaining a diversified sample, we avoided building our corpus based solely on the "tree structure" principle, in order not to confine the survey to one or more specific subgroups of the "reasoned" recruitment of participants (Gaudric et al., 2016). The goal was to diversify the cases encountered, rather than to develop a representative sample in the statistical sense. We chose three separate sites, not to conduct a comparative study, but rather to confirm that what we observed in one territory was not specific only to that area. We made sure not to exclude young people from the survey who live in priority policy neighbourhoods (QPV), which are socially disadvantaged areas. As the objective was to

What Makes Women Stop or Start Cycling?

bring out recent memories of both their childhood and adolescent practices, the choice of recruiting adolescent girls in their late teens (17–18 years) seemed relevant to us. The mothers of 14 of them were also interviewed, which helped compare with the information disclosed by their daughters and study the influence of educational practices with greater precision. The interview method used was intended to allow the participants to explore the topic in their own way (Bonham & Wilson, 2012; Crotty, 1998). All interviews first aimed to reconstruct, *ex post*, their life trajectories as women with respect to their bicycle practices and perceptions. Although priority was given to questions based on what the interviewees said, a semi-structured topic guide covered several themes: salient memories of cycling; obstacles encountered (and how they were overcome); change phases; evolution of the mobility habit; intents around mobility for the future; parents' mobility habits; influence of social relations; experience and perception of bicycles and other modes of transport; experience and perception of physical activity; and spatial perception. We considered respondents to have stopped cycling when they themselves felt that they had done so during a given period.

This chapter is divided into three parts. We begin by analysing why most women stop bicycling as teenagers. We then study the main social elements in favour of women's cycling, and finally show how certain breaks in women's lives prove to be particularly influential in precipitating the interruption or the resumption of cycling.

Why Do Most Women Stop Bicycling as Teenagers?
Most women in the sample stopped bicycling during most or all of their teenage years; it was at a time that they generally learned to avoid physical exertion, taking physical risks, moving alone, occupying public space and venturing out (Sayagh, 2018). Most of the time, this finding was reinforced when girls changed their perception of themselves, when they began to equate bicycling with

childhood, or with a boys' sport. As we shall see, certain events — sometimes concomitant — proved to be particularly influential in encouraging this observation and in catalysing the interruption of cycling during adolescence.

Gendered Socialization to Risk-Taking
While bicycle falls are relatively trivialized in childhood, they take on a whole new meaning in adolescence. It seems as though a strong tendency to "be careful" and not damage one's body becomes stronger with age. This observation echoes a study that found that the average cycling speed of young boys aged 8 to 12 years increased with age, while the average speed of the girls (aged 8 to 12 years) surveyed begins to follow the same trend, but drops from the age of 10 years onwards (Briem et al., 2004). Differently socialized to risk, girls are — as early as preadolescence (aged 9 to 12 years) — less inclined than boys to take risks on bicycles (Granié, 2013). It seems that this tendency is reinforced in adolescence. Many adolescent girls in the sample (aged 17 to 18 years) who rode bicycles in their childhood tended to devalue these practices later.

> [Slaloming on a tinkered course with wooden planks in the courtyard of his house)] I would not do it today. I was a kid, and I do not know, after a while, you are too old to have your knees skinned! [Laughs] (Célia, aged 17 years, high school student, intermediate middle class regarding economic capital, resident of the outer suburbs of Strasbourg)

Many women stopped cycling for several years during their adolescence, or even much longer because of a fall without any serious injury. In our sample, this was more pronounced in the working-class areas, and all the more so in immigrant families living in QPV where it is common for a fall to result in a parental ban on cycling, or even in the sale of the bicycle. The gendered norms of spatial use and transport modes in some QPVs are such that three girls in the sample claimed to have stopped cycling in France (two of them because of a fall), while continuing to do so during their summer holidays in their parents' home countries (Morocco and Algeria). These were in less dense urban contexts that offer greater tolerance to the practice of cycling among girls. The context plays a significant role, as the perceived road risk is not only reflected in the threat of an accident, strictly speaking, but also in the threat of abduction, which is itself inseparable from the threat of rape. As a result of this particularly gendered fear, adolescence is often marked by a reinforcement of gendered educational practices resulting in the supervision and limitation of girls' mobility, especially in the case of low perceived security in the neighbourhood (Carver et al., 2012; McDonald, 2012; Torres & Lewis, 2010) and when they reach puberty (Rivière, 2014).

Gendered Socialization to Body Aesthetics
The change in how parents look at their daughters and how daughters look at themselves in this period of body transformation often plays a major role in the interruption of cycling. Several mothers who were interviewed about their teenage daughters helped establish a link among (a) the onset of their daughter's first menstrual period, (b) the change in the way their daughters looked at themselves, (c) the start of their daily use of make-up, and (d) their abandonment of cycling and formal sport. Generally, the teenage girls studied were particularly prone to equating cycling with childhood and did not have any female friends in their close circle who cycled. They suggested that the acquisition of "feminine" clothing may have influenced their decision to stop cycling.

> I think she stopped [to bicycle] completely in the eighth grade [at age 13 years]. In the eighth grade, that is when she felt more ... well, she became a woman, a young woman, well, she had her first period. In fact, her friends and her sister [twin] had had them before, so when Marina had them, she was happy as hell! And she felt as if she had grown up! She started wearing make-up, etcetera. (Cécile, Marina's mother, aged 42 years, early childhood educator, resident of the outer suburbs of Montpellier)

As Aurélia Mardon (2009) showed, the first menstrual cycle is a true moment of identity transition. It marks the end of childhood and involves changes in actions and attitudes. We know that young women tend not to include physical activity in their descriptions of what it means to "become a woman" (Rees et al., 2006, p. 818). Thus, the findings we have just described are often concomitant with dropping out of sport in general. Though this observation pertained to women from all social backgrounds, it was more relevant to women from working-class backgrounds within our sample, which corroborates the trends observed with respect to physical activity and sport as a whole (Gimbert & Nehmar, 2018). Especially in these popular circles, women who report falls during adolescence tend to express regret, even guilt and emphasize the unsightly details of the marks left by the incident, often to the point of suggesting that it would not have mattered had it not left a scar. As reported by Caroline Moulin (2005), the press aimed at adolescent girls (especially *"20 ans"* and *"Girls!"*) is an ardent participant in this "socialization to bodily perfection", urging girls to put make-up on, to veil imperfections, to "hide the marks" (p. 78).

Gendered Socialization to the Street
When their bodies change, adolescent girls often experience street sexual harassment for the first time. These experiences, in combination with increased parental supervision, generally reinforce the idea that "a young girl should not be getting around alone" (de Singly, 2002, p. 29). This mode of thinking restricts opportunities for mobility. For example, several women in the sample reported that they had stopped cycling (mostly utilitarian but also recreational) after they had been harassed on the road. In many cases, they were subsequently driven by their parents, which did not encourage their autonomy and independence. For example, Sara was escorted to school in her mother's car from the eighth grade onwards (aged 12-13 years). She had been cycling to school since the fourth grade (age 8-9 years) until that point:

What Makes Women Stop or Start Cycling?

> I remember that as I had grown up, I was already more ... woman, and ... when I was biking I was often whistled at, accosted or looked at insistently, in addition as it was on a mountain bike the position was, leaning, not ... very .... comfortable ... so it bothered me a little when there were cars behind me and everything, I did not like it very much (Sara, aged 17 years, high school student, intermediate middle class regarding economic capital, resident of inner Strasbourg)

Very often, such experiences lead to a transformation in the way the public space is apprehended, and this results in particular learning and a conscious elaboration of protective strategies. Women who decide to continue cycling usually learn how to not occupy public space (Zaffran, 2016) and not to venture too much into unknown places. They also learn how not to stand leaning forward too much on their bikes (in order to avoid raising their buttocks and making them visible), to dress "like a man", to modify their itineraries by sometimes taking detours, and to avoid getting around alone, and less often, to become more "aggressive" in traffic (Heim LaFrombois, 2019).

Overall, we observe a kind of duality between girls who feel safer cycling than walking and girls who feel safer walking than cycling. While both do not feel safe walking alone, the latter tend to be accompanied during their movements. They pointed out that walking is more conducive to conversation. This aspect is enlightening insofar as the adolescent girls' sociabilities (especially those of the youngest ones) are strongly based on conversational activities, which probably helps explains why during this period, girls are as far or more likely than boys to walk to school (McDonald, 2012).

In contrast, for some adolescent girls, particularly from the middle or upper-middle class in terms of cultural capital, whose mothers are mostly cyclists, cycling helps to emancipate them from the feeling of vulnerability in public spaces. The daughters and mothers in question explained that by cycling, they were less conspicuous or that they were able to leave the area more quickly if they encountered any danger. However, this strategy, which is more often conscious for mothers than for daughters, is frequently synonymous with their dependence on cycling in contexts that are perceived as threatening. It therefore does not allow them to overcome their inclination to fear occupying public spaces (Sayagh, 2018).

Gendered Socialization with Mechanics
Finally, skills in "bicycle mechanics" are essentially transmitted from father to son (Sayagh, 2018). Mastering these skills is not without an effect on the mode of practice. It is often — especially for boys equipped with a repair kit — an opportunity to move away from home more serenely. The lack of skills among girls sometimes serves as a pretext for parents to forbid them from going far away, to inquire about their itineraries, or to request that they do not travel alone.

> Aïssata: My father did not want me to go by bike [to a friend's house] because it was a bit far away and the bike, it is true, I do not know what was wrong with it, but it kept getting punctured. It was well inflated this time, but since I do not know how to put the, what is it called, the things you have to stick on the wheel? Well, not on the wheel ... I do not know what it is called ...
>
> Us: The patches?
>
> Aïssata: Yes, the patches! As I do not know how to do it, my father said to me: "No, do not go, if you get a flat tyre, how are you going to do it?" So I wanted him to teach me, but my brother came and picked me up instead.

A "feminine" socialization to risk-taking, body aesthetics, sport, street and mechanics is a considerable obstacle to cycling in adolescence, especially in the working-class environment. We will now examine social elements that favour the return to cycling.

What Makes Women Stop or Start Cycling?

Main Social Elements in Favour of Women's Cycling
Having Cyclists in One's Social Environment
The presence of cyclists in the social environment often proves to be a determining factor especially for women with little experience and who are not inclined to cycle alone. Thus, at any age, an encounter — including a love encounter — can be a catalyst for the resumption of cycling. Sometimes, as was the case for Laïla, this triggering event occurs even during adolescence. Laïla's example illustrates how the gender and social orders can be questioned through cycling experiences between peers of the same sex, but from different social backgrounds. While she was still cycling to primary school, she moved to her current neighbourhood (QPV). She was 12 years old at the time. After moving, she began walking to school because none of her "neighbourhood friends" cycled. When she entered 11th grade (4 years later), she had a great deal of admiration for a girl in her class called Pauline who lived in a "wealthy neighbourhood". At first, the latter made her want to ride her bike to high school. Then, their exchanges and the journeys they shared (notably to Pauline's house) allowed her to develop skills and a mode of perceiving and practising cycling that are relatively unusual for a teenage girl from her social background. However, it increased her opportunities to travel:

> She showed me how to get on the pavement while staying on the bike... and I did not really know how to shift gears and adjust my brakes [...] she made me realize that cycling is good for health, for the ecology, for everything, in fact! You go faster ... you can go fast if someone is bothering you. (Laïla, aged 18 years, high school student, lower class, resident of the QPV of Strasbourg)

Higher Education and Ecological Concerns
The importance of peers and cultural capital was confirmed when we saw that several women in the sample, who had given up cycling (in some cases only utility cycling) during adolescence, returned to cycling at university. Four dimensions appear to contribute to this:

(a) having at least one close friend who rides a bicycle; (b) living less than 20 minutes by bicycle from the university; (c) not having access to a car; and (d) having used the bicycle as a utility during childhood and/or recreationally during adolescence. These points appear crucial as several other women (especially from working-class backgrounds) with little experience and who have not cycled since childhood say that they would probably dare to cycle again if they were less afraid of not being capable enough and if they had someone with whom to practise. In addition, for several women, like Marie, taking up cycling again at university is associated with a turning point in the way they perceive themselves and their "femininity":

> I am too ashamed of the girl I was in junior high and high school [...] I used to put on too much make-up and it was unnatural, it had become a ridiculous obsession, I mean, I thought about my little problems, I did not think about the environment, I have changed a lot! [...] I see some of them who live right next to the university, really next to it, and who come by car [...] When I arrive at university, I sweat, but I do not give a shit! It is better to sweat than to pollute! (Marie, aged 18 years, university student, resident of inner Montpellier)

Marie's example illustrates that the influence of ecological concerns is perhaps not to be neglected in the choice of resuming cycling, and that it deserves to be linked to the relationship with physical effort. Her case is an opportunity to recall that the environmental consideration of European adolescents is mainly apparent in urban and less present in rural areas (Drevon et al., 2019), and that adolescents who aspire to pursue a university degree tend to have a greater concern for the environment. Marie's case illustrates that if girls cycle less, they (paradoxically) tend to show lesser general interest in cars and more environmental concerns than boys (Sigurdardottir et al., 2013).

Sporting Inclinations
Beyond the ecological aspect, it is common for girls and women to

point out that cycling allows them to stay in control of their bodies and to preserve their health. Contrary to the appropriation of the bicycle with a view to losing weight—which rarely translates into a long-term practice—the appropriation with the idea of staying slim is particularly recurrent among the most experienced women. Often, this appropriation concerns fairly sporty girls and women from the middle or upper-middle class. Most show some pride in being physically active. For some, across all generations, the bicycle is an instrument of social distinction through weight control. This is clearly seen in the words of Gwenaëlle (aged 17 years, upper-middle class regarding economic capital, resident of inner Montpellier), who explained how the bicycle enabled her to distinguish herself from those who "eat too much" and "think little".

> Gwenaëlle: [Cycling] I also use it for sport, to stay in good health [...] some people eat, me I do sport, that is how it is! [laughter]
>
> Us: "There are some who eat?" Do you not eat?
>
> Gwenaëlle: Yes of course, but I mean ... some people eat too much, like those who spend their lives in McDonald's and then wonder why they are fat! I do not know if they think a lot!

In spite of the fact that sporting inclinations seem to favour the practice of cycling, girls and women (especially those from the lower class) are significantly less likely to participate in formal sports, less likely to participate in competition, and even less likely to have performance objectives when compared to boys and men (Naves & Wisnia-Waill, 2014). They are far less inclined to appropriate the bicycle as a means of physical preparation (Sayagh, 2018).

An Intergenerational Evolution Towards More Liberating Family, Social and Cultural Norms for Women

Immigrant women from developing countries are more likely to never learn to bicycle, or to stop cycling after puberty (Assum et al., 2011; Segert & Brunmayr, 2018) (see also Welsch, this volume). Thus, in the case of an intergenerational evolution towards more liberating family, social and cultural norms for women, it is common for children to try to teach or reteach their mothers to ride a bicycle. Very often, the mothers are interested in the idea, especially when they feel safer in the presence of their children than when they are by themselves (Heim LaFrombois, 2019). However, in most cases, their lack of self-confidence combined with the fact that their children are not trained to teach cycling results in failure. Yet, there are exceptions. For example, one teenage girl said that after her failure, she enrolled her mother in a bicycle school for adults while continuing to try to teach her, which meant that over several months she went on rides with her mother, before her mother finally stopped because of health problems.

In another case, Amal learned to bicycle at 44 years with the help of her then 12-year-old son. This resulted in lasting success. Beyond the strong determination of both parties, they seemed to have lived in a context in which it was commonplace for a woman to ride a bicycle (the same cannot be said in some QPVs) and the fact that Amal had already begun learning in childhood, facilitated her (re)learning.

> When I was little, I was a daredevil, so I did a lot of things with boys, and as I had this accident, my mother was very, very afraid that I would do it again, that I would get back on a bike, and that I would fall down and break something [...] I think it is mainly a cultural reason, girls in Morocco ... and I lived in Casablanca, which is a very big city, and the bike was not very usual for girls. That is why I wanted to learn at all costs, for me cycling is freedom! So, I learned very late. My son Toufik took the trouble to teach me, he had a lot of patience, because I never thought I would learn to ride a bicycle. It was unimaginable for me, it was as if I had acquired something exceptional! (Amal, aged 50 years, caregiver, resident of the outer suburbs of Montpellier)

Amal's case is a reminder of the importance of the social and cultural norms of the residential context and parental supervision in bicycle socialization. It illustrates the extent to which the positive perception of cycling proves to be a determining factor. It points to

What Makes Women Stop or Start Cycling?

a dimension that has remained under-studied in sociology, namely reverse mobility socialization (from children to parents).

We have seen how the presence of cyclists in the social environment (especially from the middle or upper-middle class), ecological concerns, sporting inclinations, and an intergenerational evolution towards more liberating family, social and cultural norms for women are proving to be particularly influential in favour of women's cycling. We will now see that certain breaks in women's lives — sometimes concomitant — are proving to be particularly influential in catalysing the interruption or resumption of cycling.

Breaks in the Life Cycle Impacting Cycling
Change in Place of Residence
A change in place of residence can precipitate the abandonment of the bicycle. It is particularly the case when women used to ride for recreational practice with a friend and are not inclined to ride alone. In terms of utilitarian practice, a change in place of residence can particularly result in the abandonment of the bicycle when the new environment is seen as less conducive to cycling and/or when women feel that they lack the skills they need to adapt to it (especially without prior experience bicycling in traffic). A few cases, including Virginie's, show that the experience of cycling in the city does not in itself guarantee the possibility of adapting to less urban contexts. Virginie travelled around a lot on her bicycle in her youth (notably to go to primary, middle, and high school, and university, and also to do her shopping, visit her friends, etc.) in a town in the inner suburbs of Montpellier. However, at 23 years, she stopped cycling definitively after moving in with her boyfriend in a village in the second ring of Montpellier. There are three main reasons for this: (a) the only shops in the village are down the road from her home; (b) she considered cycling as a means of transport (utility) and not as a leisure activity; (c) she did not feel safe in sparsely populated areas (fear of dogs, of getting lost, and of being assaulted without anyone being there to help her):

Becoming Urban Cyclists

> For me, cycling is really ... getting around, it is not leisure [...] I am from the city, in the country I am scared, I am scared alone, so if there are houses, that is fine, I am reassured, but if not, I will not enjoy it, no, I am afraid that something would happen to me and that I would get lost miles away from home! (Virginie, aged 47 years, Morgane's mother, account manager, resident of the outer suburbs of Montpellier)

Virginie's case shows that the inclination to avoid cycling alone is particularly restrictive when it is associated with the fear of getting lost, which is rather prevalent among participants, who adhere to the stereotype that women have a poor sense of direction (Varet et al., 2018). Virginie stated that she would never ride a bicycle again if she continues to live in the countryside. Thus, her case shows that studying the links between bicycle and space perception are essential to understanding the trajectories of cyclists.

In contrast, cycling may resume when the new residential environment is seen as more conducive to cycling, because of the presence of cycling facilities nearby and/or the low speed and density of traffic and/or the perceived number of cyclists.

> Really ... I did not usually ride a bike. It was when I arrived in Saint-Maur, that I saw that the school was really not far away, I said to myself, "Why not do it on a bike?" Because in Saint-Maur, I saw a lot of cyclists ... (Stéphanie, aged 30 years, schoolteacher, resident of the inner suburbs of Paris)

The effect of moves is generally less instantaneous on the resumption of cycling than on its interruption. When women have not been cycling for a long time, resumption is often by trial and error, including starting to cycle occasionally in reserved lanes and/or in parks, often using a bicycle-sharing system. Several studies echo this finding by showing, on the one hand, that the overall proportion of women among the bicycle-sharing system cyclists is higher than that among personal-bicycle cyclists (Goodman & Cheshire, 2014), and, on the other hand, that women are particularly likely to use the

What Makes Women Stop or Start Cycling?

bicycle-sharing system to cycle in large parks (Beecham & Wood, 2014; Goodman & Cheshire, 2014).

Like residential mobility, long and repeated trips to a country or region that is much more "cycling" than what was previously known sometimes plays a key role. For Laëtitia, her repeated trips to Germany and the fact that she had spent time there, were decisive:

> But afterwards, I went back and spent some time there. In Cologne, in particular, there are a lot of cycle paths. I saw that you can do almost everything by bike (Laëtitia, aged 33 years, artist, resident of the inner suburbs of Paris)

As Laëtitia's comments show, travelling can sometimes change the perception of the bicycle, notably through the realization that certain types of bicycles (like cargo bikes) can replace the car totally for the transport of goods and/or children. However, the influence of travel on daily mobility and the links between daily and residential mobility remain under-studied (Epstein, 2013).

Changing Jobs

Changing employment, like securing a first job, often precipitates a change in the mode of travel and can sometimes lead to the abandonment of cycling (especially utility bicycling). This is particularly so when the commuting distance increases and/or when the job in question requires compliance with a certain dress code.

> At work [...] when we arrive at a client meeting and have just experienced the heat while riding a bike, it is very difficult to keep going because we are soaked ... so for a woman it is a bit annoying [...] a man can change quickly, he will put on a new T-shirt and a new shirt, and that is it. But a woman would have to take the time to do her hair, put on a little make-up ... (Fanjatiana, aged 50 years, accountant, resident of the inner suburbs of Montpellier)

As Fanjatiana's comments show, adherence to the stereotype that a woman must take care of her appearance more than a man plays a key role in limiting women's access to cycling, mainly for those with a "feminine" gendered identity (Steinbach et al., 2011). This stereotype should be linked to gendered sporting norms that are often integrated or reinforced during adolescence. Some studies show that, from adolescence, the image of the "sweaty sportswoman" does not fit the image of femininity that girls want to give themselves (Davisse et al., 2000, p. 28).

A change of job (without a change in residence) can also result in an incentive to cycle, especially when the distance is short and/or the journey is perceived as safe, as well as when new colleagues are also cyclists. In the latter case, women—especially those with a "feminine" gender identity (Steinbach et al., 2011)—sometimes realize that cycling can be compatible with "feminine" clothing. Sometimes, the new work environment can also be an incentive for women to dress in a less "feminine" fashion.

> Working in the field of sport ... there are a lot of people, colleagues who wear sneakers/jeans, well, so I allowed myself a little more, I let go, I will say! (Bénédicte, aged 52 years, project assistant, resident of the inner suburbs of Paris)

The bicycle has played an important role in enforcing the right of women to wear more comfortable clothing for physical activity in France. Thanks to women from affluent backgrounds engaging in cycling, women from all backgrounds were able to free themselves from the skirt and dress in 1892, the year in which a prefectural circular was issued authorizing the wearing of trousers for women "on condition that they hold a bicycle or a horse in their hands". This observation still raises questions in terms of social inequalities insofar as clothing practices are particularly gendered among the working classes (Mardon, 2009).

A Change in Children's Autonomy
Among the events that systematically impact women's trajectories, becoming pregnant is a particularly recurrent theme. Often, the announcement of the news results in an immediate abandonment of the bicycle. In other cases, abandonment is associated with the first

What Makes Women Stop or Start Cycling?

physical transformations. These findings echo those of Fournand, who observed that, like horseback riding, tennis or skiing, cycling is often stopped "spontaneously, for fear of the jolts and falls that could trigger a miscarriage" (Fournand, 2009, p. 6). As she explained, under the effect of social representations of what a "good mother" is (largely relayed by pregnancy textbooks), the public sphere of the pregnant woman is considerably reduced, especially when bodily transformations become visible. Nathalie, for her part, continued to go on weekend walks for "two or three weeks" but she immediately stopped the bike to go to work:

> I bought a new bike just before I got pregnant, so I did not use it for a long time, just at the very beginning for rides [...] when you know you are not alone anymore and when you see the traffic, the cars grazing you, the pollution, you quickly feel guilty! (Nathalie, Alice's mother, aged 40 years, nurse, resident of inner Montpellier)

Like Bonham and Wilson (2012), we find that the absence and birth of children, followed by their autonomy or departure are events that structure the trajectory of women cyclists. As mothers continue to be more responsible for both childcare and eldercare, and for escorting them (Motte-Baumvol et al., 2012)—especially in popular circles—this translates into complex travel chains that often complicate cycling. As a result, certain events cause a change in organization and no longer make cycling possible. This is often the case with a divorce, a change in the husband's professional activity, the need to take care of a sick parent, or a return to school with new extracurricular activities for children. However, stopping utilitarian cycling does not necessarily imply stopping bicycling altogether.

> I think she [her mother] stopped when my little sister went to middle school, because she had to take us in the mornings to take the bus, in the evenings, she would take us for our sports, piano classes, and dancing lessons. She could not take her bike to work anymore [...] On weekends, sometimes, we went on bike rides. (Johanna, aged 17 years, intermediate middle class regarding economic capital, resident of the outer suburbs of Strasbourg)

Becoming Urban Cyclists

As soon as their children gain autonomy, some women feel far freer around their choice of mode of transport and return to cycling as happened in the case of Bénédicte, who had to give up cycling when her first daughter was born. However, since her daughters have become independent in their daily mobility, she resumed cycling.

> Now I am free again! If I want to go to work by bike, I am free to do it. No need to anticipate or take precautions for the journey. In the evenings, I know I am not rushed to meet my daughter at the crèche at 6. I no longer have any time constraints related to my children. They are in high school, they come home alone. (Bénédicte, aged 52 years, project assistant, resident of the inner suburbs of Paris)

Health Problems

Finally, several women in the sample stopped cycling because of health problems. For some—especially the youngest—this interruption was temporary (e.g. because of a broken wrist), but for others—especially the older ones—abandonment seemed permanent. In the latter case, this abandonment was often linked to the lack of confidence combined with the fear of falling than to the physical inability to ride a bicycle.

> I was diagnosed with osteoporosis and never dared to bicycle again ... (Carol, aged 70 years, trade union pensioner, resident of the inner suburbs of Paris)

The gendered dimension of the fear of falling is neither specific to France nor to cycling (Gaxatte et al., 2011) but it may partly explain why cycling in France falls among women aged between 50 and 70 years while it increases among men in the same age group (Papon & de Solère, 2010). For older people, the fear of falling is all the more problematic as it results in a sharp reduction in mobility (Pin & Vuillemin, 2014). The interviewees, especially those from the working class, seem less informed of the fact that physical activity is strongly encouraged at this age, including in the case of osteoporosis.

What Makes Women Stop or Start Cycling?

Whereas health problems may precipitate the abandonment of cycling, they may also produce the opposite effect. In our sample, this is mainly the case among women who have a taste for physical activity. Two of them were strongly reminiscent of the women interviewed by Jennifer Bonham and Anne Wilson, who "could no longer participate in their usual exercise routines, as shoulder injuries and knee injuries prevented them swimming, running or playing sport, so they shifted to cycling" (p. 207). Roxane (aged 18 years, high school student, intermediate middle class regarding economic capital, resident of inner Strasbourg), is the only woman in the sample who got back on a bicycle in a sustainable manner under the advice of her doctor. Despite her love for sport, she had stopped cycling (with her family) because of knee problems. Two years later, her doctor felt that cycling could help her with her problem, so she began cycling again, even more often than before (still with her family), which allowed her to "heal and strengthen her legs and knees".

Conclusion

The main objective of this chapter was to identify and analyse the factors that make women stop or start cycling in France. We first saw how a "feminine" socialization to risk-taking, body aesthetics, sport, street and mechanics is a considerable obstacle to cycling during adolescence, especially in the working-class environment. Certain events may be particularly influential in this period in catalysing the interruption of cycling, such as a fall, entry into secondary school, bodily changes, identity transition, street sexual harassment, abandonment of formal sport, and losing the opportunity to bicycle with a friend.

We then showed how the presence of cyclists in the social environment (especially from the middle or upper-middle class), ecological concerns, sporting inclinations, and an intergenerational evolution towards more liberating family social and cultural norms for women are proving to be particularly influential in favour of women's cycling. In the third phase, we saw that certain breaks in women's lives—sometimes concomitant—are proving to be particularly influential in precipitating the interruption or resumption of cycling, in particular changing a place of residence, securing a new job, getting pregnant, a change in child autonomy and health problems.

These events may trigger the ceasing or resumption of cycling, and are very diverse, complex and embedded in the course of women's personal lives, which cannot be studied in isolation from the gender and social order. Our results corroborate those of Jennifer Bonham and Anne Wilson (2012) and underline the interest in integrating into the analysis the influences of gendered contextual norms; changes in the perceptions of transport modes, space for oneself; gendered corporeal and spatial inclinations (propensity to move alone, to venture and occupy public space; taste for physical effort and for risk); competencies and feelings of competence (to ride and repair a bike); and ecological and health awareness and concerns. Thus, our results highlight the importance of studying both the links among urban, ecological, health, sport and mobility socialization in a systematic manner and the links among daily mobility, moving, travel and migration.

Our results encourage the study of bicycles in an intersectional manner. They suggest that middle- and upper-class women, especially those with strong cultural capital, including adolescents, are in the best position to respond to the prevailing health and environmental injunctions. In light of this observation, the challenge is to prevent the promotion of cycling among women from becoming a stigmatizing moral enterprise for those from the most underprivileged social and spatial backgrounds, that turn out to be the least inclined towards cycling.

Our chapter also shows that the promotion of cycling among women cannot be limited to the search for gender parity in terms of the number of cycling trips, as it is far from being synonymous with equal opportunities between men and women. This would be the case if women felt as free as men to cycle alone at night, to venture off the routes they know and to occupy space. Gendered differences in cycling correspond to wider gendered social inequities.

More and more "good practice" guides for city planning advocate accessibility for all, including an emphasis on the participation of women in decision making and planning, and the training of educators on gender issues. What is currently missing is sufficient identification and analysis of the areas, places and infrastructures deserted by women. Our study begins the analysis of these factors and points to some positive ways forward for future intervention. The "savoir rouler" plan set up by the French government in 2018 ensures that children leave primary school having mastered the art of riding their bikes independently and safely. Our results indicate that these actions should continue in middle and high school, as it is during this period that gender inequalities in opportunities for practice increase. Similarly, the considerable work of the adult bicycle schools that have flourished in recent years and that mainly welcome women from sub-Saharan Africa and the Maghreb should be encouraged as a further continuance. Finally, it is also necessary, at least initially, to encourage non-mixed bicycle self-repair workshops, as a necessary step towards making most women aware that they are capable of maintaining their bicycles (see also Abord de Chatillon in this volume).

References

Assum, T., Panian, T., Pfaffenbichler, P., Christiaens, J., Nordbakke, S., Davoody, H., & Wixey, S. (2011). *Immigrants in Europe, their travel behaviour and possibilities for energy efficient travel*. Deliverable D2.1. Together on the move. https://www.toi.no/andre-publikasjoner-8000-serie/immigrants-in-europe-their-travel-behaviour-and-possibilities-for-energy-efficient-travel-deliverable-d2-1-together-on-the-move-article31600-236.html

Beecham, R., & Wood, J. (2014). Exploring gendered cycling behaviours within a large-scale behavioural data-set. *Transportation Planning and Technology, 37*(1), 83–97. https://doi.org/10.1080/03081060.2013.844903

Bolusset, A., & Rafraf, C. (2019). Sept salariés sur dix vont travailler en voiture. *Insee Focus*, *143*. https://www.insee.fr/fr/statistiques/3714237#consulter

Bonham, J., & Wilson, A. (2012). Bicycling and the life course: The start-stop-start experiences of women cycling. *International Journal of Sustainable Transportation*, *6*(4), 195–213. https://doi.org/10.1080/15568318.2011.585219

Briem, V., Radeborg, K., Salo, I., & Bengtsson, H. (2004). Developmental aspects of children's behavior and safety while cycling. *Journal of Pediatric Psychology*, *29*(5), 369–377. https://doi.org/10.1093/jpepsy/jsh040

Carver, A., Timperio, A. F., Hesketh, K., & Crawford, D. (2012). How does perceived risk mediate associations between perceived safety and parental restriction of adolescents' physical activity in their neighborhood? *International Journal of Behavioral Nutrition and Physical Activity*, *9*. https://doi.org/10.1186/1479-5868-9-57

Crotty, M. (1998). *The foundations of social research*. Sage.

Davisse, A., Dechavanne, N., & Labridy, F. (2000). La mixité est-elle garante d'une réelle égalité des sexes en Education Physique ? *Hyper EPS*, *210*, 24–28.

de Singly, F. (2002). La « liberté de circulation » : Un droit aussi de la jeunesse. *Revue des politiques sociales et familiales*, *67*(1), 21–36. https://doi.org/10.3406/caf.2002.1002

Drevon, G., Ravalet, E., & Kaufmann, V. (2019). Quel imaginaire de la voiture chez les adolescents européens ? *Espace populations sociétés*, *2019-1*. https://doi.org/10.4000/eps.8774

Epstein, D. M. (2013). *La mobilité spatiale locale : L'influence de la mobilité quotidienne sur la mobilité résidentielle : L'exemple des résidants actifs luxembourgeois*. Université de Strasbourg.

Fournand, A. (2009). La femme enceinte, la jeune mère et son bébé dans l'espace public. *Géographie et cultures*, *70*, 79–98. https://doi.org/10.4000/gc.2320

Garrard, J., Handy, S., & Dill, J. (2012). Women and cycling. In J. R. Pucher & R. Buehler (Eds.), *City cycling* (pp. 211–234). MIT Press.

Garrard, J., Rose, G., & Lo, S. K. (2008). Promoting transportation cycling for women: The role of bicycle infrastructure. *Preventive Medicine*, *46*(1), 55–59. https://doi.org/10.1016/j.ypmed.2007.07.010

Gaudric, P., Mauger, G., & Zunigo, X. (2016). Lectures numériques : Une enquête sur les grands lecteurs. *Éditions de la Bibliothèque publique d'information*. http://books.openedition.org/bibpompidou/1862

Gaxatte, C., Nguyen, T., Chourabi, F., Salleron, J., Pardessus, V., Delabrière, I., Thévenon, A., & Puisieux, F. (2011). Fear of falling as seen in the multidisciplinary falls consultation. *Annals of Physical and Rehabilitation Medicine*, 54(4), 248–258. https://doi.org/10.1016/j.rehab.2011.04.002

Gimbert, V., & Nehmar, K. (2018). *Activité physique et pratique sportive pour toutes et tous* (p. 140). France Stratégie.

Goodman, A., & Cheshire, J. (2014). Inequalities in the London bicycle sharing system revisited: Impacts of extending the scheme to poorer areas but then doubling prices. *Journal of Transport Geography*, 41, 272–279. https://doi.org/10.1016/j.jtrangeo.2014.04.004

Granié, M.-A. (2013). Différences de sexe et rôle de l'internalisation des règles sur la propension des enfants à prendre des risques à vélo. *Recherche Transports sécurité*, 2011(01), 34–41.

Griffin, W. M. (2015). *Male and female, cyclist and driver perceptions of crash risk in critical road situations*. Queensland University of Technology.

Harms, L. (2007). Mobility among ethnic minorities in the urban Netherlands. *German Journal of Urban Studies*, 46(2). https://difu.de/publikationen/mobility-among-ethnic-minorities-in-the-urban-netherlands.html

Heim LaFrombois, M. (2019). (Re)Producing and challenging gender in and through urban space: Women bicyclists' experiences in Chicago. *Gender Place and Culture: A Journal of Feminist Geography*, 26(5), 659–679. https://doi.org/10.1080/0966369X.2018.1555142

Heinen, E., van Wee, B., & Maat, K. (2010). Commuting by bicycle: An overview of the literature. *Transport Reviews*, 30(1), 59–96. https://doi.org/10.1080/01441640903187001

Jones, H., Chatterjee, K., & Gray, S. (2014). A biographical approach to studying individual change and continuity in walking and cycling over the life course. *Journal of Transport & Health*, 1(3), 182–189. https://doi.org/10.1016/j.jth.2014.07.004

Krizek, K. J., Handy, S. L., & Forsyth, A. (2009). Explaining changes in walking and bicycling behavior: Challenges for transportation research. *Environment and Planning B: Planning and Design*, 36(4), 725–740. https://doi.org/10.1068/b34023

Kunieda, M., & Gauthier, A. (2007). *Sustainable transport: A sourcebook for policy-makers in developing cities*. (Module 7a: Gender and Urban Transport: Smart and Affordable). GTZ. https://trid.trb.org/view/844422

Le Vine, S., Miranda-Moreno, L., Lee-Gosselin, M., & Waygood, E. O. D. (2014). Gender and the growth of cycling in a megacity region: Emerging evidence from London. *"Bridging the Gap": 5th International Conference on Women's Issues in Transportation Proceedings* (pp. 497–509). https://trid.trb.org/view/1343638

Lusk, A. C., Wen, X., & Zhou, L. (2014). Gender and used/preferred differences of bicycle routes, parking, intersection signals, and bicycle type: Professional middle class preferences in Hangzhou, China. *Journal of Transport & Health, 1*(2), 124–133. https://doi.org/10.1016/j.jth.2014.04.001

Mardon, A. (2009). Les premières règles des jeunes filles : Puberté et entrée dans l'adolescence. *Sociétés contemporaines, 75*(3), 109–129. https://doi.org/10.3917/soco.075.0109

McDonald, N. C. (2012). Is there a gender gap in school travel? An examination of US children and adolescents. *Journal of Transport Geography, 20*(1), 80–86. https://doi.org/10.1016/j.jtrangeo.2011.07.005

McGuckin, N., Zmud, J., & Nakamoto, Y. (2005). Trip-chaining trends in the United States: Understanding travel behavior for policy making. *Transportation Research Record, 1917*, 199–204. https://doi.org/10.1177/0361198105191700122

Motte-Baumvol, B., Bonin, O., & Belton-Chevallier, L. (2012). *Gender differences for escorting children among dual earners families in the Paris Region*. 13th International Conference of the International Association for Travel Behaviour Research (IATBR). 12 July 2012. Toronto, Canada. https://hal.archives-ouvertes.fr/hal-00852990

Moulin, C. (2005). *Féminités adolescentes : Itinéraires personnels et fabrication des identités sexuées*. Presses universitaires de Rennes.

Naves, M.-C., & Wisnia-Waill, V. (2014). *Lutter contre les stéréotypes filles-garçons* (p. 236). Commissariat général à la stratégie et à la prospective.

Papon, F., & de Solère, R. (2010). Les modes actifs : Marche et vélo de retour en ville. *La revue, Commissariat général au développement durable. Service de l'observation et des statistiques*, 65–82. https://www.researchgate.net/profile/Francis_Papon/publication/258155348_Les_modes_actifs_marche_et_velo_de_retour_en_ville/links/54c26cb50cf256ed5a8d5791/Les-modes-actifs-marche-et-velo-de-retour-en-ville.pdf

Pierre, J., Caluzio, C., & Schut, P.-O. (2015). La pratique sportive des seniors : Des profils et besoins variés. *Retraite et societe*, *71*(2), 75–90. https://www.cairn.info/revue-retraite-et-societe1-2015-2-page-75.htm

Pin, S., & Vuillemin, A. (2014). Accidents de la vie courante et chutes. In C. Léon & F. Beck (Éds.), *Les comportements de santé des 55-85 ans : analyses du Baromètre santé 2010* (pp. 101–116). Editions INPES.

Pucher, J., & Buehler, R. (2008). Making cycling irresistible: Lessons from The Netherlands, Denmark and Germany. *Transport Reviews*, *28*(4), 495–528. https://doi.org/10.1080/01441640701806612

Rees, R., Kavanagh, J., Harden, A., Shepherd, J., Brunton, G., Oliver, S., & Oakley, A. (2006). Young people and physical activity: A systematic review matching their views to effective interventions. *Health Education Research*, *21*(6), 806–825. https://doi.org/10.1093/her/cyl120

Rivière, C. (2014). *Ce que tous les parents disent ? : Approche compréhensive de l'encadrement parental des pratiques urbaines des enfants en contexte de mixité sociale (Paris–Milan)*. [Thèse]. Institut d'études politiques de Paris. http://www.theses.fr/2014IEPP0001

Sayagh, D. (2018). *Pourquoi les adolescentes ont moins de possibilités réelles de faire du vélo que les adolescents* [Thèse]. Université Paris-Est.

Segert, A., & Brunmayr, E. (2018). *Can public bike sharing systems encourage migrant women to use bicycles?* (Working Paper 123). Institut für Höhere Studien (IHS). https://irihs.ihs.ac.at/id/eprint/4847/1/segert-brunmayr-2018-bike-sharing-rs123.pdf

Sigurdardottir, S. B., Kaplan, S., Møller, M., & Teasdale, T. W. (2013). Understanding adolescents' intentions to commute by car or bicycle as adults. *Transportation Research Part D: Transport and Environment*, *24*, 1–9. https://doi.org/10.1016/j.trd.2013.04.008

Soemers, J. (2016). *Steps towards an active future. A study on the influences on transport mode choice to school among Dutch adolescents* [Unpublished Master's thesis]. Utrecht University.

Song, L., Kirschen, M., & Taylor, J. (2019). Women on wheels: Gender and cycling in Solo, Indonesia. *Singapore Journal of Tropical Geography*, *40*(1), 140–157. https://doi.org/10.1111/sjtg.12257

Steinbach, R., Green, J., Datta, J., & Edwards, P. (2011). Cycling and the city: A case study of how gendered, ethnic and class identities can shape healthy transport choices. *Social Science & Medicine*, *72*(7), 1123–1130. https://doi.org/10.1016/j.socscimed.2011.01.033

Torres, J., & Lewis, P. (2010). Proximité et transport actif : Le cas des déplacements entre l'école et la maison. À Montréal et à Trois-Rivières. *Environnement Urbain / Urban Environment*, *4*. http://journals.openedition.org/eue/760

Varet, F., Degraeve, B., & Granié, M.-A. (2018). Comportements dans l'espace routier : Le rôle des attentes sociales. *Le Journal des psychologues*, *360*(8), 24–29. https://www.cairn.info/revue-le-journal-des-psychologues-2018-8-page-24.htm

Winters, M., & Teschke, K. (2010). Route preferences among adults in the near market for bicycling: Findings of the cycling in cities study. *American Journal of Health Promotion*, *25*(1), 40–47. https://doi.org/10.4278/ajhp.081006-QUAN-236

Zaffran, J. (2016). Bouger pour grandir. Défection et mobilité des adolescents. *Les Annales de la recherche urbaine*, *111*(1), 68–77. https://doi.org/10.3406/aru.2016.3224

CHAPTER 9
APPROPRIATING THE BICYCLE: REPAIR AND MAINTENANCE SKILLS AND THE BICYCLE–CYCLIST RELATIONSHIP

Margot Abord de Chatillon

Introduction

Sooner or later all cyclists are faced with a puncture or another mechanical issue, and becoming an urban cyclist results in the need to learn ways to deal with these issues. For cyclists, mastering repair and maintenance skills contributes to safer riding and to higher confidence on the road, especially for longer or unusual trips. These skills are also related to their identity as a cyclist (Aldred, 2013). They are not only useful when cyclists engage in the repair and maintenance of their bicycle but also when they choose to outsource these operations to a professional bicycle mechanic, since it allows them to be confident and informed during the commercial transaction that it entails (Akerlof, 1978). The acquisition of repair and maintenance skills is thus a major step for individuals aiming to become urban cyclists, a step made more difficult by the fact that many people only become frequent cyclists as adults (Buhler, this volume). Despite this, the mechanisms at play when learning these skills have not yet been explored in scientific literature.

To understand how urban cyclists learn how to repair and maintain their machines, it is necessary to understand the relationship between cyclists and their bicycles. When involved in repair or maintenance, individuals engage with the material object in an embodied practice (Dant, 2010) in which competences play a major role (Shove et al., 2007). This material interaction of repair and maintenance echoes the material interaction which occurs in the course of riding and the overall bicycle–cyclist interaction which is at the core of cycling practices (Spinney, 2006). It is thus important to understand how the relationship between the cyclist and their bicycle is transformed by learning bicycle repair and maintenance, and reciprocally how bicycle repair and maintenance skills can be acquired through the bicycle–cyclist relationship.

In this chapter, I follow Daniel Miller's theoretization of appropriation as a framework to argue that the development of repair and maintenance skills can be seen as an appropriation of the bicycle (1987). The relationship that cyclists maintain with their bicycle is different according to their repair and maintenance skills. As cyclists develop bicycle repair and maintenance skills, their instrumental relationship with their bicycle is transformed. By acknowledging the central role that the bicycle–cyclist relationship plays in the acquisition of bicycle repair skills, we can reframe our perspective of what it means to become an urban cyclist.

To this end, I utilize data collected in the cities of Lyon and Melbourne. These two cities have a similar cycling modal share and similar goals in the development of cycling practices, but belong to countries where different cycling cultures prevail, and where different infrastructures for cycle repair and maintenance are available. Interviews were conducted with urban cyclists who were either very inexperienced or very experienced regarding repair and maintenance skills. This allows a better understanding of the skill-learning processes and their mechanisms within cyclists' daily lives. This data allows the intertwining of repair and maintenance skills and the bicycle–cyclist relationship to show, and to identify the bicycle–cyclist relationship as a place where repair and maintenance skills are acquired, whether on or with the bicycle.

Theoretical Framework: The Bicycle–Cyclist Relationship and Appropriation

The chapter focuses on bicycle repair and maintenance as a means of appropriating the bicycle. In this section, I first argue that researching repair requires considering the materiality of bicycles and the nature of the bicycle–cyclist relationship. I then review the existing literature on the bicycle–cyclist relationship and introduce Daniel

Appropriating the Bicycle

Miller's theory of appropriation (1987) as a relevant framework for analysing the development of cycle repair and maintenance skills within the bicycle–cyclist relationship.

Repair Practices and the Materiality of Cycling

In European and Australian cities, urban cycling has been rising in the last two decades (Héran, 2015). This was followed by the expansion of bicycle shops catering for urban cyclists unable or unwilling to engage in repair and maintenance themselves. Despite this, it is still widely considered among cyclists that a good cyclist should be able to repair and maintain their own machine, to the extent that cyclists with low repair and maintenance skills may not feel legitimate (Aldred, 2013). The boom of community workshops, places where it is possible to repair one's cycle oneself with the help of available tools and a volunteer, show that repair and maintenance are still valued as essential skills for most cyclists. Therefore, a thorough understanding of how individuals become urban cyclists has to include the processes through which they acquire repair and maintenance skills.

An investigation of the acquisition of repair and maintenance skills requires looking at the bicycle differently. Indeed, transportation research, which is increasingly concerned with cycling and its adoption by urban dwellers (Dill, 2019), does not focus on the materiality of the bicycle as an object, or on the relationship between the cyclist and the bicycle. With some noticeable exceptions (Cook & Edensor, 2017; Spinney, 2006; Strömberg & Karlsson, 2016), it overwhelmingly assumes that all cyclists ride a standard two-wheeled bicycle with similar average speed, and in good condition. However, when walking in urban areas, it is not uncommon to see a bicycle parked for months, lacking a wheel or a seat (Larsen & Christensen, 2015). It is also usual to hear the rattling chain of a cyclist on the move, or to see that someone is riding a bicycle with deflated tyres. These common observations act as reminders that bicycles are not only a way to get from A to B, but that they are also material objects with specific aesthetic or technical characteristics, with a specific history, carrying the name of a given manufacturer, and that they may or may not be in good condition. Bicycles can break down, they age and decay. Considering repairs and maintenance processes means focusing on the material world and its underlying order (Graham & Thrift, 2007). A focus on bicycle repair and maintenance can allow us to rethink our relationship with the material goods surrounding us.

The Bicycle-Cyclist Relationship
Understanding bicycle repair and maintenance practices and the acquisition of the related skills requires considering the materiality of the bicycle as well as the nature of the bicycle-cyclist relationship. Research in social psychology argued that the relationship between car drivers and their cars included three main dimensions: an instrumental one, an affective one and a symbolic one (Steg, 2005). The relevance of the affective (Coleman, 2015) and symbolic (Ashmore et al., 2018) components of this relationship is increasingly recognized, and these dimensions seem to be affected by the development of repair and maintenance skills (Abord de Chatillon, 2019). Here, I focus on the instrumental dimension of the bicycle-cyclist hybrid, most relevant when discussing repair and maintenance. That is, this chapter only reflects on the relationship of the cyclist with the bicycle as a tool, and not as an object of affection, pride or a way to acquire social status.

One way of understanding the instrumental relationship between the cyclist and their bicycle is provided by Warnier's research on techniques and tools (1999). According to Warnier, when using a tool, an individual integrates it into their "corporal scheme". This is illustrated by the case of someone using a hammer. The hammer becomes an extension of this person's hand; they do not focus on the contact between their body and the hammer but on how the head of the hammer can hit the nail. This subject-object integration was also described in the field of mobilities research,

Appropriating the Bicycle

with for instance the case of windsurfing (Dant, 1998; Dant & Wheaton, 2007) and of car driving (Dant, 2004; Urry, 2006). When it comes to cycling, the bicycle-cyclist hybrid is described by Spinney (2006). Following Ingold, he argues that "The bike and body are thus produced as one: refined and maintained in conjunction with each other through and within movement." As an example of the way the hybrid expresses itself in action, Spinney adds: "Gearing is felt by the rider—the machine asking the rider to maintain a circular movement, perhaps lower or raise the speed of the rider but maintaining movement of the legs and lungs at a manageable pace." (2006, p. 719). To some extent, within the bicycle-cyclist hybrid, the rider experiences mechanical issues of the bicycle as if they were their own.

While the cyclist is on the bicycle, the complex matter of the instrumental relationship they maintain with their bicycle is expressed through the bicycle-cyclist hybrid. However, the bicycle-cyclist relationship also exists in a wider context, for instance when the cyclist considers cycling for keeping fit or plans to get their groceries by bicycle; the bicycle-cyclist relationship does not disappear when the cyclist dismounts. Bicycle repair and maintenance is likely to affect this relationship at both levels. For instance, if a gear cable of the bicycle is damaged, it means that while on the bicycle, the cyclist is unable to change gears and may struggle when riding uphill, but also that their choice of where to ride and what activities to conduct with the bicycle will be different (the cyclist may choose to avoid some hilly areas, to carry a lower weight or to stop riding the bicycle at all).

As argued above, studying repair and maintenance practices requires considering the bicycle-cyclist relationship. However, the nature of the link between these two things is yet to be explored. The following section introduces the theory of appropriation, a framework that allows considering the acquisition of repair and maintenance skills, together with the development of the bicycle-cyclist relationship, as part of the same process of consumption.

Becoming Urban Cyclists

Appropriation and Seeing Cycling as a Form of Consumption
In *Material Culture and Mass Consumption*, Miller (1987) applied theories developed by Hegel, Marx and Simmel in order to describe the relationships that individuals in our society maintain with manufactured objects surrounding them. Miller argues that objects constitute society: they act as bricks of our social lives and frame social interactions. The industrial era gave rise to the mass production of everyday objects, from which we may feel alienated if we consider the conditions in which they were produced. However, this mass production goes together with mass consumption, and we must regard the acquisition and use of manufactured objects as a true work of consumption, through which meaning can be transferred back into the objects while they are reintroduced into the social lives of the subjects.

> Consumption as work translates the object [...] from being a symbol of estrangement and price value to being an artefact invested with particular inseparable connotations. [...] The object is transformed by its intimate association with a particular individual or social group, or with the relationship between these. (Miller, 1987, p. 190)

This act of consumption as a process, that Miller successively calls "objectification" and "recontextualisation" will be termed "appropriation" here, for the argument of this chapter. It allows consideration of the daily use of objects, and their consumption, as belonging to a more general process through which individuals or social groups shape and appropriate material culture, instead of considering it as "alien". It also allows the consideration of bicycle repair and cycling as practices that, despite their differences, are both constituted of an interaction between the cyclist and their bicycle, and therefore both contribute to the cyclist appropriating their bicycle.

This paper uses the theory of appropriation as a framework through which the development of bicycle repair skills is discussed. It explores bicycle repair and maintenance as an appropriation of the bicycle as well as how this process unfolds within the instrumental aspect of the bicycle–cyclist relationship. I argue that when acquiring bicycle repair and maintenance skills, a cyclist sees the instrumental relationship they have with their bicycle transformed. The theory of appropriation allows the integration of this interrelation between repair and maintenance skills and cycling practices into a new understanding of learning repair skills.

Method
This chapter draws from data collected in the frame of an ongoing global research project in the cities of Lyon, France, and Melbourne, Australia; two cities with a cycling modal share below 4%. A mixed methods methodology was used, integrating qualitative and quantitative data. A survey was distributed to local cyclists of both cities, asking them about their repair skills and experiences, producing more than 450 survey responses in each city. Further, semi-structured interviews were conducted with 100 individuals involved with repair: among which were bicycle mechanics, bicycle shop owners, community workshop volunteers or employees and regular cyclists with diverse repair and maintenance experience and skills. This data was completed with regular participant observation in three community workshops (two in Melbourne, one in Lyon) and with the regular repair and maintenance of my own bicycle in both cities.

The main materials used in this chapter are the interviews conducted with 35 regular cyclists, recruited either for their very low or high experience of repair and maintenance according to their responses to the survey (among those who had consented to leave their contact details). An account of cyclists interviewed according to their city of residence and their experience regarding repair and maintenance can be found in Table 9.1 (overleaf). The interview extracts present in this chapter were translated from French to English when necessary.

Becoming Urban Cyclists

Table 9.1: Interviews conducted in Lyon and Melbourne.

		Melbourne	Lyon	Total
Cyclists interviewed on their repair history	Total	25	10	35
	High experience in repair and maintenance	10	6	16
	Low experience in repair and maintenance	15	4	19

Although both cities have similar cycling mode shares and evolution, with a trend towards the development of electric bicycles, they differ when it comes to the type of bicycles used. Among others, Melbourne's cyclists are more likely to ride road (sports) bikes than Lyon cyclists, who favour hybrid or city bicycles. This is due to a more widespread sports culture and the lower density of the urban area, which results in the longer average distances ridden. Furthermore, with an older cycling culture, Lyon has a larger second-hand market for bicycles, and Lyon cyclists are more likely to have purchased their bicycle second-hand rather than new (50% of them did so, in comparison with 29% of Melbourne cyclists surveyed). As a result, Lyon cyclists tend to ride on bicycles that are in less good condition than those of Melbourne's cyclists, as illustrated in Figure 9.1.

Another important difference between the two cities is the resources available to residents of each of them in terms of repair. Indeed, the important rise of community workshops in France had little equivalent in Australia: in Melbourne, there were only two workshops of this kind whereas there were eight of them in Lyon, a city with half as many inhabitants. Furthermore, French community

Appropriating the Bicycle

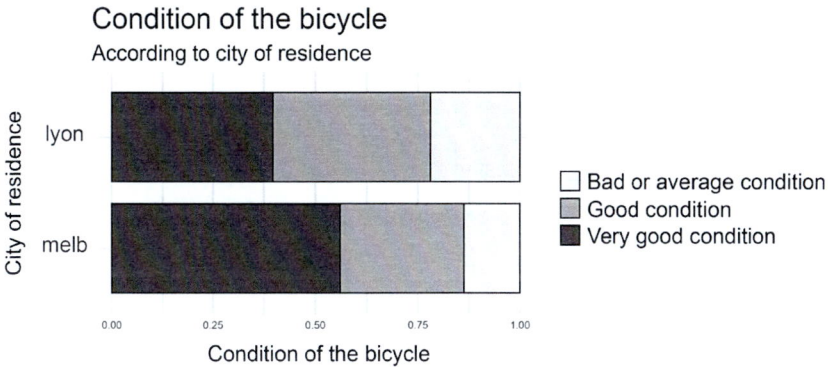

Figure 9.1: Self-assessment by survey participants of the condition of their most used bicycle according to the city of residence.

workshops benefit from a strong local and national network for support, which was not the case with Australian workshops at the time of this study.

Throughout this chapter, this international case study is not developed comparatively because the arguments introduced here include general attitudes regarding cycling, repair and maintenance and the processes of learning within these practices. However, the international setting in which this study was conducted helped to highlight a diversity of repair ecosystems and affordances, which may affect repair and maintenance practices. This allowed me to meet interviewees with more diverse backgrounds and attitudes related to repair for a more thorough understanding of the acquisition of repair skills. In the two following sections, I use the appropriation framework to describe different attitudes regarding repair and the bicycle–cyclist relationship. The first one is devoted to highlighting the difference between cyclists who have appropriated their bicycle and others who, at the other end of the spectrum, feel alienated from them. The second one focuses more precisely on the processes behind the appropriation of the bicycle.

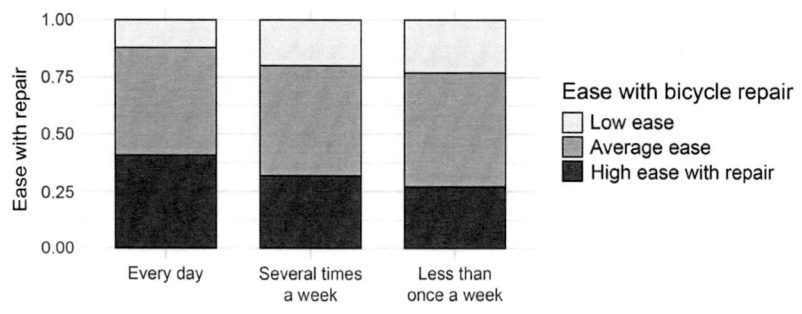

Figure 9.2: Self-assessment by survey participants of how at ease they are with bicycle repair according to their frequency of bicycle use.

The Different Stages of Appropriation

A first analysis of the survey results shows that the self-assessed ease with repair operations and frequency of bicycle use are positively correlated among cyclists ($\chi2 = 15.84$, $p = 0.003$). This result is illustrated in the graph below. This highlights a relationship between the ease with the bicycle and the ease with repair and maintenance operations, which together constitute what we call "appropriation".

In this section, I draw extreme cases of alienation from, and appropriation of, the bicycle to emphasize the nature of this process and the way it unfolds both on the bicycle and with the bicycle. This allows a better understanding of how the bicycle–cyclist relationship and repair and maintenance skills are intertwined.

The Bicycle as an Alien: Lack of Appropriation of the Bicycle

The cyclists who were the least experienced in bicycle repair and maintenance often had a lower instrumental relationship with their bicycle. Although some of them cycled very frequently, they did not know their bicycle either. They used it in ways that were less adapted to their practices and felt less comfortable overall while on their bicycle, which was to some extent considered as alien to them. This lack of repair and maintenance skills constitutes, together with a different relationship with their bicycle, a lack of appropriation. I describe below some aspects of this alienation through the example of Ellie, one cyclist who is very inexperienced in bicycle repair and maintenance. Ellie's situation is comparatively extreme and should not be considered as widespread among cyclists, but it illustrates some forms this lack of appropriation may take.

One aspect of Ellie's low experience with bicycle repair is her fear to engage with anything mechanical, and what she called a general "phobia of tyres".

> I push myself to learn lots of other things but when it comes to the bike ... anything mechanical is quite intimidating. [Ellie, Melbourne]

Below, Ellie's example is used in order to identify four aspects of the alienation that a cyclist may experience from their bicycle. These aspects are the lack of anticipation, the shortage of vocabulary, the lower social integration as a cyclist and the dependency on others.

Lack of Anticipation

One thing that many cyclists who are inexperienced in bicycle repair and maintenance describe is a lack of anticipation of mechanical issues. Like many other cyclists in her situation, Ellie often experienced mechanical issues that she did not anticipate. For instance, she recalled an accident which could have been avoided if she had understood the warning signs:

> For several years, my handlebars would rock. [...] One day, my handlebars completely fell off! I was riding and they just flew off into the air [laughs], luckily I got off my bike, I didn't fall or anything.

She also mentioned a period of several months during which her tyres kept deflating day after day, something that must have made her riding extremely uncomfortable and could have been solved easily if she had addressed this issue. These examples show how a lack of repair and maintenance skills can prevent a cyclist from detecting, understanding and treating the warning signs from their bicycle. Being inexperienced in bicycle repair and maintenance does not only mean that an incident is less likely to be anticipated, but also that cyclists are more likely to ride an ill-adjusted and uncomfortable bicycle, because they are less aware of the condition of their bicycle.

Socializing to Bicycle Repair Through Vocabulary
One aspect of this lack of appropriation is the shortage of precise vocabulary to talk about her bicycle.

> I say "left and right brake" instead of "front and back brake", that kind of thing.

> So he actually fixed the tyres, he gave me new brake cables, he gave me new ... something else, and something else, at the same time.

Ellie has the feeling that she does not understand how a bicycle works and does not know the right vocabulary. As discussed by several material culture scholars, procedural knowledge is very difficult to put into words (Watson, 2006) and in some manual professions, it is considered inappropriate to describe or explain a technical action (Delbos & Jorion, 1990). Despite this, the knowledge of a specific vocabulary and way of speaking is often key to the socialization to a new practice, as illustrated by Agnès Jeanjean's work with construction workers (Jeanjean, 2009). This is also the case for cyclists who, as a community, find themselves united around a common vocabulary (Caimotto, this volume). In this context, Ellie's feeling of alienation is thus driven not only by a lesser knowledge of how things work, but also by a lower mastery of specific vocabulary.

Socialization and Social Integration
In a paper dedicated to women weaving carpets in the Sirwa region of Morocco, Naji shows that the women engaging with practices

of weaving use this material interaction in order to redefine their feminine identity, give themselves self-worth and position themselves in society (Naji, 2009). Similarly, the practice of bicycle repair and maintenance contributes to feeling legitimate as a cyclist (Aldred, 2013). This is expressed by Ellie, who regularly mentions friends of hers who are more knowledgeable than she is at repair:

> I have a friend who welds bikes together. By contrast, I would never touch the gears.

The same thing happens to her in her workplace:

> As an avid cycler, people talk to me about how bikes work but when they talk to me ... I just smile. Because where I work is a depot, it's rather uncommon to cycle there so people talk to me about bikes all the time and I'm just like "Oh yes, I understand."

Ellie thinks that it would be easier to bond with her colleagues if she was more knowledgeable about bicycles. She sometimes even pretends that she understands what they are talking about in order to fit in the conversation.

Dependency on Others
One aspect of the alienation from one's bicycle is the dependency on others that it creates. Ellie describes how, for a long time, her father used to maintain her bicycle.

> Yes, and I wasn't riding it that much, and then my dad would come over and all he would do, now I do understand, he tightened with an Allen key.

As illustrated in this quote, Ellie used to depend on her father not only for the repair of her bicycle, but also for knowing what to do and when; she herself did not understand why he used an Allen key on her bicycle until her handlebars eventually fell off.

Ellie also mentions going to the bicycle shop and hearing that many more things were in need of repair than she first thought:

Becoming Urban Cyclists

> For the last two years, I've usually taken it in when it's in like destruction mode, like in term of the tyres, I take it in for the tyres and they will be like "Oh okay, you actually need new brake pads, you need this and this and this", and it is legitimate.

Many interviewees for this project expressed similar views, not all of whom feeling that the bill they were handed after a visit to the bicycle shop was "legitimate". The feeling of being swindled is common when doing a transaction with someone more skilled about the product being negotiated (Akerlof, 1978), a situation in which cyclists have no choice but to trust the shop employees.

Ellie's description is one of someone who has not appropriated her bicycle. Indeed, she feels very uncomfortable with the mechanical aspects of her bicycle. She does not know the names of bicycle parts well and is sometimes reluctant to touch or attempt to repair them. This is detrimental to her ability to ride comfortably and leads to unexpected breakdowns and costs. She also depends on other people more than she would otherwise. Ellie's extreme example shows the diverse ways repair and maintenance skills constitute a relationship with the bicycle as a material object embedded in social relations. In the next section, practices of cyclists who are experienced in bicycle repair and maintenance are discussed to shed more light on the process of appropriation.

An Appropriated Bicycle

At the opposite end of the spectrum, some people who have acquired cycle repair and maintenance skills have a very different instrumental relationship with their machines: they have appropriated their bicycle. This appropriation constitutes a different relationship between the cyclist and the bicycle, but also with the social environment of the cyclist.

Knowing One's Bicycle

By learning bicycle repair and maintenance skills, cyclists appropriate the bicycle and their relationship with this object changes. The knowledge of how a bicycle works informs the cyclist's experience of the ride. This is most obvious when diagnosing a mechanical issue, as shown in the example of Chloé, a cyclist who considers herself autonomous with most operations with which she engages.

> One gear cable broke down inside the gear shifter [...]. But that had started becoming noticeable, it is true that I had previously noticed that it was harder to shift gears and I think that the cable had started loosening already, maybe some threads had started breaking. [Chloé, Lyon]

Chloé is knowledgeable about the composition of brake cables (made of threads) and can apply this knowledge to understanding and anticipating mechanical issues that she faces. She also masters the adequate vocabulary (shifter, gear cable) and is able to describe precisely what she experienced. This echoes the argument brought up by Harper (1987) who shows how a very thorough understanding of the materials and of the purpose for which the machine will be used is central to conducting repair operations.

Feeling the Bicycle
In the previous example, Chloé felt that the gears were shifting less easily than usual and, thanks to her knowledge of how a bicycle works, was able to interpret from where this feeling came. Her sensory experience of riding a bicycle is informed by her repair and maintenance skills. In this case, the diagnosis occurred within the bicycle–cyclist hybrid. The mechanical specificities and the condition of the bicycle affect this hybrid, defined above as "the bicycle and the rider being produced as one". Like Chloé, cyclists experienced in repair and maintenance often diagnose mechanical issues while on the bicycle and can anticipate a mechanical issue before it occurs. This diagnosis is based on sensory appreciations, as illustrated by Samuel:

> Usually, the first thing is hearing the chain, you can hear the chain squeak, yeah, and then you check the bike over again. And [...] when I'm riding I'll listen to it, so you can usually hear when a spoke is

loose, it goes "queek, queek" so then I'll just flick the spokes just to listen to that, to adjust ... keep the spokes tight. [Samuel, Melbourne]

Samuel uses the sounds that he hears while riding (squeaky chain or loose spokes) to know what bicycle part needs to be repaired or maintained.

Appropriating the Bicycle and the Environment
Learning bicycle repair and maintenance is not only a relationship between the cyclist and the bicycle, but also with the surrounding environment. An example of this concerns two older road cyclists encountered while inflating their tyres at a public bicycle pump in a park. Asked about why they thought inflating their tyres was necessary, they answered that they were out on a ride but suddenly realized that one of them was "unusually slow". "I usually beat him!" said the second cyclist, laughing. This reply shows the way the bicycle-cyclist hybrid works, through habit. The cyclists described here are experienced enough to know their respective rhythms as allowed by the physical efforts they invest, and thus know that any variation in those rhythms can only be caused by a mechanical issue such as deflated tyres. This example reveals how developing repair and maintenance skills does not only mean appropriating the bicycle, but also the direct environment in which the repair and riding occur.

With the Bicycle
Appropriation does not only happen within the restricted frame of the bicycle-cyclist hybrid or at the scale of a bicycle trip only. Another aspect of it is the integration of the object into one's cycling practices. This is what Miller terms "recontextualisation". One example of such a thing is the following extract of a conversation with Aline, a woman who often carries groceries and her daughter as well on her Dutch bicycle.

Appropriating the Bicycle

> I have a small hand pump. It works, but it has more limited capacity and takes longer to inflate. And you know, you cannot see the air pressure displayed so you cannot be truly sure of where you're at. Even if, I do not need something that [...] I just need it to ride, to brake and when I ride my bike I usually plan my trip based on the lowest speed. I never worry about the time or think, "oh I have to be fast", and even if the tyre isn't inflated perfectly at 3 bars as it should, well it's not so bad, it will just be harder for me but there isn't much at stake. [Aline, Lyon]

Aline says that she does not mind her bicycle pump not being of high capacity since she does not cycle with the aim to perform. Her habit of inflating her tyres as well as the resources she regularly uses are thus not ideal but adapted to what she considers her riding practices should be. Aline's confidence that she knows exactly what uses she has for her bicycle allow her to feel comfortable with her repair and maintenance practices in their current state. In this way, she has appropriated her bicycle since her repair and maintenance practices fit her identity, as experienced individually and socially. Aline's situation is similar to that of people engaging in DIY attempts to renovate their kitchen described by Shove et al. (2007); indeed, the researchers show that DIY home renovation practices aim to align the material conditions of dwelling with a desirable life and social practices, such as having dinner together as a family.

The examples cited above show how cyclists with experience in repair and maintenance relate differently, not only with their bicycle but also within their surrounding environment. Taken together, examples of cyclists with extremely different experiences of bicycle repair and maintenance allow an understanding of the process of appropriation of the bicycle to be gained. They demonstrate that bicycle repair and maintenance is not a skill that is carried by the cyclist, but that is shared between the cyclist, the bicycle and the social environment in which they find themselves. Learning bicycle repair and maintenance is thus a form of socialization, both to one's bicycle and to the surrounding environment.

Becoming Urban Cyclists

Appropriation in Action
If, as argued above, repair and maintenance skills cannot be separated from the relationship that cyclists maintain with their bicycle and the environment, we must consider riding practices and experiences as central to the acquisition of repair and maintenance skills. In other words, bicycle repair and maintenance are not only learned in a classroom but also on the bicycle itself. The constant interaction between the bicycle and the cyclist in the frame of the bicycle–cyclist hybrid and in the course of riding practices in general is also one of learning, it is part of the work which constitutes the appropriation of the bicycle by the cyclist. Reciprocally, acquiring repair and maintenance skills transforms the relationship between the cyclist and their bicycle which occurs in the course of riding practices, but also inside the bicycle–cyclist hybrid.

In this final section, I show the diverse ways in which appropriation occurs, and the diverse ways in which cyclists become familiar with bicycles in general, and more specifically with their own bicycle, in time.

Development of Repair Skills Through the Bicycle–Cyclist Relationship
The theory of appropriation allows the consideration of the learning of repair and maintenance skills and the bicycle–cyclist relationship as intertwined. Consequently, the bicycle–cyclist relationship is one place where the acquisition of repair and maintenance skills occurs. In this subsection, I explore the learning of bicycle repair and maintenance as it happens within cycling practices, whether it is on or with the bicycle.

Learning on the Bicycle: Within the Bicycle–Cyclist Hybrid
The first example of the acquisition of skills through riding is the one mentioned above. Ellie's bad experience with the bicycle handlebars falling off was one that she did not forget. It made her reconsider things she had not previously cared about and understand them

differently. Acts of repair and maintenance, such as her father regularly maintaining her bike, were understood differently after the incident.

More generally, it is common for cyclists to discover something about how their bicycle works after a sudden breakdown. An example of this is Daniel, a cyclist who recounts a bicycle trip across New Zealand 25 years ago: this tour was an important life experience, but also a time where he learned a lot about how bicycles work, as shown in the following extract:

> Thinking about that, when I did the trip, I learned a lot as I went. So, I actually got a new chain when I came over to Australia, I had brought the bike with me, but I didn't realize that the shop that did it hadn't put on a new cassette. So, I found out the hard way as I was going up in Kangaroo Valley, New South Wales, and it just kept slipping. Because it's a new chain and an old cassette, [...] it was slippery, it would come and go. I have learned since then that you've gotta pay for the whole thing. And I don't know why the shop didn't just do it. [Daniel, Melbourne]

When his bicycle started changing gears without reason, Daniel identified this situation as wrong. It is only afterwards that he understood where the issue came from and learned that changing a bicycle chain must be done in complementarity with the condition of the cassette. After this event, he had updated his bicycle repair and maintenance knowledge. Daniel recounted another frightening experience that occurred during this same trip. He had attempted to fit a new pair of brake pads on his bicycle and thought he had done it right. However, it did not work and as he was cycling downhill, the brake pads got loose and shredded the rubber of his tyre.

Both examples given here are very dramatic, but they demonstrate how the appropriation of the bicycle proceeds backwards and forwards between the application of mechanical principles in how the bicycle, as a machine, operates, and the sensory experiences of riding that occur within the bicycle–cyclist hybrid. In both cases, what Daniel initially thought was right turned out to be wrong once he was actually riding, and the bicycle–cyclist hybrid was the place for a lesson of bicycle repair and maintenance. This phenomenon is what Freud termed "afterwardsness" (nachträglichkeit), and it highlights the way learning is not a linear experience but one where each new event recontextualizes the previous ones (Delbos & Jorion, 1990).

Learning with the Bicycle: Beyond the Bicycle–Cyclist Hybrid
The bicycle–cyclist hybrid is not the only example of bicycle riding practices in which repair and maintenance skills are learned. Indeed, similar to the way people eventually decide to purchase an electric bicycle, the acquisition of repair skills can also be triggered by diverse events related to the general cycling life and projects of individuals (Marincek, this volume; Müggenburg et al., 2015). We can sort these events into three categories, each of which can be an opportunity for learning about repair: the intensification of riding practices, the transformation of riding practices and the continuation of riding practices.

A first category of key events is when cyclists intensify their riding practices. This can take the form of a house move, which extends the length of a commute, or of an upcoming trip. For instance, Caitlyn attended the basic bicycle maintenance workshop as a way to prepare for touring New Zealand by bicycle. "I didn't know how to change a tyre and I thought it would be important to learn before I went," she explained.

A second category of key events in the riding life of a cyclist is that related to a transformation of their riding practices. One example is the case of Florent, a man who, when his grandfather died and left him his old bicycle, decided to turn it into a fixed-gear bicycle as a new project. In the course of doing so, he ended up visiting numerous bicycle shops and asked them for advice about the mechanical aspects of fixed-gear bicycles. He learned enough repair and maintenance skills then to decide to become a bicycle mechanic.

Appropriating the Bicycle

Another example of learning repair skills through the transformation of riding practices is the purchase of a new bicycle. For instance, Aline was once given money to purchase a good quality bicycle. She then searched for one that would have a similar braking system as the bicycle she used to ride as a child, pedal brakes. She recounted how this search made her aware of some new technical aspects of the bicycle:

> It happened when I was looking for a pedal brake bicycle. The thing is, we often confuse pedal brakes with fixed gear or freewheel, but it is not the same. That's it, this is how I have been confronted to, how I learned the difference between both and what I wanted and all. [...] I don't know how I could have learned otherwise. [Aline, Lyon]

A third category of key events in cycling practices which led to the acquisition of repair and maintenance skills is through the continuation of riding practices. One example of this is Karen, a middle-aged e-bicycle rider who regularly goes to the bicycle shop for a service. Karen progressively established a relationship with the mechanics working there, who often give her advice on how to maintain her bicycle. For instance, as she recalls, they advised her to change gears more often, despite her not feeling the need to do so on her electric bicycle: "When the bike chain had to be changed, the guys tried to explain to me how to use it better so that it would not happen that often, and I think I've got better at it now."

Another case of such an interaction is when she got advice from them on how to inflate her tyres better: "So again I went back and then they said, 'you got a lot of wear on your tyres because you are not pumping them up enough' and blah blah blah. I said, 'no I've pressed them and they're fine!' but no, it was not as pumped up as supposedly it needs to be." According to Karen, frequent visits to her local bicycle shop contributed to a good relationship with the staff who then started giving her mechanical advice. Her regular riding habits and her social integration with the bicycle shop staff are two factors that contributed to her acquiring bicycle repair and maintenance skills, among which is the ability to guess whether the tension of her tyres is sufficient by squeezing them.

These examples demonstrate how the acquisition of repair and maintenance skills may happen not only through formal learning in a classroom or a workshop, but also through the bicycle-cyclist relationship. It can occur on the bicycle, within the bicycle-cyclist hybrid, like when the bicycle breaks down unexpectedly, revealing a problem that existed before and could have been detected. It can also occur with the bicycle, when cyclists decide to intensify their practices, to transform them or while continuing them. One important point highlighted in this is the role that bicycle shops can play in the appropriation of bicycles by their owners. Indeed, even if this is not their primary aim, they can be an environment in which people learn about repair and acquire new cycling habits.

Development of the Bicycle-Cyclist Relationship Through the Acquisition of Repair and Maintenance Skills
The bicycle-cyclist relationship is central to repair and maintenance skills and practices. Reciprocally, developing repair and maintenance skills, as well as repairing and maintaining one's bicycle, contribute to the appropriation since it transforms the relationship that the cyclist maintains with the bicycle. This appropriation occurs both at the level of the bicycle-cyclist hybrid and generally, in strengthening the relationship that the cyclist maintains with the bicycle.

On the Bicycle: Development of the Bicycle-Cyclist Hybrid
Cyclists who learn repair and maintenance skills transform their relationship with their bicycle in many ways. One way in which this transformation is visible is during a bicycle ride, when the cyclist and the bicycle assemble into a hybrid. An example of this is the testimony of Caitlyn, the cyclist who attended a bicycle maintenance workshop in anticipation of her New Zealand trip. According to her, her riding behaviour changed since she attended that workshop:

Appropriating the Bicycle

> I probably inflate my tyres more regularly now. I didn't realize that I needed to do it so often. I was riding around with probably close to flat tyres, let's be honest. I had to change my brake pads myself as well [...] And that was good like, I felt confident to do that, to adjust the brake pads. That was fun. And now ... I had a crash recently and now my brake pads need replacing again, on the front end, and I feel confident to do that, to just tinker. [Caitlyn, Melbourne]

Caitlyn's testimony shows that developing repair skills affected much more than her ability to intervene when her bicycle breaks down; indeed, the way she considers her bicycle was also transformed. She feels more confident when engaging with repair but also with experimenting. The workshop contributed to transforming Caitlyn's attitude to her bicycle and to her appropriation of it. Furthermore, the workshop led her to reconsider what is, to her, adequate air pressure in her tyres: she now feels less comfortable riding with deflated tyres than she used to. This illustrates a transformation of the experience of a cyclist within the bicycle–cyclist hybrid. Once again, acquiring repair skills contributed to the appropriation of the bicycle, as expressed in the bicycle–cyclist hybrid.

With the Bicycle: Development of Cycling Practices
Through learning repair and maintenance skills, cyclists see the instrumental relationship that they have with their bicycle transform, not only while riding but also in general. One example of this is Barbara, a cyclist who decided to have some training on bicycle repair and maintenance, with the aim to become a professional bicycle mechanic. When asked about what changed in her cycling practices since then, she replied:

> One of the main things is to not be too quick to throw away my bike. Now I know how to maintain my bikes, so it's okay. Particularly in bike shops, they're always quick to go "get rid of that bike", but actually I'm finding that I don't want an upgrade. I'm quite connected to my old vintage bike, and I just want to maintain it to a point where it rides fine, it gets me from A to B. It's been a big shift, just knowing

that you don't always have to upgrade. And also, I guess I'm more confident riding around, and I always carry around a tool set and stuff so if something happens, I'll be able to do the repairs on the road. [Barbara, Melbourne]

Barbara's case shows that the relationship with the bicycle is transformed by the acquisition of bicycle repair and maintenance skills. Indeed, acquiring knowledge affected the confidence with which she rides, and therefore the distance she rides. Besides, learning these skills affected how long she keeps a bicycle instead of throwing it away, and allowed her to use her bicycle the way she wants, instead of having to submit to what bicycle mechanics think is best for her. These skills therefore brought some autonomy into her riding practices.

The process of appropriation goes both ways; the acquisition of bicycle repair and maintenance skills transforms the instrumental relationship that a cyclist has with their bicycle, and the development of the instrumental relationship between a cyclist and their bicycle contributes to them acquiring new repair and maintenance skills. This happens at the level of the bicycle ride and of the bicycle-cyclist hybrid, but also at the general level of the cycling practices in which the cyclist engages.

Conclusion

Learning how to repair one's bicycle is still a major step for anyone wishing to become an urban cyclist (Aldred, 2013) but no previous research work has yet dwelled on this learning process. I argued that bicycle repair and maintenance practices must be understood together with the relationship between the cyclist, their bicycle and their environment. Indeed, cyclists who are experienced in bicycle repair and maintenance show a different relationship to their bicycle and their environment than inexperienced ones. Riders who are less skilled at repair and maintenance may feel alienated from their bicycle, as they depend on others to keep it in good condition. They are more often subject to unexpected breakdowns and costs.

Conversely, those who are experienced in repair and maintenance are able to diagnose a mechanical issue while riding and to anticipate mechanical issues. As a rider acquires new repair and maintenance skills, they see their instrumental relationship with their bicycle transform and reciprocally, cyclists learn about bicycle repair and maintenance in the course of their cycling practices. This double movement constitutes a process of appropriation (Miller, 1987). Furthermore, the acquisition of repair and maintenance skills transforms the social relations in which cyclists are involved.

Highlighting this intertwining of cycling practices and repair skills allows a better understanding of what it means to learn how to repair a bicycle and of how this process occurs both on and off the bicycle. The acquisition of repair and maintenance skills can occur on the bicycle or at the level of usual or changing cycling practices, for instance when planning a bicycle trip abroad, or when purchasing a new bicycle. On the other hand, learning repair and maintenance skills transforms the sensory experience of a bicycle ride and changes the opportunities and choices made in the course of general cycling practices.

This chapter shows the relevance of the theory of appropriation for reintegrating the materiality of the bicycle into the consideration of cycling practices, something that is often overlooked in scientific discussions of cycling. It also allows a focus on the embodied nature of cycling and the sensory aspects of such a practice. This study has wide implications for policy makers aiming to develop cycling modal share, since it locates this mode of transportation as the interconnection between cyclists, bicycles as material objects, and their environment. Riding and repairing a bicycle are two skills that complete and strengthen each other in a process of appropriation of a bicycle. This chapter therefore highlights the importance of including bicycle repair and maintenance in the scope of cycling policies and makes a point for designing bicycle repair and maintenance courses that take the cycling practices and lived experiences of their attendees into account. It shows that several aspects of cycling practices that are not usually seen as educational, such as riding one's bicycle or even falling off it, can actually contribute to the acquisition of repair and maintenance skills. As France and the UK recently released national bicycle repair vouchers in the context of the Covid-19 pandemic, it is relevant to note that such visits also contribute to cyclists appropriating their bicycle.

This chapter shows how the relationship between a cyclist, their bicycle and the environment can be better understood through a theory of appropriation. Of course, there is much more to say on this topic. I deliberately did not dwell on issues of diversity and differential impact, which requires its own study. Women's ease in engaging with, and learning about, bicycle repair and maintenance, for example, is inhibited by various mechanisms of exclusion (Abord de Chatillon, 2021). Similarly, the frequent obstacles faced by members of ethnic and class minorities when engaging with cycling contribute to deterring them from gaining cycle repair and maintenance skills and appropriating their bicycle (Lubitow, 2017; Steinbach et al., 2011). There is much scope for further research to explore the diverse meanings invested by cyclists in bicycle repair and maintenance practices using the framework analysis presented here.

References
Abord de Chatillon, M. (2019). "We care for each other" — Pratiques mécaniques et relation cycliste-vélo. *Rencontres Doctorales de l'APERAU*. Strasbourg.
Abord de Chatillon, M. (2021). Feminine velonomy: Women's Experiences of bicycle repair and maintenance within patriarchal contexts (in France and Australia). In D. Zuev, K. Psarikidou, & C. Popan (Eds.), *Cycling societies: Emerging innovations, inequalities and governance*. Routledge.
Akerlof, G. A. (1978). The market for "lemons": Quality uncertainty and the market mechanism. *Uncertainty in Economics, 84*(3), 235–251.

Aldred, R. (2013). Incompetent or too competent? Negotiating everyday cycling identities in a motor dominated society. *Mobilities*, *8*(2), 252–271. https://doi.org/10.1080/17450101.2012.696342

Ashmore, D. P., Thoreau, R., Kwami, C., Christie, N., & Tyler, N. A. (2018). Using thematic analysis to explore symbolism in transport choice across national cultures. *Transportation*. https://doi.org/10.1007/s11116-018-9902-7

Coleman, K. A. (2015). *Bicycles as objects: Identity, attachment, and membership categorization devices*. [Unpublished MA thesis]. University of Alberta. https://doi.org/10.7939/R3QV3C865

Cook, M., & Edensor, T. (2017). Cycling through dark space: Apprehending landscape otherwise. *Mobilities*, *12*(1), 1–19. https://doi.org/10.1080/17450101.2014.956417

Dant, T. (1998). Playing with things: Objects and subjects in windsurfing. *Journal of Material Culture*, *3*(1), 77–95. https://doi.org/10.1177/135918359800300104

Dant, T. (2004). The driver-car. *Theory, Culture & Society*, *21*(4–5), 61–79. https://doi.org/10.1177/0263276404046061

Dant, T. (2010). The work of repair: Gesture, emotion and sensual knowledge. *Sociological Research Online*, *15*(3), 1–22. https://doi.org/10.5153/sro.2158

Dant, T., & Wheaton, B. (2007). Windsurfing: An extreme form of material and embodied interaction? *Anthropology Today*, *23*(6), 8–12.

Delbos, G., & Jorion, P. (1990). *La transmission des savoirs*. Éd. de la Maison des sciences de l'homme.

Dill, J. (2019, 14 August). Bicycle research 2019: More than helmets and head injuries [Blog]. https://jenniferdill.net/2019/08/14/bicycle-research-2019-more-than-helmets-and-head-injuries/

Graham, S., & Thrift, N. (2007). Out of order: Understanding repair and maintenance. *Theory, Culture & Society*, *24*(3), 1–25. https://doi.org/10.1177/0263276407075954

Harper, D. (1987). *Working knowledge: Skill and community in a small shop*. University of Chicago Press.

Héran, F. (2015). *Le retour de la bicyclette : Une histoire des déplacements urbains en Europe, de 1817 à 2050*. La Découverte.

Jeanjean, A. (2009). Corps en chantier. In M.-P. Julien & C. Rosselin (Éds.), *Le sujet contre ses objets... Tout contre : Ethnographies de cultures matérielles*. Editions du comité des travaux historiques et scientifiques.

Larsen, J., & Christensen, M. D. (2015). The unstable lives of bicycles: The "unbecoming" of design objects. *Environment and Planning A, 47*(4), 922–938. https://doi.org/10.1068/a140282p

Lubitow, A. (2017). Narratives of marginalized cyclists: Understanding obstacles to utilitarian cycling among women and minorities in Portland, OR. *TREC Final Reports*. https://doi.org/10.15760/trec.171

Miller, D. (1987). *Material culture and mass consumption*. Blackwell.

Müggenburg, H., Busch-Geertsema, A., & Lanzendorf, M. (2015). Mobility biographies: A review of achievements and challenges of the mobility biographies approach and a framework for further research. *Journal of Transport Geography, 46*, 151–163. https://doi.org/10.1016/j.jtrangeo.2015.06.004

Naji, M. (2009). La formation de féminités à travers le tissage dans le Sirwa (Maroc). In M.-P. Julien & C. Rosselin (Éds.), *Le sujet contre ses objets... Tout contre : Ethnographies de cultures matérielles*. Éditions du comité des travaux historiques et scientifiques.

Shove, E., Watson, M., Hand, M., & Ingram, J. (2007). *The design of everyday life*. Berg.

Spinney, J. (2006). A place of sense: A kinaesthetic ethnography of cyclists on Mont Ventoux. *Environment and Planning D: Society and Space, 24*(5), 709–732. https://doi.org/10.1068/d66j

Steg, L. (2005). Car use: Lust and must. Instrumental, symbolic and affective motives for car use. *Transportation Research Part A: Policy and Practice, 39*(2), 147–162. https://doi.org/10.1016/j.tra.2004.07.001

Steinbach, R., Green, J., Datta, J., & Edwards, P. (2011). Cycling and the city: A case study of how gendered, ethnic and class identities can shape healthy transport choices. *Social Science & Medicine, 72*(7), 1123–1130. https://doi.org/10.1016/j.socscimed.2011.01.033

Strömberg, H., & Karlsson, I. C. M. (2016). Enhancing utilitarian cycling: A case study. *Transportation Research Procedia, 14*, 2352–2361. https://doi.org/10.1016/j.trpro.2016.05.264

Urry, J. (2006). Inhabiting the car. *The Sociological Review, 54*(s1), 17–31. https://doi.org/10.1111/j.1467-954X.2006.00635.x

Warnier, J.-P. (1999). *Construire la culture matérielle.* Presses Universitaires de France. https://doi.org/10.3917/puf.warni.1999.01

Watson, R. (2006). Tacit knowledge. *Theory, Culture & Society, 23*(2–3), 208–210. https://doi.org/10.1177/026327640602300244

AFTERWORD

Rachel Aldred

Coming back to these chapters reminded me of pre-Covid times — the February symposium in Lyon seems a long time ago now! I very much enjoyed the chance to learn from and listen to the variety of mixed methods research looking at urban cycling. In this afterword, prompted by re-reading the material, I reflect on the concept of "skills", referred to by various authors, and highlight some possible tensions over how we understand skills in relation to urban cycling.

Thinking about cycling skills also takes me back to one particular visit, some years ago, to The Netherlands. Already an experienced London cyclist, I found cycling in The Netherlands relaxing and pleasant. I no longer had to worry constantly about being tailgated, or about "taking the lane" in order to turn right across multiple traffic lanes.

It seemed to me that part of the success of The Netherlands was that, in practice theory terms, cycling skills had been incorporated (to some extent neutralized) within the cycling environment, rather than being expected of the individual cyclist. Such themes are related to those discussed in Peter Cox's chapter in this volume, where he explores relationships between infrastructure, cycling practices and cycling advocacy. My cycling experience had been very different in the UK, where to cycle I felt I had to "skill up", learning not only to ride with motor traffic (Bikeability Level 3) but also some maintenance basics. I managed to just about get to grips with changing an inner tube, but gave up on anything more advanced.

I learnt how to read a set of 14 Transport for London cycling maps to help me plan any unfamiliar journeys. These highlighted London Cycle Network routes (in blue: this could mean anything from an occasional navigational sign on a busy road, to bus lanes and advisory white lines, or if you had really won the jackpot, a

Afterword

just-about-ok track on the footway), and "recommended by other cyclists" routes (in yellow: generally quite wiggly, and ranging from truly quiet backstreets to popular short cuts for London's taxi drivers). Somehow, I still often got horribly lost finding new destinations, winding up on nightmarish urban highways like Park Lane, or sometimes exactly where I started, after a mess of confusing one-way streets.

Still, I cycled across the busy and intimidating Old Street roundabout several times a week (my motto: "if they're beeping, they've seen you"), and repaired my own punctures (anything beyond that went to the local bike shop). By contrast, Dutch cyclists seemed to have it easy. The skills I struggled to learn were embedded in their local infrastructure, policy environment, and cycling cultures. In The Netherlands, I was not expected to ride with motor traffic, unless on very quiet streets. Dutch cyclists seemed to rely on clunky but reliable steeds, and to take their bikes to the local shop when punctures did strike, avoiding oily hands from changing an inner tube. And my advanced bike map-reading skills were redundant: in general, all main roads had decent infrastructure, making navigating much easier.

In other words, Dutch route infrastructure negated the need for advanced traffic-interaction skills; the dense network of Dutch bike shops negated the need for advanced maintenance and repair skills; and the dense network of high-quality cycle infrastructure negated the need for advanced navigational skills. In practice theory terms, these themes were resolved within the environment rather than needing to be located in the individual.

One could extend this to the bicycle itself. In the UK, the most commonly sold types of bicycle are cheap mountain bikes, lacking mudguards or carriers, without integral locking or lights. For these bicycles to be half-way functional in an everyday cycling context, additional items need to be purchased, attached and removed from the bike when parked (to avoid returning to your bike at night, to find the lights missing — a common complaint). It is a stark contrast with how driving—an inherently riskier and more difficult practice—has been simplified and made easy for mass use.

Practice theorists like Elizabeth Shove describe practices—like cycling—as being made up of meanings and stuff, alongside skills. In a UK context—and many other low-cycling contexts—certain skills are needed, as is specialist "stuff"; to add to the bike, and to adorn the rider (e.g. helmets, to guard against the perceived high risk of cycling in motor traffic). This is all bound up with the understanding of cycling as a dangerous activity, attracting "cyclists" who are "keen" and "enthusiastic"—but also obsessive "Lycra Louts", the stereotype's closely related flip side.

So back to The Netherlands, and to me, at a conference with two colleagues a decade or so ago. Between us, we had two bikes, three people. Not a problem—unlike in the UK, Dutch cycling is constructed as a sociable practice, and bikes have rear carriers specifically so you can give your friend or colleague a lift, as needed. By contrast, giving someone a "backie" in the UK can be illegal (the law is not entirely clear) and often frowned upon.

The obvious thing then seemed to be for one of my colleagues to give me a lift. In the university car park, I sat gingerly on the rear carrier. My colleague set off. I slid off the side, and she nearly fell off. We tried again, with similar results. A Dutch woman going to her car paused to watch us, obviously thinking we were enacting some comedy routine. We tried again. Finally, we gave up and walked to our destination, pushing the bikes.

Reflecting on my own incompetence, it struck me that if Dutch cyclists were not expected to change a puncture, or weave between lorries and buses, they were still expected to be able to balance effectively on the back of a bicycle. This was something that I, by contrast, had never learnt (or perhaps I had, but had forgotten in my years of solo cycling across Old Street).

Thinking about this now, I am reminded of a very different literature—on de-skilling and work practices. Do Dutch cyclists require a lower level of individual cycling skills than cyclists in

Afterword

more hostile contexts, or is it the case that thinking this implies still prioritizing "vehicular cycling", even when we are also saying that people should not need to learn those skills?

What might happen if we made other types of skills (which might not be inherently any "easier" in technical terms) more visible? If for adult beginner cycle training, for instance, we were able not just to orient around interactions with cars (and avoiding being injured), but to focus more on having positive interactions with other people cycling, and people walking? On skills required to carry shopping and other people, rather than seeing solo and unencumbered cycling as a default?

The concept of "skills" in relation to cycling is then somewhat complicated, as illustrated by Rérat and by Adam et al., who discuss the need for new methods that can embrace both socialization and the body in action. It would be immensely interesting to study how the concept varies in different cycling contexts, including looking both at expert and public definitions. It's easy to interpret everyday activities as not requiring skill (because it seems everyone can do them). But perhaps those activities that have successfully become widespread are not necessarily easy, but rather incorporate skills that many users find more enjoyable to acquire and crucially, to perform: rather than my daily dash across Old Street, representing an enjoyable exercise of skill for 25-year-old me but clearly not for many others.

The above discussion may suggest a counter-argument to some of the papers, perhaps particularly Margot Abord de Chatillon's piece, which I very much enjoyed reading. However, to me it instead raises questions of what we expect cycling to do. Is it enough for it to be a mass consumer product, made easy and enjoyable? Should we expect it to be part of a movement whereby people become more than consumers, part of a wider social change? These questions are discussed in the chapters by Peter Cox and Maria Cristina Caimotto, who both address the gap that can exist between cycling as a convivial activity and a planning logic based on productivity and speed. Focusing on the e-bike, Marincek documents how this ambiguous technical object can facilitate cycling trajectories with the potential to change the social status of cycling and the audiences it addresses.

This then links to the questions raised at the beginning about equity by Matthieu Adam and Nathalie Ortar, also highlighted in the papers by Thomas Buhler and Janina Welsch. Cycling equity has not had enough attention in high- and low-cycling contexts alike. There are increasingly studies of socio-spatial equity, particularly from North and Latin America (for instance, analysing locations of bike hire stations, or bike infrastructure) that help contribute to our understanding of why some groups feel excluded from cycling. With better spatial planning, we can help address these inequalities and hence hope to redress some of the under-representation among groups such as women, older people and some ethnic minority groups.

However, it is important to understand tensions between equity and other goals. Cycling is sometimes seen as a magic bullet or miracle cure for all policy ills. Yet we need to be clear about which objectives are being prioritized and measured. For instance, cycling uptake can help reduce carbon emissions — if it represents mode shift from the car. However, if we focus on getting current car users cycling, this will mean we disproportionately target affluent, white men — who are over-represented among drivers. By contrast (and as per David Sayagh et al.'s chapter), women tend to make more trips by bus and on foot, so getting them to cycle (for instance, by prioritizing school run infrastructure, given women are much more likely than men to make those trips) may mean a lower carbon reduction — but may address equity and access goals more effectively.